D0073119

The Poetics of Indeterminacy

The Poetics of Indeterminacy:
Rimbaud to Cage

MARJORIE PERLOFF

PRINCETON UNIVERSITY PRESS
Princeton, New Jersey

Published by Princeton University Press, Princeton, New Jersey
In the United Kingdom: Princeton University Press, Guildford, Surrey

Library of Congress Cataloging in Publication Data will be
found on the last printed page of this book

Publication of this book has been aided by a grant
from the Andrew W. Mellon Fund of Princeton University Press

This book has been composed in Linotron Baskerville

Clothbound editions of Princeton University Press books
are printed on acid-free paper, and binding materials are
chosen for strength and durability

Printed in the United States of America by Princeton
University Press, Princeton, New Jersey

For Joseph, Nancy, and Carey

Preface

THIS BOOK had its inception some eight years ago when I was writing a book about the poetry of Robert Lowell. In studying Lowell's "imitations" of Rimbaud, it occurred to me, and I have not changed my mind, that what we loosely call "Modernism" in Anglo-American poetry is really made up of two separate though often interwoven strands: the Symbolist mode that Lowell inherited from Eliot and Baudelaire and, beyond them, from the great Romantic poets, and the "anti-Symbolist" mode of indeterminacy or "undecidability," of literalness and free play, whose first real exemplar was the Rimbaud of the *Illuminations.* While some of the ideas that went into this study were crystallizing, I accepted an assignment to write a book on the poetry of Frank O'Hara. This particular project, completed in 1977, reenforced my conviction that we cannot really come to terms with the major poetic experiments occurring in our own time without some understanding of what we might call "the French connection"—the line that goes from Rimbaud to Stein, Pound, and Williams by way of Cubist, Dada, and early Surrealist art, a line that also includes the great French/English verbal compositions of Beckett. It is this "other tradition" (I take the phrase from the title of a poem by John Ashbery) in twentieth-century poetry that is the subject of my book.

My debt to colleagues, students, and friends is a large one. Portions of this study in their earlier versions have been tried and tested on audiences at the following institutions: the University of Wisconsin-Madison, the University of California-Irvine, the State University of New York at Binghamton, the University of New Mexico, Oberlin College, Cambridge University, the University of Warwick, the Academy of Literary Studies at Princeton University, the Huntington Library Research Seminar, and the NEH-Folger Library Conference, "After the Flood" in Washington, D.C. The criticism as well as the support I have received at these institutions has been invaluable.

The following people read part or all of the manuscript and made helpful suggestions: Charles Altieri, David Antin, Gerda Blumenthal, James Breslin, Jackson I. Cope, Donald Davie, L. S. Dembo, David Fite, Geoffrey Green, Lawrence Kramer, James Laughlin, David Lehman, Douglas Messerli, C. J. Rawson, Michael Riffaterre, Thomas Whitaker, and George T. Wright. I have also profited from long hours of discussion on the relationship of Symbolism to "The Other Tradition" with the following critics and poets: Daniel Aaron, Calvin Bedient, Jo Brantley Berryman, Tim Dlugos, Kathleen Fraser, Renée Riese Hubert, Lucille Kerr, Herbert Leibowitz, William McPherson, Peter Manning, Roy Harvey Pearce, Jerome Rothenberg, David St. John, Catharine R. Stimpson, David Shapiro, James Thorpe, Arthur Vogelsang, Emily Wallace, Charles Wright, and Harriet Zinnes.

I am especially grateful to Herbert Lindenberger, whose enthusiasm, erudition, critical insight, and painstaking reading of the manuscript helped to make the whole enterprise possible.

Marjorie Sherwood of the Princeton University Press has been, from first to last, an exemplary editor. Christina Stough helped me to prepare the manuscript for the press.

My greatest debt is to my husband, Joseph Perloff, and to my daughters, Nancy and Carey. This is not the usual sort of acknowledgment one makes to one's family for forbearance and understanding during a period of intensive writing. I want to note here that my husband read every word of the manuscript in its many versions, urged me to make specific changes, cautioned me against certain sweeping generalizations, and improved any number of awkward transitions or obscure passages. His knowledge of the visual arts was especially helpful. Nancy, a graduate student in

Musicology, and Carey, a student of Classics and Comparative Literature, were enthusiastic readers but also, at times, vociferous critics. Unlike my earlier books this one is, in a real sense, a family enterprise, and accordingly it is dedicated to a very remarkable—and surprisingly determinate—family.

January 1980 Marjorie Perloff

Contents

List of Illustrations

Acknowledgments

Parts of the following chapters and sections of this book have been published, previously, usually in considerably different form:

Chapter One (an early version) in *Centrum*, 4, no. 2 (Spring 1975).

Chapter Three in *American Poetry Review*, 8 (September-October 1979).

Chapter Four in *The Missouri Review*, 2, no. 1 (Fall 1978).

Chapter Five, part iii in *The Iowa Review*, 6 (Winter 1975).

Chapter Six, part ii in *Parnassus: Poetry in Review*, 6 (Fall/Winter 1978).

Chapter Seven, portions in *American Poetry Review*, 7, no. 5 (September-October 1978) and *Beyond Amazement: New Essays on the Poetry of John Ashbery* (Cornell University Press, 1980).

I am grateful to the editors of these journals and of *Beyond Amazement* for permission to use this material.

For permission to include material published by them, grateful acknowledgment is made to the following:

David Antin, for permission to quote from his unpublished manuscripts and letters as well as from *Definitions* by David Antin, copyright © 1967 by David Antin; "Go for Broke" in *The Poetry of Surrealism,* edited by Michael Benedikt, copyright © 1974 by David Antin; "The Death of the Platypus," *Trobar,* 1 (1960), copyright © 1960 by David Antin; "constructions and discoveries," *Chelsea* 16 (March 1965) by David Antin, copyright © 1965 by David Antin.

Georges Borchardt, Inc., for permission to quote from *Some Trees* by John Ashbery, copyright © 1956 by John Ashbery; from *Rivers and Mountains* by John Ashbery, copyright © 1962, 1963, 1964, 1966 by John Ashbery; from *Collected Poems in English and French* by Samuel Beckett, copyright © 1977 by Samuel Beckett. David Lehman, *Beyond Amazement: New Essays on John Ashbery*. Copyright © 1980 by Cornell University. Used by permission of the publisher, Cornell University Press.

University of Chicago Press, for permission to quote from *Rimbaud, Complete Works, Selected Letters,* translated by Wallace Fowlie, copyright © 1967 by Wallace Fowlie.

Farrar, Straus and Giroux, Inc., for permission to quote from Robert Lowell's translation of "The Drunken Boat" by Arthur Rimbaud, from *Imitations* by Robert Lowell, copyright © 1958, 1959, 1960, 1961 by Robert Lowell.

Grove Press, Inc. and John Calder, Ltd., for permission to quote from *Watt* by Samuel Beckett, copyright © 1953 by Samuel Beckett; *How It Is* by Samuel Beckett, copyright © 1964 by Samuel Beckett; *First Love and Other Shorts,* by Samuel Beckett, copyright © 1974 by Samuel Beckett; *Fizzles* by Samuel Beckett, copyright © 1976 by Samuel Beckett; *Collected Poems in English and French* by Samuel Beckett, copyright © 1977 by Samuel Beckett.

Harcourt Brace Jovanovich, Inc. and Faber & Faber Ltd., for permission to quote from *Collected Poems 1909-1962* by T. S. Eliot, copyright © 1936 by Harcourt Brace Jovanovich, Inc.; copyright © 1963, 1964 by T. S. Eliot.

Harper & Row, Publishers, Inc., for permission to quote from *Arthur Rimbaud, Complete Works,* translated by Paul Schmidt, copyright © 1975 by Paul Schmidt.

David Higham Associates Ltd., for permission to quote from *Collected Poems* of Edith Sitwell, copyright © 1957 by Edith Sitwell.

Liveright Publishing Corporation, for permission to quote from

Fernhurst, Q.E.D. and Other Early Writings by Gertrude Stein, copyright © Liveright Publishing Corp., 1971.

Macmillan Publishing Co., Inc. and A. P. Watt Ltd., for permission to quote from *Collected Poems* of William Butler Yeats, copyright © 1928 by Macmillan Publishing Co., Inc., renewed 1956 by Georgie Yeats.

New Directions Publishing Corporation, for permission to quote from *Talking at the Boundaries* by David Antin, copyright © 1974, 1975, 1976 by David Antin; from *A Season in Hell and the Drunken Boat* by Arthur Rimbaud, translated by Louise Varese, copyright © 1945, 1952 by New Directions; from *Splendide Hotel* by Gilbert Sorrentino, copyright © 1973 by Gilbert Sorrentino; from *Collected Earlier Poems* by William Carlos Williams, copyright © 1938 by William Carlos Williams; from *Paterson, Book II* by William Carlos Williams, copyright © 1948 by William Carlos Williams.

New Directions Publishing Corporation and Faber & Faber, Ltd., for permission to quote from *The Cantos* by Ezra Pound, copyright © 1934, 1938 by Ezra Pound; *Personae* by Ezra Pound, copyright © 1926 by Ezra Pound; from *Selected Prose 1909-1965* by Ezra Pound, copyright © 1973 by the Trustees of the Ezra Pound Literary Property Trust.

New Directions Publishing Corporation and Laurence Pollinger, Ltd., for permission to quote from *Imaginations* by William Carlos Williams, copyright © 1920 by The Four Seas Company, copyright © 1923, 1951, 1957 by William Carlos Williams, copyright © 1970 by Florence H. Williams.

New Rivers Press, for permission to quote from *The Book of Rimbaud* by Keith Abbott, copyright © 1977 by Keith Abbott.

Random House Inc./Alfred A. Knopf, Inc., for permission to quote from the *Collected Poems* of Wallace Stevens, copyright © 1954 by Wallace Stevens; from *Collected Poems* of W. H. Auden, copyright © 1976 by Edward Mendelson; from *Portraits and Prayers* by Gertrude Stein, copyright © 1934 by Gertrude Stein; from *Selected Writings of Gertrude Stein,* copyright © 1962 by Random House, Inc.

Viking Penguin, Inc., for permission to quote from *Three Poems* by John Ashbery, copyright © 1970, 1971, 1972 by John Ashbery; from *Self-Portrait in a Convex Mirror* by John Ashbery, copyright © 1972, 1973, 1974, 1975 by John Ashbery; from *Houseboat Days* by John Ashbery, copyright © 1975, 1976 by John Ashbery; from *As We Know* by John Ashbery, copyright © 1979 by John Ashbery.

Wesleyan University Press, for permission to quote from *Hard Freight* by Charles Wright, copyright © 1973 by Charles Wright; from *The Tennis Court Oath* by John Ashbery, copyright © 1957, 1959, 1961, 1962 by John Ashbery.

Wesleyan University Press and Marion Boyars Publishers, Ltd., for permission to quote from *Silence* by John Cage, copyright © 1961 by John Cage; *A Year from Monday,* copyright © 1967 by John Cage; *M, Writings '67-72* by John Cage, copyright © 1973 by John Cage.

The Poetics of Indeterminacy

CHAPTER ONE

Unreal Cities

Rimbaud est le premier poète d'une civilisation non encore apparue.

—René Char

In the reaction of Rimbaud to Baudelaire lies the germ of half the subsequent history of French poetry.

—Charles Tomlinson

. . . la poésie moderne, celle qui part, non de Baudelaire, mais de Rimbaud. . . . détruisait les rapports du langage et ramenait le discours à des stations de mots. . . . La Nature y devient un discontinu d'objets solitaires et terribles, parce qu'ils n'ont que des liaisons virtuelles. . . .

(. . . modern poetry, that which stems not from Baudelaire but from Rimbaud. . . . destroyed relationships in language and reduced discourse to words as static things. . . . In it, Nature becomes a fragmented space, made of objects solitary and terrible, because the links between them are only potential. . . .)

—Roland Barthes

. . . aucune oeuvre particulière n'a déterminé plus que les *Illuminations* l'histoire de la littérature moderne. . . . Rimbaud a découvert le langage dans son (dis)fonctionnement autonome, libéré de ses obligations expressive et représentative, où l'initiative est réelement cédée aux mots. . . .

(. . . no single work has had more influence on the history of modern literature than the *Illuminations*. . . . Rimbaud discovered language in its autonomous (dis)functioning, freed from its obligations to express and to represent, a language in which the initiative is truly surrendered to the words. . . .)

—Tzvetan Todorov[1]

[1] René Char, *Recherche de la base et du sommet* (Paris: Gallimard, Collection "Poésie," 1965), p. 130. Charles Tomlinson, "Rimbaud Today," *Essays in Criticism*, 9 (1959), 94. Roland Barthes, *Le Degré zero de l'écriture* (1953; rpt. Paris: Éditions du Seuil, 1973), p. 39 and cf. p. 34; *Writing Degree Zero*,

I

I BEGIN with four quotations, two of them from contemporary poets, two from literary theorists.

If these statements sound exaggerated or extreme, it is only because we have not yet followed up their implications. The issue is not the relative "greatness" of Rimbaud and Baudelaire. Rather, what Char and Tomlinson, Barthes and Todorov are, in their various ways, telling us is that, when we try to situate the poetry of the present, not only in France where Rimbaud's unsurpassed influence—on Apollinaire and Jacob, Reverdy and Char, the Dada and Surrealist poets—has long been recognized, but in Anglo-America, the Rimbaldian context becomes increasingly important. For Rimbaud was probably the first to write what I shall call here the poetry of indeterminacy. And whereas Baudelaire and Mallarmé point the way to the "High Modernism" of Yeats and Eliot and Auden, Stevens and Frost and Crane, and their Symbolist heirs like Lowell and Berryman, it is Rimbaud who strikes the first note of that "undecidability"[2] we find in Gertrude Stein, in Pound and Williams, as well as in the short prose works of Beckett's later years, an undecidability that has become marked in the poetry of the last decades.

Indeed, the presence of Rimbaud in contemporary poetry is remarkable even in the literal sense. Not only does his work continue to challenge the translator;[3] Rimbaud

---

trans. Annette Lavers and Colin Smith (Boston: Beacon Press, 1970), pp. 49-50. Tzvetan Todorov, "Une Complication de texte: les *Illuminations*," *Poétique*, 34 (April 1978), 252-253. The translation is my own.

[2] For this term, see Tzvetan Todorov, *Symbolisme et intérpretation* (Paris: Éditions du Seuil, 1978), p. 82.

[3] I compare some of the major translations in Chapter Six. Since 1975, two poets have undertaken large-scale translations of Rimbaud's work: Paul Schmidt, *Arthur Rimbaud, Complete Works* (New York: Harper and Row, 1975); and Bertrand Matthieu, *A Season in Hell* (Cambridge, Mass.: Pomegranate Press, 1976), and *Illuminations*, with a foreword by Henry Miller (Brockport, N.Y.: BOA Edition, 1979). Schmidt includes a large selection of letters, arranged chronologically with the appropriate poems.

is also the subject of dozens of homages, whether in the form of poems addressed to or about him, or in the prose poems that deliberately play on the mode of the *Illuminations*. In the former group, we find poems ranging from Charles Wright's carefully wrought imagistic lyric, "Homage to Arthur Rimbaud" (1973), which begins:

Laying our eggs like moths
In the cold cracks of your eyes,
Brushing your hands with our dark wings

—Desperate to attempt
An entrance, to touch that light
Which buoys you like a flame,
That it might warm our own lives. . . .[4]

to the irreverent collaborations of William Burroughs and Gregory Corso, who cut up Rimbaud's "A une raison" and produced two disjointed, fragmentary texts called "Everywhere March Your Head" and "Sons of Yours In."[5] For the Beats, it was, of course, Rimbaud's life rather than his art that was exemplary (his experimentation with drugs, his homosexuality, his hatred of the Establishment, and so on); Ginsberg's Rimbaud is still essentially Henry Miller's.[6]

[4] *Hard Freight* (Middletown, Conn.: Wesleyan University Press, 1973), p. 13. See also Marilyn Hacker, "Letter from Charleville, 1871: Rimbaud to Verlaine," *Columbia University Forum*, Spring 1974, p. 32; Gilbert Sorrentino, "Arthur Rimbaud," *A Dozen Oranges* (Santa Barbara: Black Sparrow Press, 1976), unpaginated; René Char, "Tu as bien fait de partir, Arthur Rimbaud!", in *Fureur et mystère*, ed. Yves Berger (Paris: Gallimard, 1967), p. 212; Helmut Maria Soik, "To Arthur Rimbaud" ("An Arthur Rimbaud"), *Rimbaud under the Steel Helmet* (*Rimbaud unterm Stahlhelm*), bilingual edition, trans. Georg M. Gugelberger and Lydia Perera (Los Angeles: Red Hill Press, 1976), unpaginated.

[5] "Two Cut Ups," *Locus Solus*, II (Summer 1961), 148-151.

[6] See Henry Miller, *The Time of the Assassins, A Study of Rimbaud* (1946; rpt. New York: New Directions, 1962). In the foreword to Bertrand Matthieu's translations of the *Illuminations* (see note 3 above), Miller writes: "There is no doubt in my mind that Rimbaud's life-expanding vision of things has never been more desperately needed than it is today." In "Advice to Youth" (with Robert Duncan), a Writing Class held at Kent State University, 5 April 1971, Allen Ginsberg says:

Nevertheless, even a versified biography like Jack Kerouac's "Rimbaud" shows familiarity with the poetry itself:

—Illuminations! Stuttgart!
Study of Languages!
On foot Rimbaud walks
& looks thru the Alpine
passes into Italy, looking
    for clover bells, rabbits,
    Genie Kingdoms. . . .[7]

The more interesting "homages" are the long prose poems based on the Rimbaldian model: for example, Jack Spicer's *Fake Novel About the Life of Arthur Rimbaud* (1962), Gilbert Sorrentino's *Splendide Hotel* (1973), and Keith Abbott's *Book of Rimbaud* (1977). Of these, Abbott's is the most conventional; his announced aim is to "take images from Rimbaud" and "send them into the trance state." But the resultant dream poems have none of Rimbaud's evocativeness and mystery:

> Inside a long corridor I could see the lean white figure of Rimbaud's mother. For a moment I thought she was a scarecrow but the walls and floors were so dull, not even a glimmer of light along the molding, it was all flat grey, I couldn't imagine the least bit of greenery there. She had her mouth open and periodically I heard a steam whistle, very loud and very full.[8]

> I kept thinking I was in love with Kerouac and I also was in love with somebody else, another cat who looked exactly like Rimbaud. . . . So I immediately transferred the same erotic *schwärmerei*, the same erotic pleasure, to Rimbaud, and then I fell in love with Rimbaud's writing because it was the manifestation of his seed, so to speak. . . .

Ginsberg, *Allen Verbatim, Lectures on Poetry, Politics, Consciousness*, ed. Gordon Ball (New York: McGraw-Hill, 1975), p. 111. See also the selections from Ginsberg's critical prose in *The Poetics of the New American Poetry*, ed. Donald M. Allen and Warren Tallman (New York: Grove Press, 1973), pp. 326-327, 336, 348.

[7] *Yugen*, 6 (1960), 42.

[8] (Cathedral Station: New Rivers Press, 1977), pp. 9, 24.

Spicer's *Fake Novel* is much more original than this. He takes as his starting point the actual events of Rimbaud's life—his birth in Charleville (here called "Charleyville"), his escape to Paris, the "Frank terrors" (the Franco-Prussian War), and the Zanzibar slave trade—and weaves them into a verbal collage in which fact and fantasy collide: the dead-letter office where Rimbaud was ostensibly born is juxtaposed to the streets of Laredo, Gambetta's balloon, and President Buchanan's "letter to Cordell Hull." In both verse and prose passages, Spicer imaginatively reinvents Rimbaud's life and art: "If Rimbaud had died there in the cabbage patch," he remarks at one point, "before we imagined he existed, there would be no history."[9]

A similar play on Rimbaud's fabled life and his enigmatic utterances is found in Sorrentino's *Splendide Hotel.* The origin of this alphabet fantasy in which each of the twenty-six letters generates a separate prose poem, is the sentence from "Après le déluge," "Et le Splendide-Hôtel fut bâti dans le chaos de glaces et de nuit du pôle."[10] Sorrentino's Splendide Hotel becomes a kind of last European resort, closer to Marienbad than to Rimbaud's dream landscape. The prose poems and occasional lyrics interweave allusions to Rimbaud with playful catalogues of persons and places, puns, and reflections on poetry, especially that of Williams. Under the letter "W," Sorrentino writes: "William Carlos Williams was eight years old when Arthur Rimbaud died. It pleases me to see a slender but absolute continuity between the work of the damned Frenchman and the patronized American."[11]

This "slender but absolute continuity" is one I shall take

[9] *A Fake Novel about the Life of Arthur Rimbaud* is part of a longer work called *The Heads of the Town Up to the Aether*; see *The Collected Books of Jack Spicer*, ed. Robin Blaser (Santa Barbara: Black Sparrow Press, 1975), p. 161; and cf. Michael Davidson, "Incarnations of Jack Spicer: *Heads of the Town up to the Aether*," *Boundary 2*, 6 (Fall 1977), 119-125.

[10] Rimbaud, *Oeuvres complètes*, ed. Suzanne Bernard (Paris: Garnier, 1960), p. 253. All further references to Rimbaud are to this edition unless otherwise noted. Subsequently cited as "Rimbaud."

[11] (New York: New Directions, 1973), p. 56.

up later but from a rather different point of view. For my concern is not with the romance of Rimbaud's life, as that life has been understood by later poets, but with those structural and modal inventions that have significantly altered our way of writing and reading poetry. Let me begin with a poem that does not allude to Rimbaud in any direct way but which nevertheless bears his indelible imprint:

These Lacustrine Cities
—John Ashbery

These lacustrine cities grew out of loathing
Into something forgetful, although angry with history.
They are the product of an idea: that man is horrible, for instance,
Though this is only one example.

They emerged until a tower
Controlled the sky, and with artifice dipped back
Into the past for swans and tapering branches,
Burning, until all that hate was transformed into useless love.

Then you are left with an idea of yourself
And the feeling of ascending emptiness of the afternoon
Which must be charged to the embarrassment of others
Who fly by you like beacons.

The night is a sentinel.
Much of your time has been occupied by creative games
Until now, but we have all-inclusive plans for you.
We had thought, for instance, of sending you to the middle of the desert,

To a violent sea, or of having the closeness of the others be air
To you, pressing you back into a startled dream
As sea-breezes greet a child's face.

But the past is already here, and you are nursing some
 private project.

The worst is not over, yet I know
You will be happy here. Because of the logic
Of your situation, which is something no climate can
 outsmart.
Tender and insouciant by turns, you see

You have built a mountain of something,
Thoughtfully pouring all your energy into this single
 monument,
Whose wind is desire starching a petal,
Whose disappointment broke into a rainbow of tears.[12]

Ashbery's poem begins as a mock classroom lecture on the history of lake cities; we are, it seems, to be provided with instances and "example(s)." But as we read on, we rapidly learn that these "lacustrine cities"—cities oddly emerging from lakes like underwater plants or geological deposits—seem to exist nowhere outside the text itself. For how are we to understand cities that have no streets or buildings, no recognizable inhabitants, no traffic—indeed, cities located in a semantic field that also contains desert and mountain, swan and petal? Unlike, say, Blake's London or Baudelaire's Paris or Yeats's Byzantium or even the "Unreal City / Under the brown fog of a winter noon" of Eliot's *Waste Land*, they seem to have no external referent. Suppose, for example, that we take the "lacustrine cities" of the first stanza to represent some sort of defense mechanism, erected by the poet to protect himself from the fluidity of his subconscious, from the terrible awareness "that man is horrible, for instance." In this context, the emergent "tower" of stanza 2 makes sense, but when Ashbery tells us that this tower "dipped back / Into the past for swans and tapering branches," the narrative becomes enigmatic. Why is the poet's carefully conceived "tower"

[12] *Rivers and Mountains* (1966; rpt. New York: The Ecco Press, 1977), p. 9.

arising from lacustrine depths "burning"? And who is the "you" that suddenly appears in stanza 3, or the "we" who want to relegate this "you" to "the middle of the desert" or "to a violent sea"? How does the "I" of stanza 6 know that "You will be happy here"? Is he talking to himself or to someone else? In this context, the phrase "Because of the logic / Of your situation, which is something no climate can outsmart," is particularly ironic because the "situation" has no "logic" whatever. Indeed, the poem blocks all attempts to rationalize its imagery, to make it conform to a coherent pattern.

In Ashbery's verbal landscape, fragmented images appear one by one—cities, sky, swans, tapering branches, violent sea, desert, mountain—without coalescing into a symbolic network. "These Lacustrine Cities" is framed as a series of synecdoches, but Ashbery's are not, in the words of Wallace Stevens' title, "Parts of a World." For there seems to be no world, no whole to which these parts may be said to belong. Totality is absent. Thus the "others" of stanza 3 who "fly by you like beacons" are juxtaposed to the "night" which is a "sentinel." "Beacons" and "sentinels" are related by contiguity but there is a gap between "others" and the "night." Such disjunctive metonymic relations converge to create a peculiar surface tension.

The poem's syntax contributes to this effect. Ashbery's sentences are often simple subject-predicate units ("The night is a sentinel"; "But the past is already here"), sentences whose "normal" construction makes the unrelatedness of the words placed in nominative or predicative slots all the more puzzling. What does it mean to say that "wind is a desire starching a petal"? In what sense can "the closeness of the others be air / To you"? And how are we to interpret such repeated conjunctions as "although," "for instance," "until," "then," "but," and "yet"—connectives that create expectations of causality, of relatedness that the narrative never fulfills. Reading Ashbery's text is thus rather like overhearing a conversation in which one catches an occasional word or phrase but cannot make out what the speakers are talking about.

And yet one does keep listening. For the special pleasure of reading a poem like "These Lacustrine Cities" is that disclosure of some special meaning seems perpetually imminent. Ashbery's "open field of narrative possibilities" (his phrase for Gertrude Stein's discourse) does have certain referential signposts: a painful childhood memory ("they" having "all-inclusive plans for you"), the source of creative power (the tower controlling the sky and "with artifice dipping back into the past"), an abortive love affair ("tender and insouciant by turns"). But such potential plots are rather like water spouts, rising to the surface only to dissipate again. As readers, we are thus left in a state of expectancy: just at the point where revelation might occur, the curtain suddenly comes down, "pressing you back," as Ashbery puts it, "into a startled dream."

What is the relationship of such an "enigma text"[13] to the poetry of High Modernism? How, for instance, do Ashbery's mysterious "lacustrine cities" relate to Eliot's "Unreal City"? Consider the following passage from *The Waste Land*:

> Unreal City
> Under the brown fog of a winter noon
> Mr. Eugenides, the Smyrna merchant
> Unshaven, with a pocket full of currants
> C.i.f. London: documents at sight,
> Asked me in demotic French
> To luncheon at the Cannon Street Hotel
> Followed by a weekend at the Metropole.[14]

Eliot's Unreal City is, first and foremost, a very real fog-bound London, whose inhabitants we have already met in the corresponding passage from "The Burial of the Dead," where the protagonist has a vision of "A crowd" flowing "over London Bridge, so many." We can identify the Cannon Street Hotel as a place where commercial travelers stay in the City, and the Metropole was, in Eliot's day, one of

[13] I take this phrase from Roger Cardinal, "Enigma," *20th Century Studies*: The Limits of Comprehension, 12 (December 1974), 42-62.

[14] *Collected Poems 1919-1962* (New York: Harcourt Brace, 1970), p. 61. All further references are to this edition.

the leading hotels in Brighton. It is thus immediately evident that the narrator is being propositioned by a Mr. Eugenides, who deals in currants brought "Carriage and insurance free to London" (C.i.f.).[15] This is the sort of identification we cannot make in the case of the Ashbery poem where the landscape of the "lacustrine cities" is associated, not with real hotels, city bridges, and business deals, but with such contradictory images as deserts and violent seas.

Ashbery's people are shadowy and indefinable. There may be a number of characters in his poem; on the other hand, "I," "we," and "you" may well refer to the poet himself. By contrast, Mr. Eugenides the Smyrna merchant is a figure of multiple symbolic associations. He has already been introduced in "The Burial of the Dead" as "the one-eyed merchant" of Madame Sosostris' Tarot pack; he reappears, moreover, in "Death by Water" as Phlebas the Phoenician. In ancient times, Phoenician and Syrian merchants were among those who spread the mystery cults throughout the Roman Empire; these mystery cults were, as Jessie Weston tells us, later associated with the Holy Grail. The sacred mystery of which Mr. Eugenides is the bearer, however, is only the shrivelled grape in the form of "currants," and his proposition to the narrator is thus a travesty of the Fisher King's invitation to the quester outside the Grail Castle. As the one-eyed man of the Tarot card, the merchant also symbolizes death or winter: the private monster whom the primitive hero fights in his lair.

Eliot's symbolism is always complex, and we can associate Mr. Eugenides not only with the debasement of the ancient mystery cults—and hence of religion in general—but also with the deracination of the twentieth-century city dweller. Like Hakagawa and Madame de Tornquist in the earlier "Gerontion," the Smyrna merchant is a sinister cosmopolite: he speaks "demotic" French rather than his native

[15] For this and related background information, see Grover Smith, *T. S. Eliot's Poetry and Plays, A Study of Sources and Meaning* (Chicago: University of Chicago Press, 1956), pp. 87-89.

language and operates out of London. His name, moreover, is a play on "Eugenics," a science Eliot found especially distasteful.[16] The one-eyedness of the merchant on the Tarot card also symbolizes blindness, and most of the inhabitants of the Waste Land are, of course, blind in one form or another. In this context, the invitation to luncheon can be read as a debased food ritual of the sort we find throughout Eliot's poetry, beginning with Prufrock's "taking of a toast and tea," and the Black Mass of "Gerontion," in which Christ the Tiger is "eaten . . . divided . . . drunk / Among whispers."[17] The invitation is, moreover, made against the background of "the brown fog of a winter noon," with its connotations of decay and the death of the spirit.

In submitting this eight-line passage to what one might call a "Norton Anthology reading," I am under no illusion that such explication constitutes criticism. But I do believe that, in the case of a poem like *The Waste Land*, critical inquiry can begin only after these points on the map have been established. For, unlike "These Lacustrine Cities," where tower, swan, and petal have no definable referents, *The Waste Land* has, despite its temporal and spatial dislocations and its collage form, a perfectly coherent symbolic structure.

Consider the relationship of the "Mr. Eugenides" scene to another City passage, fifty lines later in "The Fire Sermon":

> 'This music crept by me upon the waters'
> Along the Strand, up Queen Victoria Street.
> O City city, I can sometimes hear
> Beside a public bar in Lower Thames Street,
> The pleasant whining of a mandoline

[16] See Eliot, *After Strange Gods* (London: Faber and Faber, 1934), pp. 69-71.

[17] On the symbolism of the Eucharist in its debased version as meaningless food ritual, see Genesius Jones, *Approach to the Purpose: The Poetry of T. S. Eliot* (New York: Barnes and Noble, 1965), pp. 101-108.

And a clatter and a chatter from within
Where fishmen lounge at noon: where the walls
Of Magnus Martyr hold
Inexplicable splendour of Ionian white and gold.
(pp. 62-63)

Again Eliot grounds his vision firmly in the realities of London geography: the Strand, Queen Victoria Street, Lower Thames Street, Magnus Martyr. As the protagonist walks through downtown London, he suddenly recalls Ferdinand's words from *The Tempest* (" 'This music crept by me upon the waters' "), words that point to the sea-change central to the play and, by analogy, to the poet's vision of what the "Unreal City" might be. For here is one of the speaker's rare glimpses of another better world, a world not debased by possible assignations with a Mr. Eugenides. In this connection, the symbolic value of Magnus Martyr is important. Eliot's own note tells us that this church has "one of the finest among [Christopher] Wren's interiors." Situated at the foot of London Bridge, St. Magnus Martyr was rebuilt after the Great Fire destroyed the one for parishioners dwelling on the bridge itself. Known as "St. Magnus ad pontem," it was especially the fishmen's church. So the fishmen who lounge at noon in the neighboring bar, listening to the pleasant whining of a mandoline, are symbolically linked both to the Fisher King of ancient myth and to Christ.

Even if we did not know the history of Magnus Martyr, the name immediately reminds us of the martyrdom of Christ, and its "Ionian white and gold" (the allusion is both to the liturgy and to classical Greece) is symbolically opposed to the decayed London of brown fog and winter in which the speaker is propositioned by the unsavory Smyrna merchant. Indeed, a whole network of symbolic links now manifests itself. The poem opposes the one-eyed merchant to the fishmen, his demotic French to the pleasant whining of a mandoline and to Ferdinand's water music, his invitation to luncheon to the momentary vision, near the end of the poem, of true communion:

Damyata: The boat responded
Gaily, to the hand expert with sail and oar
The sea was calm, your heart would have responded
Gaily, when invited, beating obedient
To controlling hands

(p. 69)

These are polarities that all readers of *The Waste Land* have recognized. No one would argue, for instance, that brown is Eliot's color for spiritual renewal—that to be "under the brown fog" is a good thing—or that "Ionian white and gold" is to be feared and avoided. Again, it is quite clear that the "pleasant whining of a mandoline," like the *Parsifal* reference earlier in "The Fire Sermon" ("*Et O ces voix d'enfants, chantant dans la coupole!*") is to be preferred to the "Jug Jug" of the nightingale or the "murmur of maternal lamentation" of the "hooded hordes" in "What the Thunder Said." Again, whether or not Eliot himself had homosexual leanings, there can be little doubt that Mr. Eugenides' proposition is to be regarded as an instance of debased sex, along with Lil's attempted abortions, the typist's mechanical lovemaking, and the mindless couplings the three Thames Daughters recall. Eliot's context is so carefully established that when we come to the line

Burning burning burning burning

we can be certain, whether we relate these words primarily to the fires of lust ("To Carthage then I came") or to the fire of purgation (the Buddha's sermon) or to the conflagration of London, that the reference is not to food burning on the kitchen stove. This is again a certainty we do not have in reading a poem like "These Lacustrine Cities," where the burning tower is an arresting but unanchored image, whose evocations are indeterminate. For although Ashbery's references to a burning tower and swans immediately recall "The broken wall, the burning roof and tower" of Yeats's "Leda and the Swan," the connection between the two texts is left suspended. Moreover, we cannot determine the meaning of Ashbery's image by going to his other poems, whereas the "burning" of "The Fire Sermon" clearly points ahead to Arnaut Daniel's "foco que gli affina" in the final lines of *The Waste Land*, as well as to the purgatorial fires of "Little Gidding."

What makes *The Waste Land* such a thickly textured poem is that the symbolic threads are woven and designed so intricately that the whole becomes a reverberating echo chamber of meanings. The "Unreal City" passage discussed above points in many directions. The opening phrase picks up the "Unreal City" motif from the London Bridge sequence in Part I. The "brown fog of a winter noon" (in the earlier passage, a "winter dawn") is the persistent climate of *The Waste Land*; nature in this poem still wears the colors of the spirit. Mr. Eugenides is related, along the axis of metaphor or substitution,[18] to all the other sinister charlatans in the poem, just as every woman in *The Waste Land* is a version of "Belladonna, the Lady of the Rocks / the Lady of Situations." Yet the merchant's Tarot card is closely linked to that of the "drowned Phoenician sailor," which is the protagonist's own card, and so when Phlebas the Phoenician undergoes "Death by Water" in Part IV, the merchant's fate is linked to the narrator's own as well as to the fate of the "hypocrite lecteur":

[18] I am referring to Roman Jakobson's famous distinction between metaphor and metonymy, the axis of selection and the axis of combination, in "Two Aspects of Language and Two Types of Aphasic Disturbances," *Fundamentals of Language* (1956); rpt. in *Selected Writings of Roman Jakobson*, II: *Word and Language* (The Hague, Mouton & Co., 1971), pp. 239-259. The distinction between the two axes was first made by Saussure in the classic *Cours de linguistique générale* (1916); Jakobson's formulation has been further refined by Levi-Strauss, Barthes, and Lacan: see Elmar Holenstein, *Roman Jakobson's Approach to Language* (Bloomington: Indiana University Press, 1976), pp. 137-52; David Lodge, *The Modes of Modern Writing: Metaphor, Metonymy, and the Typology of Modern Literature* (London: Edward Arnold, 1977), pp. 73-124.

O you who turn the wheel and look to windward,
Consider Phlebas, who was once handsome and tall as
 you.

(p. 65)

Of *The Waste Land*, one might therefore say, as Eliot was to put it in "Burnt Norton," "Footfalls echo down the memory." Indeed, the echoes are so richly orchestrated that images and allusions are constantly intensified. When we come, for example, to the climactic line in Part V: "I sat fishing with the arid plain behind me," we have a complex sense of what it means to "fish" in such circumstances, and the "arid plain" brings up memories of all the places we have traveled through in order to get where we are: the "stony rubbish" and "dead tree that gives no shelter" of Ezekiel's Valley of Dry Bones (Part I), the "brown land" of "The Fire Sermon" which "The wind / Crosses . . . unheard," and the "endless plains" of "cracked earth / Ringed by the flat horizon only" of "What the Thunder Said." However difficult it may be to decode this complex poem, the relationship of the word to its referents, of signifier to signified, remains essentially intact.[19] It is, I shall argue

[19] I am aware that here I take issue with Derridean theory. "Indeterminacy," as I use that term in this book, is taken to be the quality of particular art works in a particular period of history rather than as the central characteristic of all texts at all times. Thus I regard Derrida's own *Glas* (Éditions Galilée, 1974), with its intricate "dédoublement du moi" into two columns—"Hegel" and "Genet"—as a fascinating example of a literary text belonging to "The Other Tradition"; indeed, it could profitably be compared to Ashbery's double-column "Litany," a poem I discuss in Chapter Seven. But to apply what Derrida himself calls the "hallucinatory" *dialectique-galactique* of a work like *Glas* to poetry in general is an enterprise of a very different kind. This is not the place to take up the question of whether or not the sign can bring forth the presence of the signified or whether it is merely the *trace* of that other which is forever absent. I refer the reader to three valuable recent critiques of Deconstructionist theory: Charles Altieri, "The Hermeneutics of Literary Indeterminacy: A Dissent from the New Orthodoxy," *New Literary History*, 10 (Autumn 1978), 71-99; James S. Hans, "Derrida and Freeplay," *Modern Language Notes*, 94 (May 1979), 809-826; and Maria Ruegg, "The End(s)

later, the undermining of precisely this relationship that characterizes the poetry of Rimbaud and his heirs. For what happens in Pound's *Cantos*, as in Stein's *Tender Buttons* or Williams' *Spring and All* or Beckett's *How It Is* or John Cage's *Silence*, is that the symbolic evocations generated by words on the page are no longer grounded in a coherent discourse, so that it becomes impossible to decide which of these associations are relevant and which are not. This is the "undecidability" of the text I spoke of earlier.

But before I turn to the larger question of the relationship of such *undecidability* or indeterminacy to Symbolist discourse, let us look at the work of two very different Modernist poets whose legacy to Ashbery and to his fellow-poets is generally considered important: Wallace Stevens and W. H. Auden. Here is Part II of Stevens' late great poem, "The Auroras of Autumn" (1947):

Farewell to an idea . . . A cabin stands,
Deserted, on a beach. It is white,
As by a custom or according to

An ancestral theme or as a consequence
Of an infinite course. The flowers against the wall
Are white, a little dried, a kind of mark

Reminding, trying to remind, of a white
That was different, something else, last year
Or before, not the white of an aging afternoon,

---

of French Style: Structuralism and Post-Structuralism in the American Context," *Criticism*, 21 (Summer 1979), 189-216. Hans is especially persuasive in arguing that, even if the Deconstructionists are right about the nature of language, they have nevertheless created a critical climate in which all texts look exactly alike. Derridean readings of specific texts, in other words, have a way of obscuring those essential differences (as opposed to "*différance*") that must, after all, concern those of us who are still interested in the relationships of particular literary works to each other. Moreover, as Maria Ruegg argues, the "devaluation of values" of Post-Structuralism, the insistence that the text "whitewashes itself—by undecidably affirming and negating its own values" (p. 216), raises some formidable problems for Derridean theory.

Whether fresher or duller, whether of winter cloud
Or of winter sky, from horizon to horizon.
The wind is blowing the sand across the floor.

Here, being visible is being white,
Is being of the solid of white, the accomplishment
Of an extremist in an exercise . . .

The season changes. A cold wind chills the beach.
The long lines of it grow longer, emptier,
A darkness gathers though it does not fall

And the whiteness grows less vivid on the wall.
The man who is walking turns blankly on the sand.
He observes how the north is always enlarging the
change,

With its frigid brilliances, its blue-red sweeps
And gusts of great enkindlings, its polar green,
The color of ice and fire and solitude.[20]

Stevens' poetic landscape is, on the face of it, far removed from Eliot's reverberating echo chamber. Gone are the references to symbolic figures like Mr. Eugenides and symbolic places like the Church of Magnus Martyr. Stevens, as has been often remarked, rejects the belief in a transcendent realm above and beyond what man can see, although he retains Baudelaire's "soif insatiable" for it.[21] He would never, for instance, have endorsed Yeats's famous statement that "A symbol is the only possible expression of some invisible essence, a transparent lamp around a spiritual flame," or "a hand pointing the way into some divine labyrinth."[22] For Stevens, being must ultimately re-

[20] *The Palm at the End of the Mind, Selected Poems and a Play*, ed. Holly Stevens (New York: Alfred A. Knopf, 1971), p. 308. All subsequent references are to this edition.

[21] See Baudelaire, *Oeuvres complètes*, ed. Y. G. Le Dantec et revisée par Claude Pichois (Paris: Bibliothèque de la Pléiade, 1968), p. 686. Subsequently cited as Baudelaire, OC.

[22] "William Blake and His Illustrations to *The Divine Comedy*" (1924), in *Essays and Introductions* (New York: Macmillan, 1961), pp. 116-117.

side, not in "some divine labyrinth" beyond the sense world, but only here and now, within "things as they are."[23]

But if Stevens rejects one form of Romantic dualism, that between natural and supernatural, the "real" and the transcendent worlds, he remains committed to the other, perhaps more central Romantic and Symbolist dualism between the "I" and the other, self and world. "The dialogue between subject and object," writes Hillis Miller, "is Stevens' central theme."[24] And inevitably, if the poet regards the landscape as external to himself, he reads meanings into it.

Generically, Part II of "The Auroras" is a dirge for the powers of the imagination. Helen Vendler writes:

> Stevens' tendency in the first elegiac canto is to match unequivocal notations of skeletal whiteness against extremely conjectural modifiers of that whiteness: his mind, in other words, must admit the phenomenon, but will not for a long time admit its significance. Instead, it casts around for ways of explaining this whiteness, or ways of softening its harshness.[25]

The minimal landscape the poet tries to evade is one of total bareness: the deserted white cabin on the empty beach, the dried white flowers against the wall, the wind that blows sand across the floor. Stevens cannot avoid this autumnal truth, but, having confronted it "blankly" in all its desolation, he turns to the night sky and observes "how the north is always enlarging the change," witnessing, for a brief moment, the "blue-red sweeps" and "great enkindlings" of the Northern Lights. This vision is, as Vendler notes, "exhilarating," but, as she rightly concludes, "the celestial aurora and the chilling earthly wind . . . are two

[23] See J. Hillis Miller, "Wallace Stevens," in *Poets of Reality, Six Twentieth-Century Writers* (1965; rpt. New York: Atheneum, 1969), pp. 217-284, esp. pp. 221, 228.

[24] *Poets of Reality*, p. 224.

[25] *On Extended Wings, Wallace Stevens' Longer Poems* (Cambridge, Mass.: Harvard University Press, 1969), p. 252.

manifestations of the same force. The identification is first made syntactically: 'The wind is blowing' and 'the north is enlarging the change'. . . . Later the parallel is made metaphorically, as Stevens borrows the vocabulary of wind in composing his auroras of 'sweeps' and 'gusts'."[26]

Such reconciliation of seeming opposites is squarely within the Romantic tradition. To argue, as have a number of Derridean critics, that "Farewell to an idea" is "a farewell to the hierarchical metaphysics of the origin and the center,"[27] is, I think, wishful thinking. Michael T. Beehler writes: "The trope of the sourceless auroral lights, of a light that has no central origin of radiation but which is always already diffused and radiated, undoes the classical trope of the sun as source and divine center of light and truth."[28] Against this, we might consult the dictionary:

> *aurora borealis.* A radiant emission from the upper atmosphere that occurs sporadically over the middle and high latitudes of both hemispheres in the form of luminous bands, streamers, or the like, caused by the bombardment of the atmosphere with charged solar particles that are being guided along the earth's magnetic lines of force. (*Random House*)

The actual dependency of the auroras on the sun provides us with a nice parable. Stevens' poem may well be *about* absence and decentering (although that theme is, as

[26] Vendler, *On Extended Wings*, p. 255. Cf. Harold Bloom, *Wallace Stevens, The Poems of our Climate* (Ithaca and London: Cornell University Press, 1977), pp. 262-265.

[27] Michael T. Beehler, "Inversion/Subversion: Strategy in Stevens' 'The Auroras of Autumn'," *Genre*, 11, no. 4 (Winter 1978), 632. Cf. Joseph N. Riddel, "Interpreting Stevens: An Essay on Poetry and Thinking," *Boundary 2*, 1 (Fall 1972), 79-95; and Riddel, "Bloom—A Commentary—Stevens," *The Wallace Stevens Journal*, 1 (Fall/Winter 1977), 111-119.

[28] Beehler, *Genre*, 634; cf. Michel Benamou, *L'Oeuvre→Monde de Wallace Stevens*, diss. Paris, 1973 (Lille: Reproduction des Thèses, 1973), pp. 348-349; Joseph N. Riddel, *Boundary 2*, 90: "The 'flaring lights' of 'Auroras' . . . are centerless like the ever-receding 'ideas' of the poem to which the old poet is repeatedly saying 'Farewell.' "

Vendler shows, qualified in complex ways), but there is a big difference between the reference to indeterminacy and the creation of indeterminate forms. Indeed, "Farewell to an idea," as I read it, is almost a textbook exemplar of Eliot's Objective Correlative:

> The only way of expressing emotion in the form of art is by finding "an objective correlative"; in other words, a set of objects, a situation, a chain of events which shall be the formula of that *particular* emotion. . . .[29]

In this case, the images of whiteness and bareness—empty cabin, deserted beach, dried flowers, winter cloud and winter sky, cold wind blowing sand across the floor and chilling the beach—become the symbolic embodiments of Stevens' emotional state, the sense of inner desolation that comes upon a man in his autumn years when he has said "Farewell to an idea." Again, the "blue-red sweeps / and gusts of great enkindlings," as they are perceived in the final tercet of the canto, are clearly symbolic of momentary enlightenment, a spiritual renewal when the mind once again perceives the world as able to manifest color: "polar green, / The color of fire and ice." But the color is also that of "solitude" just as the "brilliances" are "frigid," and so the epiphany has an ambiguous cast.

The landscape of "The Auroras of Autumn" is thus the externalization of the poet's psyche; its configurations and equivocations point always to his interiority. We are so accustomed to such Symbolist landscapes in Romantic and Modernist poetry that we tend to forget that there was a time when poetry did not function in this way, and that, at least since the 1910s, Anglo-American poetry has had a counter-tradition that has held up the formula, most succinctly stated by Beckett in *Watt*: "No symbols where none intended."[30] Consider the opening of Beckett's short prose piece called "Ping":

[29] "Hamlet," *Selected Essays* (London: Faber and Faber, 1953), p. 145.
[30] "Addenda," *Watt* (1953; rpt. New York: Grove Press, 1977), p. 254.

> All known all white bare white body fixed one yard legs joined like sewn. Light heat white floor one square yard never seen. White walls one yard by two white ceiling one square yard never seen. Bare white body fixed only the eyes only just. Traces blurs light grey almost white on white. Hands hanging palms front white feet heels together right angle. Light heat white planes shining white bare body fixed ping fixed elsewhere.[31]

Beckett's white-on-white composition superficially resembles Stevens'. But here words like "white" and "bare," which have specific connotations in Stevens' text, have no definable meaning. Their value is compositional rather than referential, and the focus shifts from signification to the play of signifiers. In Beckett's later texts, the referent becomes increasingly inaccessible. Indeterminacy, in works like "Ping," is not thematic motif; it exists in the very fabric of the discourse. Seen from this viewpoint, "These Lacustrine Cities" is perhaps closer to Beckett than it is to Stevens.

W. H. Auden gives us yet another version of Symbolist poetic. "Lakes," one of the *Bucolics* Auden wrote in the early 50s, may well have been Ashbery's model when he wrote "These Lacustrine Cities." It begins:

> A lake allows an average father, walking slowly,
>   To circumvent it in an afternoon,
> And any healthy mother to halloo the children
>   Back to her bedtime from their games across:
> (Anything bigger than that, like Michigan or Baikal,
>   Though potable, is an 'estranging sea').
>
> Lake-folk require no fiend to keep them on their toes;
>   They leave aggression to ill-bred romantics
> Who duel with their shadows over blasted heaths:
>   A month in a lacustrine atmosphere

[31] "Ping," *First Love and Other Shorts* (New York: Grove Press, 1974), p. 966. In its French version, "Bing," this text was published in 1966 by Éditions de Minuit (Paris).

Would find the fluvial rivals waltzing not exchanging
  The rhyming insults of their great-great-uncles.

No wonder Christendom did not get really started
  Till, scarred by torture, white from caves and jails,
Her pensive chiefs converged on the Ascanian Lake
  And by that stork-infested shore invented
The life of Godhead, making catholic the figure
  Of three small fishes in a triangle.

Sly Foreign Ministers should always meet beside one,
  For, whether they walk widdershins or deasil,
The path will yoke their shoulders to one liquid centre
  Like two old donkeys pumping as they plod;
Such physical compassion may not guarantee
  A marriage for their armies, but it helps.[32]

Auden's strategy in "Lakes" is to assemble a set of symbolic properties and then to deflate the whole symbol-making process. To read meanings into the landscape is, he implies, a natural human tendency, but it will not do to take the process too seriously. For the judgments one makes about natural phenomena and the social attitudes that surround them have a way of backfiring and implicating the judge. Such comic distancing from the objects to be contemplated allies Auden to Ashbery, who can similarly say of his "lacustrine cities" (perhaps an echo of Auden's "lacustrine atmosphere"): "They are the product of an idea: that man is horrible, for instance, / Though this is only one example."

Auden's witty *paysage moralisé* takes its starting point from the simple fact that a lake is an enclosed, circumscribed "liquid centre." Like Eliot, Auden begins with the literal, but his literal references are more abstract and conceptual. He does not envision a particular lake that then becomes an objective correlative of a particular set of emotions, as does Stevens in his image of the empty white cabin on the

[32] *Collected Poems*, ed. Edward Mendelson (New York: Random House, 1976), p. 430.

deserted beach. Rather, he plays upon the possible human qualities that lakes call to mind: domesticity (the ease and safety of family life on the lakefront); non-aggression ("fluvial rivals" turn from thoughts of duelling to the waltz); good fellowship (the first ecumenical council of churches, at which Arianism was decreed heretical, was held on the "Ascanian Lake" at Nicaea); and diplomacy (lakes are the ideal setting for peace talks). It all sounds reassuring and pleasant: lakes symbolize such things as decency, goodness, safety, family happiness—the ability to control one's destiny.

But as the poem unfolds stanza by stanza, both poet and reader begin to have second thoughts. Modesty is perhaps just another word for complacency. Lake-dwellers start to take themselves too seriously; even the drowning man flatters himself that his death must have been fated. Again, the circumscribed existence associated with lakes breeds a curious defensiveness: lake-lovers want their Edenic retreats all to themselves:

> I'm sorry;
> Why should I give Lake Eden to the Nation
> Just because every mortal Jack and Jill has been
> The genius of some amniotic mere?

Too much exposure to a "lacustrine atmosphere" makes one a bit stuffy and provincial. Here is Auden's final stanza:

> It is unlikely I shall ever keep a swan
> Or build a tower on any small tombolo,
> But that's not going to stop me wondering what sort
> Of lake I would decide on if I should.
> Moraine, pot, oxbow, glint, sink, crater, piedmont,
> dimple . . . ?
> Just reeling off their names is ever so comfy.

Swan and tower,[33] images that reappear in "These Lacustrine Cities" in the context of dream, here represent the

[33] An interesting comparison could be made between Auden's treatment of these images and that of Yeats, for whom swan and tower are, of

comic fantasy of the would-be owner of lakes, who contemplates settling in on a sandbar (tombolo) and "keeping" swans much as one keeps chickens down on the farm. The whole notion of such a safe paradisal retreat is, Auden implies, mere illusion. And so the catalogue of "lake-types"—a false catalogue because the items presented seriatim are not parallel, some referring to shape ("oxbow," "sink," "dimple"), some to geological formation ("moraine," "crater"), some to appearance ("glint"), and some to setting ("piedmont")—is purposely absurd. "Reeling off their names is ever so comfy" because, in the end, the poet has become the victim of his own account of "lakes"; he seems to have absorbed their impulse toward smugness and caution. To settle for such charming but undemanding forms of nature is to take the coward's path. And a very "comfy" path it is.

What starts as a series of casual ruminations on a certain character type thus turns out to be a meditation on what Stevens calls, in one of his cryptic titles, "How to Live. What to Do." Auden opts for the "estranging sea" rather than the "potable" lake; he regards struggle as valuable. But because "a poem is a rite,"[34] it will not do to say these things directly. A few years after writing "Lakes," Auden told an audience at Oxford, where he had just been appointed to the Poetry Chair:

> . . . it is from the sacred encounters of his imagination that a poet's impulse to write a poem arises. Thanks to the language, he need not name them directly unless he wishes; he can describe one in terms of another and translate those that are private or irrational or socially unacceptable into such as are acceptable to reason and society.[35]

---

course, central symbols. Quite possibly, Auden's use of these images may be a tongue-in-cheek allusion to Yeats's emblem-making powers.

[34] "Making, Knowing and Judging" (1956), in *The Dyer's Hand and Other Essays* (1962; rpt. New York: Vintage Books, 1968), p. 58.

[35] "Making, Knowing and Judging," p. 59.

Here Auden, who has the reputation of making much more modest claims for poetry than, say, Yeats or Eliot,[36] reveals himself to be surprisingly close to their common precursor, Baudelaire:

> Tout l'univers visible n'est qu'un magasin d'images et de signes auxquels l'imagination donnera une place et une valeur relative; c'est une espèce de pâture que l'imagination doit digérer et transformer.

> (The whole visible universe is but a storehouse of images and signs to which the imagination will give a relative place and value; it is a sort of fodder which the imagination must digest or transform.)[37]

For Auden, the act of writing poetry is a kind of inspired translation, a rendering of the "irrational," ineffable, incommensurable through the concretion of the symbol. For only by means of the symbol are the "sacred encounters of [the poet's] imagination" made accessible. Auden's is still essentially the poetic of Baudelaire and of the Romantics before him; its emphasis is on organic unity, coherence, indirection, multiplicity of meanings.[38] As Tzvetan Todo-

[36] See Richard Ellmann, *Eminent Domain: Yeats among Wilde, Joyce, Pound, Eliot, and Auden* (New York: Oxford, 1967), pp. 97-126.

[37] "Salon de 1859," OC, p. 1044. My translation.

[38] The best single discussion of the gradual evolution of a Symbolist aesthetic in the nineteenth century is Tzvetan Todorov's "La Crise Romantique," *Théories du symbole* (Paris: Editions du Seuil, 1977), pp. 179-260. In taking as his exemplar the German theorist, Karl-Philip Moritz, Todorov is able to trace the origin and development of such criteria as "organic unity," "totality," "coherence," and so on; all these, he shows, are subsumed under the single word "Symbol." This historical treatment of Symbolism is supplemented by the more practical applications found in Todorov's *Symbolisme et interprétation* (1978)—see note 2 above.

Among the countless treatments of Symbolism, those that have been especially helpful to me are listed below in chronological order:

Marcel Raymond, *From Baudelaire to Surrealism*, trans. from the French (1933; rpt. London: University Paperbacks, 1970), esp. pp. 1-14.

Hugo Friedrich, *The Structure of Modern Poetry*, trans. Joachim Neugroschel (1956; Evanston: Northwestern University Press, 1974), esp. pp. 3-38.

rov puts it: "La vérité existe; seulement la voie y conduisant est difficile à suivre" ("Truth exists; only the path leading to it is difficult to follow").[39] In this context, Rimbaud's obstinate insistence that in his poetry, "J'ai voulu dire ce que ça dit, littéralement et dans tous les sens"[40] strikes a very different note. It is this difference to which I now turn.

II

In an interesting essay called "Enigma," Roger Cardinal outlines a three-stage cycle which poetry has undergone in the last 150 years:

Anna Balakian, *The Symbolist Movement, A Critical Appraisal* (New York: Random House, 1967).

Walter Hinderer, "Theory, Conception and Interpretation of the Symbol," in *Perspectives in Literary Symbolism*, ed. Joseph Strelka, Yearbook of Comparative Criticism, I (University Park: Pennsylvania State University Press, 1968), 83-127.

René Wellek, "The Term and Concept of Symbolism in Literary History," *Discriminations, Further Concepts of Criticism* (New Haven: Yale University Press, 1970), pp. 90-121.

Donald Davie, "Pound and Eliot: a distinction," in *Eliot in Perspective, A Symposium*, ed. Graham Martin (New York: Humanities Press, 1970), 62-82.

Hugh Kenner, *The Pound Era* (Berkeley and Los Angeles: University of California Press, 1971), esp. pp. 121-144.

Charles Altieri, "From Symbolist Thought to Immanence: The Ground of Postmodern American Poetics," *Boundary 2*, i (Spring 1973), 605-641; and, in somewhat different form, Chapter I, "Modern and Postmodern: Symbolist and Immanentist Modes of Poetic Thought," *Enlarging the Temple* (Lewisburg: Bucknell University Press, 1979).

Michael Riffaterre, *Semiotics of Poetry* (Bloomington: Indiana University Press, 1978), esp. pp. 1-22.

J. Hillis Miller's *Poets of Reality* and David Lodge's *The Modes of Modern Writing* (see notes 18, 23, above) also belong on this short list.

[39] *Symbolisme et interprétation*, p. 78. All translations from Todorov are mine.

[40] "Paroles attribués à Rimbaud," in Rimbaud, *Oeuvres complètes*, ed. Roland de Renéville et Jules Mouquet (Paris: Bibliothèque de la Pleiade, 1946), p. xxvii. According to Paterne Berrichon, this was Rimbaud's reply to his mother when she asked him, at Roches in 1873, what the *Saison en enfer* meant.

> Firstly, art finds itself becoming mysterious because it begins to treat of mysteries. Secondly, it deliberately chooses to be mysterious, because the mysteries of which it treats need to be kept from the profane. Lastly, art is mysterious because its capacity to attract attention depends precisely upon its sustaining an air of mystery. Now the first stage of such a cycle must be dated from the period of early Romanticism. . . . The mysteriousness of a work like [Novalis'] *Hymnen an die Nacht* is then a function of the mysteriousness of its subject matter. At the second stage in our imagined cycle, the mystery invoked in the work of art is deepened by artistic procedures designed to make access into the work difficult. The difficulty of Mallarmé's sonnets is then not a question of their subject-matter . . . but of their being clothed in 'une ombre exprès' that veils any clear meaning that might otherwise peep through. Our pleasure in such works has to do with our enjoyment in glimpsing meanings below the surface. . . .[41]

This is the end of the second stage. In our own time, Cardinal posits, the concern for the "meanings below the surface" has given way to increasing interest in the play of the surface itself. "At the final stage of our cycle, a . . . sensibility may be said to emerge that is prepared to occupy itself with the gestures of mystery and defer clarification of the content of that mystery." Such a "work of enigma" is "poised between sense and nonsense"; it is "a *revelation* which is equally a *re-veiling*" (p. 45). A similar, and perhaps clearer, distinction between these two stages is made by James McFarlane, in a comment on Yeats's famous lines: "Things fall apart; the centre cannot hold, / Mere anarchy is loosed upon the world":

> The very vocabulary of chaos—disintegration, fragmentation, dislocation—implies a breaking away or a breaking apart. But the defining thing in the Modernist mode is not so much that things fall *apart* but that they fall

[41] "Enigma," *20th Century Studies*, p. 44.

> *together* (recalling appropriately the derivation of "symbol" from *symballein,* to throw together). In Modernism, the centre is seen exerting not a centrifugal but a centripetal force; and the consequence is not disintegration but (as it were) superintegration.[42]

It is thus when "things" refuse to "fall together," that the "superintegration" of Symbolism breaks down and a new mode evolves.

Such a three-stage cycle is, of course, a simplified model of historical change but it is helpful in numerous ways. For one thing, it regards "the New Poetry" less as the total revolution its proponents sometimes claim it to be,[43] than as the natural outcome of a revolution that occurred much earlier, at the turn of the nineteenth century. On the other hand, both Cardinal and McFarlane insist that there *is* a real difference between Modern or Symbolist poetry (stage two of the cycle) and what is called, for want of a better term, the "postmodernism" of the third stage, although the difference is not, of course, a matter of simple chronology.

This difference has been minimized in current Anglo-American criticism, which regards as axiomatic the proposition that twentieth-century poetry is a belated version of Romanticism. "Modernism in literature has not passed,"

[42] "The Mind of Modernism," in *Modernism 1840-1930,* ed. Malcolm Bradbury and James McFarlane, Pelican Guides to English Literature (New York: Penguin Books, 1976), p. 92.

[43] *Postmodernism,* which has replaced the term *avant-garde* as a designation for all that is new, exciting, innovative and different about the art of our own time, as distinct from *Modernism,* is a slippery term. In "Towards a Postmodern Hermeneutics of Performance," in *Performance in Postmodern Culture* (Milwaukee: Center for Twentieth-Century Studies, 1977), pp. 19-32, Richard Palmer draws up charts in which he places categories like "Time" and "Space" under the headings *Pre-Modern, Modern,* and *Postmodern.* Such categorization is bound to be reductive; the question also arises whether Postmodern is just a period label or whether it designates what is worthwhile in the period. See Ihab Hassan, *Paracriticisms: Seven Speculations of the Times* (Urbana: University of Illinois Press, 1975), and the Symposium on Postmodernism in *Bucknell Review* 26 (Winter 1980). The contributors include Ihab Hassan, David Antin, Julia Kristeva, Wallace Martin, Matei Calinescu, Charles Russell, and myself.

writes Harold Bloom in *A Map of Misreading*. "Rather it has been exposed as never having been there."[44] Robert Pinsky's important study, *The Situation of Poetry* (1977), begins with the premise that "contemporary poetry is by and large traditional."[45] Pinsky's longest chapter, "The Romantic Persistence," argues that the best poets of our time have learned the lessons laid down by Keats's "Ode to a Nightingale," namely that poetry must mediate between solipsism and "absorption in unconscious nature," that neither "the pure nominalist's perception," found in such poems as Ashbery's "Definition of Blue," nor, at the other extreme, the "cool imagism" of Robert Bly or Gary Snyder is satisfactory.[46] And, in an otherwise fascinating essay (1979) on the difference between the *mimetic* (the imitation of "what is there") and the *meontic* (the imitation of "what is not there") modes in art, Thomas McFarland makes no allowance for a poetic that does not ground the "transcendent" in the "real." Thus he finds "an inherent weakness in all surrealistic practice," in that Surrealism "tends to abandon the reality of this world":

> The greatest meontic art does not abandon the forms of this world in its quest for the place beyond the heavens. Rather, it unfolds, as it were, from those forms to point toward hyperouranic being. . . . Symbolic extensions are

[44] *A Map of Misreading* (New York: Oxford, 1974), p. 28. Bloom has been writing on the nature of "belated Romanticism" in a series of books that begins with *The Anxiety of Influence, A Theory of Poetry* (New York: Oxford, 1973).

[45] *The Situation of Poetry, Contemporary Poetry and its Traditions* (Princeton: Princeton University Press, 1976), p. 6.

[46] From John Bayley's *Romantic Survival, A Study in Poetic Evolution* (1957; rpt. London: Chatto & Windus, 1969), Frank Kermode's *Romantic Image* (1957; rpt. New York: Vintage Books, 1964), and Robert Langbaum's *The Poetry of Experience, The Dramatic Monologue in Modern Literary Tradition* (1957; rpt. New York: Norton, 1963); to such studies as George Bornstein's *Transformations in Romanticism in Yeats, Eliot and Stevens* (Chicago: University of Chicago Press, 1976) and Helen Reguero's *The Limits of Imagination: Wordsworth, Yeats, and Stevens* (Ithaca: Cornell University Press, 1976), studies of the Romantic "survival" in modern poetry have been legion.

> thus hinged, inextricably involved with the objects presented in an artistic discourse.

And McFarland now goes on to cite Coleridge's famous definition of the Symbol: "It always partakes of the Reality which it renders intelligible; and while it enunciates the whole, abides itself a living part in that Unity, of which it is representative."[47]

What is wrong with Surrealism, it would seem, is that it rejects Symbolist dualism, the bifurcation of sense and spirit worlds, of subject and object. In Roger Cardinal's scheme, on the other hand, Surrealism is seen as simply a characteristic mode occurring at the third stage of the cycle, neither better nor worse than its Romantic or Symbolist predecessors. A similar case is made by Todorov in a brief, illuminating discussion on the difference between the poetry of Nerval and Rimbaud. "El Desdichado" (which Todorov would place at the second or Symbolist stage of Cardinal's cycle),[48] is an extremely difficult poem to interpret, but when we track down Nerval's allusions to myth, literature, and hermetic lore, we are able to interpret, at least in broad outlines, what the text means:

> "La fée" ou "Amour" ne sont pas des termes indéterminés, dont la spécification est laissée à la volonté du lecteur, incité à associer librement là-dessus, mais, bien au contraire, des termes aux évocations strictement contrôlées.
>
> ("The fairy" or "Love" are not indeterminate expressions, whose specification is left up to the reader, encouraged to make whatever free associations he wishes, but, on the contrary, expressions whose evocations are strictly controlled.)[49]

[47] See "The Place beyond the Heavens: True Being, Transcendence, and the Symbolic Indication of Wholeness," *Boundary 2*, 7 (Winter 1979), 301-302. The Coleridge passage occurs in *Lay Sermons*, ed. R. J. White (Princeton: Princeton University Press, 1972), p. 30.

[48] Ironically, Cardinal himself uses Nerval's sonnet as an example of an early enigma-poem; see pp. 46-48. But he recognizes that later poets took the concept of enigma much further.

[49] *Symbolisme et interprétation*, p. 78.

By contrast, in Rimbaud's *Illuminations*:

> Les phrases elles-mêmes qui composent le texte sont bien compréhensibles, mais l'objet qu'elles évoquent n'est jamais nommé et l'on peut donc hésiter sur son identification. . . . le processus interprétatif est radicalement changé lorsque les évocations symboliques, aussi ingénieuses soient-elles, se trouvent privées de piédestal. . . .
>
> (The phrases themselves that constitute the text are quite comprehensible, but the object that they evoke is never named and one therefore hesitates as to their identification. . . . the interpretative process is radically changed when symbolic evocations, however ingenious, find themselves deprived of a pedestal.)[50]

Perhaps Todorov and Cardinal read the map of modern poetry differently from Bloom or Pinsky or McFarland because their generalizations are derived from Continental (and especially French) rather than Anglo-American models. Perhaps America really *is* different, and the poets of the sixties and seventies are, in fact, still writing in the tradition of Wordsworth or Emerson or Keats. If so, poets must be fundamentally different from, say, novelists and painters, for surely no one would argue that the novels of William Gass or John Hawkes are belated versions of Jane Austen or that Jasper Johns is to be understood as an ephebe of Turner or Constable.

Or perhaps, as I think, Modernism was itself a time of tension between rival strains, the Symbolist or "High Modern" and the "Other Tradition" which is the subject of my book. And here the "French connection" does provide an important missing link. I am thinking not only of Rimbaud and later French poets but also of the visual arts. For in painting and sculpture, Cardinal's third stage, the stage in which surface is preferred to "depth," *process* to *structure*, is much more readily identifiable than it is in poetry. From the early days of Cubism in 1910 through Vorticism and

[50] *Symbolisme et interprétation*, p. 79.

Futurism, Dada and Surrealism, down to the Abstract Expressionism of the fifties, and the Conceptual Art, Super-Realism, assemblages, and performance art of the present, visual artists have consistently resisted the Symbolist model in favor of the creation of a world in which forms can exist "littéralement et dans tous les sens," an oscillation between representational reference and compositional game. To put it another way, William Empson's famous "seven types of ambiguity"—that is, the multiple layers of meaning words have in poetry (and, by analogy, images in painting)—give way to what we might call an "irreducible ambiguity"—the creation of labyrinths that have no exit.[51]

Duchamp's enigmatic *Large Glass* (*La Mariée mise à nu par ses célibataires, même*), for example, exerts a special fascination for the viewer who keeps trying to extract meanings that the art work blocks at every turn. Art becomes play, endlessly frustrating our longing for certainty. A composition like the *Large Glass* is also a critique of the very criticism it inspires, mocking the solemnity of the explicator who is determined to find *the* key. In the same way, poetic texts like "These Lacustrine Cities" or "Ping" derive force from their refusal to "mean" in conventional ways. To refer to lacustrine cities that emerge until a tower controls the sky is, in itself, a judgment on the poet's ability to depict a coherent, recognizable landscape. Again, to use, as does Ashbery, shifting pronouns and false causal connectives is itself an implicit commentary on the nature of identity and causality. Here intertextual relationships become especially important: we read an Ashbery against an Eliot or an Auden just as Duchamp's *Large Glass* acts to defamiliarize our sense of what a painting or sculpture should be.

Contemporary poets have often commented on this situation, but no one has paid much attention, perhaps because readers seem bent on absorbing the unfamiliar into familiar patterns. From Charles Olson's "Projective Verse" (1950), with its call for "objectism" ("the getting rid of the

[51] See David Lodge, *The Modes of Modern Writing*, p. 226.

lyrical interference of the individual as ego . . . for man is himself an object"[52]); to John Cage's remark in *Silence* (1961) that "I'd never been interested in symbolism . . . I preferred just taking things in themselves, not as standing for other things";[53] to Frank O'Hara's praise for Jasper Johns' "meticulously and sensually painted rituals of imagery" which "express a profound boredom with the symbols of an oversymbolic society" (1962);[54] and David Antin's definition, in the mid-seventies, of poetry as "the language art," a form of discourse which, rather than "saying one thing and meaning something else," returns to the literal but with the recognition that "phenomenological reality is itself 'discovered' and 'constructed' by poets,"[55] the question of how to create poetry in a post-Symbolist age has been a primary concern. It is interesting that even Robert Lowell, whose roots are deep in the Symbolist tradition, could declare, in the Afterword to *Notebook 1967-68*: "I lean heavily on the rational, but am devoted to surrealism. . . . it is a natural way to write our fictions,"[56] and Lowell's last book, *Day by Day* (1977) can be said to follow Rimbaud's dictum of "saying" what it "says" "littéralement et dans tous les sens."

One of the most telling assessments of the hegemony of Symbolism, as it looked to a poet coming of age in the fifties, is John Ashbery's essay on Pierre Reverdy, written in French for the *Mercure de France* (1962):

D'une façon générale, la plus grande partie de la

[52] *Human Universe and Other Essays*, ed. Donald Allen (New York: Grove Press, 1967), pp. 59-60.

[53] (Middletown: Wesleyan University Press, 1961), p. 58.

[54] *Art Chronicles 1954-1966* (New York: George Braziller, 1975), p. 11; cf. my *Frank O'Hara: Poet among Painters* (New York: George Braziller, 1977), pp. 19-30.

[55] See "Modernism and Postmodernism: Approaching the Present in American Poetry," *Boundary 2*, 1 (Fall 1972), 132-133; "Some Questions about Modernism," *Occident*, 8 (Spring 1974), 27.

[56] (New York: Farrar, Straus & Giroux, 1969), p. 159. In the second *Notebook* (New York: Farrar, Straus & Giroux, 1970), p. 262, Lowell calls it "unrealism" rather than "surrealism."

poésie américaine actuelle (et celle de l'Angleterre aussi) languit à l'ombre de T. S. Eliot. Les poètes qui lui ont succédé ont affaibli ou dénaturé le contenu intellectuel de la poésie d'Eliot, mais ils en ont retenu certains aspects superficiels: le langage sec et digne, ou le ton de J. Alfred Prufrock. . . .

Ce genre de poésie est à l'opposé de celle de Reverdy: *transparente, sans "signification" philosophique*. . . . Reverdy parvient à restituer aux choses leur vrai nom, à abolir *l'eternel poids mort de symbolisme* et d'allégorie. . . . Dans *The Waste Land* d'Eliot, le monde réel apparaît avec les rêves qui lui sont propres, mais il est toujours artificiellement lié à une signification allégorique—l'usine à gaz et le "dull canal," par exemple. Tandis que chez Reverdy un canal ou une usine sont des *phénomènes vivants*, ils font partie du monde qui nous entoure. . . . C'est comme si on voyait pour la première fois un paysage naturel, n'ayant vu jusque là que des paysages peints.

J'ai toujours regretté que les rythmes sombres d'Eliot et de Yeats, par exemple, soient au service d'une signification précise, et que leurs élans poétiques . . . soient comme un cerf-volant dont le fil est fermement tenu par le poète rivé à sa terre. Ce qui nous enchante chez Reverdy, c'est la pureté de sa poésie, faite de changements, fluctuations, archétypes d'événements, situations idéales, mouvements de *formes transparentes*, aussi naturels et variés que les vagues de la mer.[57] (my italics)

For Ashbery, the world is no longer a half-open dictionary. Nature no longer wears the colors of the spirit. Rather, the poet's desire is to "abolish the eternal dead weight of symbolism," to give back to things their "true name." In Reverdy's poetry, as Ashbery sees it, images, both concrete and arresting, that are no longer grounded in what To-

[57] "Reverdy en Amérique," *Mercure de France*: Pierre Reverdy Issue, 344 (January/April 1962), 111-112. Since Ashbery is writing a careful, almost a "schoolboy" French, I have thought it best to leave the passage untranslated.

dorov calls "*un* discours," are placed in fluid relationships so that they appear as "living phenomena." The kite analogy is especially apt: the poet, Ashbery suggests, must be willing to release the string, at least partly, so as to give his invented "kite" the opportunity to float freely. The poem thus becomes, as Ashbery said of Gertrude Stein's *Stanzas in Meditation*, a "hymn to possibility."[58]

A similar case for the poetry of "unmediated presentation" was made by Jerome Rothenberg in a 1973 interview with William Spanos:

> My own discomfort isn't with symbols *per se* . . . but with that "symbolism" which substitutes *interpretation* for *presentation*: the kind of distinction that puts the surrealists into conflict with the symbolists & the New Critics with the surrealists. . . . The surrealist "image" is unmediated, its associations implicit & directly perceived, as in the experience of "dream," which was of course their model. In that sense, I've always assumed a continuity between the surrealists & the absurdists—with someone like Kafka or Breton, say, in his collections of "black humor," as an intermediary figure. For the absurdists the idea of the absurd itself (like "dream" for the surrealists) serves as the great simplifying image, which allows for *direct presentation* of conflicting impulses. . . . I think the move away from symbolism is characteristic of modern poetry from World War I to World War II, though not clearly articulated or divested of symbolist traces until the 1950s.[59] (my italics)

In distinguishing between a "symbolism" that demands "interpretation" and the "direct presentation" of the image, Rothenberg is, of course, echoing Pound's famous Imagist Manifesto (1913), with its call for "Direct treatment of the 'thing,' whether subjective or objective." The "move away from symbolism," as Rothenberg reminds us, was already

[58] "The Impossible," a review of Gertrude Stein's *Stanzas in Meditation*, *Poetry*, 90 (July 1957), 251.

[59] "A Dialogue with William Spanos," *Boundary 2*, 3 (Spring 1975), 539.

going on in the period between the wars. And here the distinction between Pound and Eliot, names that continue to be paired in almost all discussions of "modern poetry," is crucial. For after *Mauberley* (1920) and *The Waste Land*, Pound and Eliot began to move in different directions. They remained, of course, lifelong friends, and in public they continued to praise each other's work, but by the late thirties, when Pound was working on the Adams Cantos and Eliot on *Four Quartets*, they no longer shared a common aesthetic.[60]

After the Second World War, when the Beats and Black Mountain poets, the New York school and the "Deep Image" group were coming on the scene, the Eliot-Pound divergence began to be recognized, by the poets if not yet the critics. "It was 1948," Rothenberg remembers in a recent autobiographical sketch, "& by year's end I was seventeen. I had been coming into poetry for two years. My head was filled with Stein and Cummings, later with Williams, Pound, and the French Surrealists, the Dada poets who made 'pure sound' three decades earlier."[61]

This passage is found in the "Pre-Face" to *Revolution of the Word, A New Gathering of American Avant-Garde Poetry, 1914-1945*. On the title page of this anthology, which appeared in 1974, Rothenberg places the following epigraph:

> Tching prayed on the mountain and
> wrote MAKE IT NEW
> on his bath tub
> Day by day make it new
> cut underbrush
> pile the logs
> keep it growing.
>
> —EZRA POUND, *Canto* 53

[60] See Hugh Kenner, *The Pound Era*, pp. 134-138; Marshall McLuhan, "Pound, Eliot, and the Rhetoric of The Waste Land," *New Literary History*, 10 (Spring 1979), 557-580.

[61] *Revolution of the Word, A New Gathering of American Avant Garde Poetry, 1914-1945* (New York: The Seabury Press, 1974), p. xi.

And the first page of the text bears the epigraph:

> Nothing changes from generation to generation
> except the thing seen
> and that makes a composition.
>
> —G. STEIN

The iconoclastic anthology begins with Walter Arensberg's short prose piece, "Dada is American" and ends with Louis Zukofsky's "A '1' "; it includes extracts from Stein's *Tender Buttons*, Williams' *Spring and All*, and Marcel Duchamp's *Rrose Sélavy*, as well as such little-known works as Walter Lowenfels' "Apollinaire an Elegy" and Eugene Jolas' "dream scenario" called "Rimbaud and the Chauffeur."

Many of these "poems," interestingly enough, are written in prose rather than verse. Of this phenomenon, Rothenberg says:

> Metrics give way to measure—"not the sequence of the metronome" (Pound) but a variable succession of sounds & silences, breath- or mind-directed, a "musical line" derived from the complex movements of actual speech. The written text becomes the poem's notation or, in the formulation of visual & concrete poets, a space which the eye reads visible shape & meaning at a single glance. Here and there too, one sees the first experiments with performance & a fusion with the other arts—towards "intermedia" & the freedom of a poetry without fixed limits, which may change at any point into something else.
>
> (p. xviii)

Such a "poetry without fixed limits" sounds more anarchic than it really is. What Rothenberg means by "the complex movements of actual speech" may be glossed by an important discussion of prosody by Northrop Frye. In *The Well-Tempered Critic* (1963), Frye distinguishes "three primary rhythms of verbal expression": prose, verse, and the "associative rhythm" of speech:

> The irregular rhythm of ordinary speech may be conventionalized in two ways. One way is to impose a pattern of recurrence on it; the other is to impose the logical and semantic pattern of the sentence. We have verse when the arrangement of words is dominated by recurrent rhythm and sound, prose when it is dominated by the syntactical relations of subject and predicate.[62]

The "associative rhythm," as it is heard in actual speech, is no more like prose than it is like verse. Its unit of rhythm is the "short phrase that contains the central word or idea aimed at, but is largely innocent of syntax. It is much more repetitive than prose, as it is in the process of working out an idea, and the repetitions are largely rhythmical filler" (p. 21). As for the poetry-verse relationship, Frye writes:

> "Poetry," however indispensable a word in literary criticism, can hardly be used in the technical sense of a verbal structure possessing a regular, recurrent and in general predictable rhythm. All verse is "poetry" as that word is generally used, except when "poetry" implies a value judgement. It does not follow that all poetry is verse. Any jingle or doggerel that approximately scans is verse in my sense, however unpoetic; no free verse, such as Whitman's, is verse in my sense, however important as poetry.
>
> (p. 24)

Instead of pigeon-holing given literary works as belonging either to prose or to poetry, we study what happens when the three primary rhythms are placed in all their possible combinations. When, for example, we begin with a "normal" form of verse equidistant from both prose and the associative rhythm we find, in English, a form like the heroic couplet:

> In Pope, for instance, the writing always makes prose sense, but there is no point at which it either leans over

[62] (1963; rpt. Bloomington: Indiana University Press, 1967), p. 21.

> toward prose or leans away from it. We hear at once the full ring of the rhyming couplet, and we know immediately what kind of thing to expect. . . . We do not know what Pope is going to say, but we know the units within which he is going to say it.
>
> (pp. 66-67)

From such a "continuous form," verse can move either closer to prose, as in the blank verse of Wordsworth or Browning, where "we find ourselves listening to a syncopated mixture of iambic pentameter and a prose semantic rhythm" (p. 67), or closer to the associative rhythm, as in the lyric of Keats or Poe, where the metrical base is obscured by incantatory sound repetition and discontinuous syntactic phrasing. The poets discussed earlier in this chapter, Eliot, Stevens, and Auden, all belong somewhere along this verse continuum. Auden's unrhymed six-line stanzas of alternating iambic pentameter and hexameter move in the direction of a prose semantic rhythm, somewhat to the left of Browning in their easy conversational flow. Stevens' approximate blank verse tercets, with their discontinuous phrasing, their word and phrasal repetition, and their use of aphorism, move in the other direction, toward the lyric. *The Waste Land* has, of course, a much more complex prosodic structure, combining the four-stress alliterative line, blank verse, heroic couplets, short rhyming stanzas, and associative rhythms, as in the case of the Pub scene in II. But Eliot's is by no means "free verse"; as he himself puts it in "Reflections on *Vers Libre*," "the ghost of some simple metre should lurk behind the arras in even the 'freest' verse; to advance menacingly as we doze, and withdraw as we rouse." And in the same essay:

> . . . the most interesting verse which has yet been written in our language has been done either by taking a very simple form, like the iambic pentameter, and constantly withdrawing from it, or taking no form at all, and constantly approximating a very simple one. It is this con-

> trast between fixity and flux, this unperceived evasion of monotony, which is the very life of verse.[63]

But that, of course, assumes that there is a *fixity*, a norm to be evaded gracefully. The Symbolist poet accepts this as a given, just as he accepts the existence of truth, however indirectly and intuitively that "truth" must be perceived and communicated. But the poets of "The Other Tradition" accept neither the metrical nor the metaphysical norm, and they therefore gravitate, quite naturally, to "free verse" or to the "prose poem."

Both of these forms, Frye suggests, are not *verse* at all, but variations on the associative rhythm. "Free verse" is a "secondary or mixed form. . . . [It] is usually a series of phrases with no fixed metrical pattern, the influence of verse being shown in the fact that the phrases are rhythmically separated from one another, not connected by syntax as in prose" (pp. 72-73). In this sense, the *Cantos* are in "free verse" whereas Eliot always retains a metrical base.

The associative rhythm can move toward prose in much the same way it moves toward verse:

> Criticism does not appear to have any such term as "free prose" to describe an associative rhythm influenced, but not quite organized, by the sentence. But that free prose exists is clear enough, and in fact it develops much earlier than free verse.
>
> (p. 81)

We find "free prose" in such subliterary forms as the personal letter or diary, but also in literature: Frye cites Swift's *Journal to Stella*, Sterne's *Tristram Shandy*, and Burton's *Anatomy of Melancholy*, "a tremendous masterpiece of free prose where quotations, references, allusions, titles of books, Latin tags, short sharp phrases, long lists and catalogues, are all swept up in one vast exuberant associative wave" (p. 83).

[63] "Reflections on *Vers Libre*" (1917), in *To Criticize the Critic and Other Essays* (New York: Farrar, Straus & Giroux, 1965), pp. 187, 185.

Rimbaud's *Saison en enfer* and *Illuminations* are regularly referred to as prose poetry, but it is interesting to see how different they both sound and look from Baudelaire's *Petits poèmes en prose*. Baudelaire's norm is still the complete sentence, and his prose poems combine the causal and sequential sequence of prose with the phrasal recurrence of lyric. Rimbaud's rhythm is much more exclamatory and fragmented; short phrases pile up and sentences having normal subject-predicate word order do not follow one another so as to form a coherent discourse. In more extreme form, we meet the same rhythmic structuring in the short prose compositions of Gertrude Stein and in Beckett's associative monologues like *The Unnamable* and *How It Is*, as well as in his condensed, impersonal "Residua" like "Imagination Dead Imagine" and "Ping."

In Williams' *Spring and All* and *The Descent of Winter*, free prose and free verse are interwoven; again, in the poetry of Ashbery, free verse (as in *Rivers and Mountains*, which contains "These Lacustrine Cities") alternates with the "free prose" of *Three Poems*. And in the experimental scores for oral poems of David Antin and John Cage, the associative rhythm of speech becomes a new vital center. To limit discussion of "modern poetry" to "modern verse" would be, accordingly, to eliminate some of the most influential verbal art of the period. Indeed, a glance at recent poetry magazines and small-press books reveals that more and more "poets" are experimenting with discontinuous "prose" forms: for example, Michael Benedikt, Michael Davidson, Russell Edson, Larry Eigner, Kathleen Fraser, Bernadette Mayer, Gilbert Sorrentino, Charles Tomlinson—the list could go on and on.

In the chapters that follow, accordingly, "poetry" is construed not as "verse" (which is not, in fact, the dominant medium of the poets concerned) but as *language art* or "word-system."[64] The poets included—Rimbaud, Stein,

[64] The phrase is Gertrude Stein's. See "Portraits and Repetition," in *Writings and Lectures 1919-1945*, ed. Patricia Meyerowitz (Baltimore: Penguin Books, 1967), p. 115.

Williams, Pound, Beckett, Ashbery, Cage, and Antin—are discussed as *representative* figures of what I take to be a central poetic tradition. Any such choice of poets as mine is bound to incur disfavor among some readers, and I hasten to say that there are many poets who could be included in a study of what we might call "the new literalism," beginning with the D. H. Lawrence of *Birds, Beasts, and Flowers* and the Louis Zukofsky of *A 1-12*, and coming down to such works of our own day as Jerome Rothenberg's *Poland/1931*, Ed Dorn's *Slinger*, and W. S. Merwin's *The Lice*. I make no claims for comprehensiveness; the poets I discuss are simply those whom I take to be the best exemplars of particular facets of the indeterminacy model. In this connection, I should say that Frank O'Hara, who surely has a place in the Rimbaud tradition, is omitted for the simple reason that I have already devoted a whole book to his work. But he is nevertheless a presence in these pages, for it is what he refers to comically as "Concrete Rimbaud obscurity of expression which is simple and definite / even lasting,"[65] that I hope to trace in all its vagaries.

One final note. To explore what I call "the mode of undecidability" in twentieth-century poetry is by no means to criticize the great Symbolist movement of our period. It is, rather, to suggest that much of the poetry now emerging has different origins and therefore makes rather different suppositions. It deserves to be read on its own terms. In the words of René Magritte:

> People who look for symbolic meanings fail to grasp the inherent poetry and mystery of the image. No doubt they sense this mystery, but they wish to get rid of it. They are afraid. By asking, "what does this mean?" they express a wish that everything is understandable. But if one does not reject the mystery, one has quite a different response. One asks other things.[66]

[65] "You are Gorgeous and I'm Coming," *The Collected Poems of Frank O'Hara*, ed. Donald Allen (New York: Alfred A. Knopf, 1971), p. 331.

[66] See Suzy Gablik, *Magritte* (Boston: New Graphic Society, 1976), p. 11.

CHAPTER TWO

"Trouver une langue" The *Anti-paysage* of Rimbaud

. . . je me flattais d'inventer un verbe poétique accessible, un jour ou l'autre, à tous les sens. Je réservais la traduction.

(. . . I flattered myself on inventing, some day, a poetic language accessible to all the senses. I withheld the translation.)

—Rimbaud, *Une Saison en enfer* (Délires II)[1]

[Rimbaud] cesse de tenir le monde pour un dictionnaire entr'ouvert, pour un recueil de significations déchiffrables. . . . Aussi son paysage n'est-il plus vraiment un paysage mais plutôt un anti-paysage, une pure vision sans témoin. . . .

([Rimbaud] no longer regards the world as a half-open dictionary, a collection of significations to be deciphered. . . . Also his landscape is no longer really a landscape but rather an anti-landscape, a pure vision without witness.)

—Jean-Pierre Richard, "Rimbaud ou la poésie du devenir"[2]

THERE is no real precedent for the *anti-paysage* of the *Illuminations*. The first thing to say about the "cities" evoked in "Les Ponts" and "Métropolitain," in "Parade" and "Promontoire," is that, in the words of Rimbaud's "Barbare," "elles n'existent pas." These dream landscapes, at once present and absent, concrete and abstract, are composed of particulars that cannot be specified, of images that refuse to cohere in a consistent referential scheme. Indeed, external reference seems peculiarly irrelevant in the case of these poems. Does "Métropolitain" refer to the

[1] Rimbaud, *Œuvres*, ed. Suzanne Bernard (Paris: Garnier, 1960), p. 292. Subsequently cited as "Rimbaud." All page numbers given in parentheses are to this edition.

[2] *Poésie et profondeur* (Paris: Éditions du Seuil, 1955), p. 240.

London "tube" or to the suburban railway that enters a tunnel and goes underground within city limits, or to neither? Is the palace described in "Promontoire" the Grand Hotel that opened in Scarborough in 1867, and, if so, how can its facades be decorated with "tarantellas"? Are the crystal and wood chalets that move on invisible rails in "Villes I" meant to evoke one of the Alpine funiculars erected in the 1870s?[3] These speculations lead nowhere, for the context in which such references are embedded repeatedly provides conflicting evidence. Why, for example, are "barges" found in the smoky underground world of "Métropolitain"?

By the same token, the attempt to find consistent psychological themes in the *Illuminations* is repeatedly blocked. The last sentence of "Les Ponts" reads:

> Un rayon blanc, tombant du haut du ciel, anéantit cette comédie.
>
> (p. 273)
>
> (A white ray, falling from the top of the sky, blots out this comedy.)

Robert Greer Cohn comments: "The avenging ray is his [Rimbaud's] own. . . . he welcomes it as a relief from his earlier inauthentic self, just as St. Paul speaks of his own conversion—the descending fire on the road to Damascus—as having killed the frivolous child in him."[4] Nothing in the text of "Les Ponts" either confirms or refutes this interpretation.[5] We can only say that the falling white

[3] These suggestions, put forward by Antoine Adam in "L'Enigme des 'Illuminations'," *Revue des Sciences Humaines* (December 1950), and by V. P. Underwood, "Rimbaud et l'Angleterre," *Revue de Littérature Comparée* (January-March 1955), are discussed by Suzanne Bernard in her detailed Notes to the Garnier edition. See esp. pp. 501, 516-517, 526-527.

[4] *The Poetry of Rimbaud* (Princeton: Princeton University Press, 1973), p. 303.

[5] This point is made about the *Illuminations* in general by Tzvetan Todorov in "Une complication de texte: les *Illuminations*," *Poétique*, 34 (April 1978), 243. Reprinted in Todorov's *Les Genres du discours* (Paris: Éditions du Seuil, 1978), pp. 204-220, but I refer to the *Poétique* text which is more

ray puts an abrupt end to the preceding spectacle, the bizarre design of bridges. Or again, when Cohn suggests that "Parade" presents "the male-dominated modern city in a Western democracy like France," and that such a city acts as a threat to the sexually insecure, fatherless Rimbaud, we have the uneasy sense that something has been added to or subtracted from the text. The tears mentioned near the end of "Parade" refer, we are told, to "the deprived boy's sorrow"; tears are "an essence of a frustrated male-male relationship."[6] But the poem itself undercuts such Freudian interpretation by associating tears with pulsing blood and eyes that are on fire, and by concluding that "Leur raillerie ou leur terreur dure une minute, ou des mois entiers" ("Their jeering or their terror lasts for a minute, or for whole months").[7]

"Une minute, ou des mois entiers." In framing this ambivalent statement, Rimbaud expresses his resistance to closure. His tears are not to be taken as symbols of something else. "Far from serving as a protective screen between us and the poet's secret psychological complexity," writes Leo Bersani, "language in the *Illuminations* would be obliterated by the very luminosity of the pictures which language evokes. . . . Everything is designed—as in a spectacularly vulgar circus number—to fascinate our eyes, to make it impossible for us to turn our glutted vision away from the hypnotic scene. These cineramic hallucinations attain a certain impersonality by the frankly excessive and improbable nature of the spectacle."[8]

Fictiveness is perhaps the central quality of Rimbaud's

---

readily available. I am indebted to this essay throughout, as well as to Todorov's related discussion in *Symbolisme et interprétation* (Paris: Éditions du Seuil, 1978), pp. 76-85.

[6] Cohn, *The Poetry of Rimbaud*, pp. 270-271.

[7] Rimbaud, p. 261.

[8] "Rimbaud's Simplicity," *A Future for Astyanax, Character and Desire in Literature* (Boston: Little, Brown and Co., 1976), p. 257. Cf. John C. Lapp, " 'Mémoire': Art et hallucination chez Rimbaud," *Cahiers de l'Association Internationale des Etudes Françaises*, 23 (1971), 163-175.

poetic landscape. Here is the first of the two prose poems called "Villes":

Villes

Ce sont des villes! C'est un peuple pour qui se sont montés ces Alleghanys et ces Libans de rêve! Des chalets de cristal et de bois qui se meuvent sur des rails et des poulies invisibles. Les vieux cratères ceints de colosses et de palmiers de cuivre rugissent mélodieusement dans les feux. Des fêtes amoureuses sonnent sur les canaux pendus derrière les chalets. La chasse des carillons crie dans les gorges. Des corporations de chanteurs géants accourent dans des vêtements et des oriflammes éclatant comme la lumière des cimes. Sur les plates-formes au milieu des gouffres les Rolands sonnent leur bravoure. Sur les passerelles de l'abîme et les toits des auberges l'ardeur du ciel pavoise les mâts. L'écroulement des apothéoses rejoint les champs des hauteurs où les centauresses séraphiques évoluent parmi les avalanches. Au-dessus du niveau des plus hautes crêtes, une mer troublée par la naissance éternelle de Vénus, chargée de flottes orphéoniques et de la rumeur des perles et des conques précieuses;—la mer s'assombrit parfois avec des éclats mortels. Sur les versants des moissons de fleurs grandes comme nos armes et nos coupes, mugissent. Des cortèges de Mabs en robes rousses, opalines, montent des ravines. Là-haut, les pieds dans la cascade et les ronces, les cerfs tettent Diane. Les Bacchantes des banlieues sanglotent et la lune brûle et hurle. Vénus entre dans les cavernes des forgerons et des ermites. Des groupes de beffrois chantent les idées des peuples. Des châteaux bâtis en os sort la musique inconnue. Toutes les légendes évoluent et les élans se ruent dans les bourgs. Le paradis des orages s'effondre. Les sauvages dansent sans cesse la fête de la nuit. Et une heure je suis descendu dans le mouvement d'un boulevard de Bagdad où des compagnies ont chanté la joie du travail nouveau, sous une brise épaisse, circulant sans pouvoir éluder les fabuleux fantômes des monts où l'on a dû se retrouver.

Quels bons bras, quelle belle heure me rendront cette région d'où viennent mes sommeils et mes moindres mouvements?

(pp. 276-277)

Cities

(What cities! What a people this is for whom these Alleghenies and these Lebanons of dream have arisen! Chalets of crystal and wood that move on invisible rails and pulleys. Ancient craters girdled by colossi and copper palm trees roar melodiously in the fires. Amorous revels ring out over the canals suspended behind chalets. The play of chimes clamors in the gorges. Guilds of giant singers congregate in robes and oriflammes as dazzling as the light of the summits. On platforms in the midst of whirlpools, the Rolands trumpet their valor. On footbridges over the abyss and on the roofs of the inns the fire of the sky adorns the masts with flags. The collapse of apotheoses joins the fields to the highlands where seraphic centauresses spin among the avalanches. Above the level of the highest crests, a sea troubled by the eternal birth of Venus, heavy with Orpheonic fleets and the murmur of pearls and precious shells;—the sea grows somber sometimes with fatal flashes. On the slopes, harvests of flowers large as our weapons and our vessels bellow. Processions of Mabs in russet dresses, opaline, ascend from the ravines. Up there, their feet in the waterfall and the brambles, stags suck at Diana's breast. The Bacchantes of the suburbs sob and the moon burns and howls. Venus enters the caves of blacksmiths and hermits. Groups of belfries sing the ideas of the peoples. From castles built of bone issues unknown music. All the legends evolve and elks rush through the towns. The paradise of storms crumbles. The savages dance ceaselessly the revels of the night. And, one hour, I went down into the bustle of a boulevard in Bagdad where companies sang the joy of the new work under a heavy breeze, circulating without being able to escape the fab-

> ulous phantoms of the mountains where we were to have met again.
>
> What strong arms, what lovely hour will give me back this region from which come my slumbers and my slightest movements?)[9]

"C'est son des villes!" the poet exclaims rapturously, but immediately the reader is thrown into confusion. For what does "ce" refer to? And where are we? The description that follows is neither that of a recognizable cityscape like Eliot's riverfront London nor an ideal city of the imagination like Yeats's Byzantium. Rather, Rimbaud evokes "cities" that are, from the start, impossible to locate in "real" space. For although the poem unfolds a metonymic network of urban images—*chalets, rails, canaux, plates-formes, passerelles, toits des auberges*—these references to a possible city are consistently canceled out by images of wild nature: *vieux cratères, gorges, cimes, gouffres, avalanches.*[10] In the sec-

[9] The special difficulty of translating Rimbaud is that it is all but impossible in English not to overspecify and hence restrict the poet's meanings. Here, for example, are four representative translations of the sentence "La chasse des carillons crie dans les gorges":

"The hunt of chimes clamors in the gorges." Louise Varèse, *Illuminations and other Prose Poems* (New York: New Directions, 1957), p. 61.

"The pack of chimes clamors in the gorges." Wallace Fowlie, *Rimbaud: Complete Works, Selected Letters* (Chicago: Phoenix Books, 1966), p. 241.

"The play of chimes clamors in the gorges." Enid Rhodes Peschel, *A Season in Hell and the Illuminations, A New Translation* (New York: Oxford, 1973), p. 137.

"The rush of pealing bells cries out in the gorges." Paul Schmidt, *Arthur Rimbaud, Complete Works* (New York: Harper & Row, 1975), p. 230.

What seems to have happened here is that the translators give us varying synecdoches for the word "chasse," which involves hunting, a pack of animals, a sport or play, a rush of activity. No English equivalent can do the original justice because Rimbaud's context, "la chasse des carillons," does not specify the word's meaning. I have tried, in my own translation, to be as faithful as possible to the original, but there is often no solution; in this case, I reluctantly use the word "play" as appropriate in the given sentence.

[10] On this point, see Todorov, *Poétique*, 244; Nathaniel Wing, *Present Appearances: Aspects of Poetic Structure in Rimbaud's Illuminations*," Romance

ond sentence, "Alleghenies" are mysteriously placed next to "Lebanons of dream" so that the modern West meets the ancient East. But in the very next sentence, Rimbaud abruptly drops this exotic mountain imagery and shifts, without any discernible logic, to crystal and wood chalets on invisible rails and pulleys. This Alpine scene is in turn replaced by a landscape of craters, colossal statues, and copper palm trees that "roar melodiously in the fires." On our imaginary map, the East-West axis is thus replaced by a North-South one. Indeed, Rimbaud's dream cities seem to be everywhere.

In the course of the poem, the sense of place becomes more and more elusive. Canals are suspended behind chalets, platforms are found in the midst of whirlpools, footbridges span the abyss. What seem to be mountain peaks turn out to be the crests of waves, and there is a constant metamorphosis of land into ocean and back again, as in the sentence:

> Sur les passerelles de l'abîme et les toits des auberges l'ardeur du ciel pavoise les mâts.

> (On footbridges over the abyss and on the roofs of the inns the fire of the sky adorns the masts with flags.)

One expects these masts to belong to ships, but, as in the case of Ashbery's "These Lacustrine Cities," Rimbaud's parts belong to no discernible whole. The image of the masts dissolves in its turn and the "collapse of apotheoses" joins fields to highlands "where seraphic centauresses spin among the avalanches." After a series of such metamorphoses, land and water finally merge in an hallucinatory image: the stags being suckled by Diana have their feet "in the waterfall and the brambles." From this point on, the mood of the poem becomes increasingly frenzied. "The Bacchantes of the suburbs sob and the moon burns and

---

Monographs, Inc. Number 9 (Oxford: University of Mississippi Press, 1974), 103-104.

howls." Venus, whose "eternal birth" has troubled the sea, now reappears, entering the caves of blacksmiths and hermits. As the oxymoronic "paradise of storms" crumbles, "savages dance ceaselessly the revels of the night." And the reader suddenly realizes that the "light of the summits" has been replaced by darkness.

In this context, the words "Et, une heure, je suis descendu dans le mouvement d'un boulevard de Bagdad" ("And, one hour, I went down into the bustle of a boulevard in Bagdad"), come as a total disruption. The eternal present, with its continuous metamorphosis of landscapes and its astonishing juxtapositions of disparate images, now gives way to one time and one place. The reference to "une heure," the past tense, the specific locale (note that Bagdad is the first actual city mentioned in the poem), and the appearance of the poet who, prior to this moment, has been seemingly absent, behind the curtain, so to speak—all these factors suggest that a spell has been broken. A "heavy breeze" fills the Bagdad night, and the mountains retreat, their "fabulous phantoms" impossible to elude and yet just as impossible to reach. To meet *there* (wherever "there" may be and whoever was supposed to meet) is now out of the question. The moment has passed. And so, in the poem's final plaintive lines, the poet asks what "strong arms" and what "lovely hour" will give him back this "region," a region that is the source not only of vision but also of sleep, and, in the oddest conjunction of all, of "my slightest movements"—of all action.

But what is the *content* of the poet's fleeting vision? It is impossible to say, for Rimbaud's historical and mythological references are at least as contradictory as are his spatial images. Proper names—Rolands, Mabs, Venus, Diana—are consistently presented in a context which does not specify their meaning. The phrase "these Alleghenies and these Lebanons of dream," for example, oddly combines two worlds: the new Western world of the American continent, with its exotic Indian names, and the Near East of the Bible and ancient history. Again, the poem blends medieval reference (the mysterious "play of chimes," the "Guilds of giant singers [who] congregate in robes and oriflammes," the "Rolands," the "castles built of bone"); faery lore viewed in Shakespearean terms (Queen Mab); the Arabian Nights (the Bagdad boulevard); and oddly inverted Greek myths (Venus born over and over again in a troubled ocean and entering caves in pursuit of blacksmiths—an oblique reference to Hephaestus; Diana, the virgin huntress, giving suck to stags). Phrases like "seraphic centauresses" combine Christian and Pagan connotations, and the element of fantasy is heightened by making the centaurs female. In another such fantastic image, the Maenads who sob under the burning, howling moon are referred to as the "Bacchantes of the suburbs."

Rimbaud's cities are full of noises. Consider the following series of verbs: "Les vieux cratères . . . *rugissent* mélodieusement," "Des fêtes amoureuses *sonnent*" "La chasse des carillons *crie*," "les Rolands *sonnent* leur bravoure," "des moissons de fleurs . . . *mugissent*," "la lune . . . *hurle*," "Des groupes de beffrois *chantent* les idées des peuples," "Les sauvages *dansent* sans cesse." But how does one describe this incessant music? Some sounds are lovely and mysterious ("a sea . . . heavy with Orpheonic fleets and the murmur of pearls and precious shells"), some dazzling ("Amorous revels resound over the canals"), some martial and heroic ("The play of chimes clamors in the gorges"; "the Rolands trumpet their valor"), some harsh and ugly ("The Bacchantes of the suburbs sob and the moon burns and howls"), some lofty and inspiring ("Groups of belfries sing the ideas of the peoples"). The divergent connotations of these images work against harmony. Each "note" retains its separate identity so that the "unknown music" rising from "castles of bone" remains an enigma.

Images of motion work in much the same way.[11] Rimbaud's landscape is characterized by constant explosive movement and shifting perspective, beginning with the

[11] See Renée Riese Hubert, "The Use of Reversals in Rimbaud's *Illuminations*," *L'Esprit Créateur*, 9, no. 1 (Spring 1969), 9-17.

dream Alleghenies and Lebanons that have risen up out of nowhere. The crystal chalets move both horizontally on rails and upward on pulleys. Platforms rise above whirlpools, footbridges span the abyss, rooftops and masts shoot upward into the sky. But just when the focus seems to be wholly on vertical movement, a "collapse of apotheoses" takes place. The perspective, shifting rapidly upward and downward, now becomes vertiginous: processions of Mabs *ascend* the ravines but Venus *descends* into the caves. All the legends *rise* but the paradise of storms *crumbles*. And then vertical and horizontal motion come together in the whirlpool of the savage dance. At this point, the poet suddenly realizes that "une heure" he descended into the Bagdad boulevard. This descent shatters existing space; as the guild of singers and the poet himself go around in aimless circles, the mountain peaks recede upward. And abruptly the poet descends downward into the self.

Rimbaud's cityscape is thus a phantasmagoria. Like a stage-set, it makes use of stylized backdrops: now a scene of craters and copper palm trees, now platforms in the midst of whirlpools, now a Bagdad boulevard. It is the landscape of fairytale, of calculated artifice. The poetic imagination becomes, as Bersani observes, "a slide projector which ejects each slide almost at the very instant it is lighted up."[12]

This is an especially apt analogy. In "Villes," Rimbaud presents a succession of briefly illuminated scenes, each one astonishingly palpable and arresting. But when we look for the relational principle that might inform these images, we come up against a wall. In a single paragraph, Rimbaud juxtaposes chalets, craters, canals, gorges, inns, avalanches, a sea, flowers, a waterfall, suburbs, caverns, chateaux, towns, a boulevard in Bagdad. "The *Illuminations*," says Tzvetan Todorov, "have established discontinuity as their fundamental rule. Rimbaud has used the absence of organization as the very principle of organization that governs these texts."[13]

[12] Bersani, *A Future for Astyanax*, p. 244.

[13] *Poétique*, p. 245: "les *Illuminations* ont érigé la discontinuité en règle

Symbolist poetry, I suggested in Chapter One, is polysemous, a poetry of multiple relational meanings. Thus Eliot's Unreal City is a crowded and oppressive modern London, that has echoes of Dante's Inferno, Baudelaire's Paris, and the "Falling towers" of "Jerusalem Athens Alexandria Vienna." It is, above all, the landscape of the mind and, as such, it exudes brown fog and a "heap of broken images." But it also contains glimpses of a hyacinth girl and fishmen lounging at noon, of "Ionian white and gold" and a calm sea.[14] In "Villes," however, the depth of Eliot's cityscape gives way to surface, to what Jean-Pierre Richard calls a "shallow screen,"[15] upon which synecdochic images, the parts of an absent whole, appear side by side without necessary connection.

In the *Illuminations*, the word thus becomes, in Barthes' phrase, "un signe sans fond"—a free-standing sign.[16] Freed from their "normal" channels of reference, words can shed their natural and conventional associations. In most contexts, for example, a "boulevard of Bagdad" would evoke exoticism, adventure, sensuality, violence. But in "Villes" the Bagdad boulevard oddly becomes the site where guilds sing of the joys of work, and, what is even stranger, it is the place where the poet's vision, far from materializing, is dissipated. A similar inversion is found in Rimbaud's music images. When Eliot, alluding to Verlaine's *Parsifal*, cites the line "*Et O ces voix d'enfants, chantant dans la coupole!*" the reader of *The Waste Land* infers that this music-image symbolizes a glimpse of the supernatural, providing an ironic commentary on "The sound of horns and motors, which shall bring / Sweeney to Mrs. Porter in the spring."[17] But what are we to make of "Groups of belfries" that "sing the ideas of the peoples"? What are the ideas of the peoples and how do they relate to the Church?

---

fondamentale. De l'absence d'organisation, Rimbaud a fait le principe d'organisation de ces textes."

[14] *Collected Poems 1909-1962* (New York: Harcourt Brace, 1970), p. 69.

[15] *Poésie et profondeur*, p. 240: "un écran sans épaisseur."

[16] *Le Degré zero de l'écriture* (Paris: Éditions du Seuil, 1953), pp. 69-70.

[17] *Collected Poems*, p. 61.

Or consider Rimbaud's color images. A phrase like "Des cortèges de Mabs en robes rousses, opalines" ("Processions of Mabs in russet dresses, opaline") does not symbolize a particular complex of values as does Eliot's Ionian white and gold or Yeats's "Miracle, bird or golden handiwork," or, say, Stevens' "The houses are haunted / By white night-gowns. / None are green, / Or purple with green rings. . . ."[18] In "Disillusionment of Ten O'Clock," the poem in which these lines occur, the speaker longs for "red weather" (vitality, passion, relief from the ennui of "white night-gowns"), but when the poet of "Métropolitain" talks of "le sable rose et orange qu'a lavé le ciel vineux" ("the rose and orange sand washed by the wine-colored sea"), in what is ostensibly a description of an urban landscape, the signification of the colors remains open. Multiplicity of meaning gives way to a strange new literalism. It makes no difference whether "Villes" or "Métropolitain" were inspired by Rimbaud's visit to the London docks or his ride on the subway, for the cityscapes he presents are pure invention. The nucleus of such invention is, as Eric Sellin has said with reference to Reverdy's poetry, "a poetic image which is not metaphor as such. . . . It is not depiction, parallelism, or analogy, although it may occur within such frameworks; it is rather . . . a confrontation with an irreducible ambiguity."[19]

Irreducible in what sense? Here E. H. Gombrich's analysis of Cubist painting is especially helpful. The Cubists, Gombrich argues, wanted to create an art form that destroys mimetic illusion. "If illusion is due to the interaction of clues and the absence of contradictory evidence, the only way to fight its transforming influence is to make the clues contradict each other and to prevent a coherent image of reality from destroying the pattern in the plane." Cubism

[18] *The Palm at the End of the Mind, Selected Poems and a Play*, ed. Holly Stevens (New York: Alfred A. Knopf, 1971), p. 11.

[19] "The Esthetics of Ambiguity: Reverdy's Use of Syntactical Simultaneity," in *About French Poetry from DADA to "TEL QUEL," Text and Theory*, ed. Mary Ann Caws (Detroit: Wayne State University Press, 1974), p. 114.

counters "the transforming effects of an illusionist reading by the introduction of contrary clues which will resist all attempts to apply the test of consistency."[20]

This is, I think, a very important perception, not just about Cubism but about non-illusionist art in general. Surrealism, for example, does not, like Cubist art, involve an unstable structure of dismembered planes in indeterminate spatial positions; it retains what seems to be a three-dimensional pictorial image. But here it is the objects themselves that provide the "contrary clues" Gombrich speaks of. In the case of landscape paintings like Magritte's *The Glass Key* or *The Battle of Argonne*, for instance, we cannot be sure whether the grayish shapes in the sky are clouds or rocks, or whether, since the law of gravity seems to be defied through levitation, these "cloud / rocks" float upwards or downwards or are merely suspended in air. Again, the fantastic dismemberment of objects one finds in the painting of Chagall or Miró counters the transforming effects of an illusionist reading.[21] Rimbaud, in any case, anticipates both Cubist and Surrealist art in his deliberate scrambling of clues, a scrambling that inhibits the working of what Jean-Louis Baudry has called "le vouloir dire."[22] A poem like "Villes" defies, at every turn, "the test of consistency," so that we perceive Rimbaud's astonishing images as what Ashbery termed, with reference to Reverdy, "des phenomènes vivants" or "formes transparentes."

Here syntax is especially revealing. In Symbolist poetry,

[20] *Art and Illusion, a Study in the Psychology of Pictorial Representation*, The A. W. Mellon Lectures in the Fine Arts, 1956 (New York: Pantheon Books, Bollingen Series 35, 1960), pp. 281-282.

[21] On the relation of Cubism to its cognates, see Robert Rosenblum, *Cubism and Twentieth-Century Art*, rev. ed. (New York: Harry Abrams, Inc., 1976), pp. 13-14, and Chapter 11, "Cubism and Fantastic Art: Chagall, Klee, Miró," pp. 259-294. On Magritte, see Suzi Gablik, *Magritte* (Boston: New York Graphic Society, 1976), esp. Chapter 7: "The Object Lesson," pp. 102-125.

[22] "Le Texte de Rimbaud," *Tel Quel*, 36 (Winter 1969), 45. This is the second of two related articles by Baudry. The first appeared in *Tel Quel*, 35 (Autumn 1968), 46-63.

syntax tends to be extremely elliptical; words are wrenched out of their "normal" contexts and call attention to themselves. In reading Mallarmé, for example, we find the syntax so difficult that we are constantly forced to *stop* reading. As Bersani observes, "An unprecedented word order makes us ponder over the materiality of the words themselves, and any meaning we may come up with will be inseparable from the physical arrangement of the words. For it is precisely in the originality with which words have been placed in relation to one another that we immediately recognize the poetic specificity of Mallarmé's language: it *is* the poetic message."[23]

Rimbaud's syntax is the very opposite. Between the brief exclamatory opening and the climactic twenty-second sentence, the poem unreels a series of straightforward subject-verb units (and an occasional noun phrase), with relatively little modification and almost no subordination:

> Des fêtes amoureuses sonnent sur les canaux pendus derrière les chalets.
> (Amorous revels ring out over the canals suspended behind chalets.)

> La chasse de carillons crie dans les gorges.
> (The play of chimes clamors in the gorges.)

> Vénus entre dans les cavernes des forgerons et des ermites.
> (Venus enters the caves of blacksmiths and hermits.)

> Les sauvages dansent sans cesse la fête de la nuit.
> (The savages dance ceaselessly the revels of the night.)

These "normal" declarative sentences are arranged in what looks like a stable narrative sequence, but the very stability of word order and sequence works against the possibility of complex signification. The reader can assign each word to its proper slot, but the slots often turn out to be empty. Proceeding through the first sentence cited above in a linear fashion, we can assign meanings to "fêtes,"

[23] Bersani, *Future for Astyanax*, p. 248.

"amoureuses," "sonnent," and "canaux"; we know, moreover, that "fêtes" is the subject of the verb "sonnent," which is in turn followed by an adverbial modifier of place. But such information doesn't really help because we don't know what these "fêtes amoureuses" signify. As in the case of Ashbery's "Lacustrine Cities," the reader understands what is being said but not what is being talked about.

The indeterminacy of persons and places in the *Illuminations* is made all the more startling by Rimbaud's peculiar reliance upon demonstrative pronouns and definite articles. The narrator of "Villes" repeatedly points to things as if he assumes that we know what they are: "*Ce* sont des villes!," "*C'est* un peuple," "*ces* Alleghanys et *ces* Libans de rêve," "*les* feux," "*La* chasse des carillons," "*la* lumière des cimes," "*les* Rolands," "*les* passerelles de *l*'abîme," and so on. To talk of "Toutes les légendes" or "Le paradis des orages" or "les fabuleux fantômes" is to make the reader an accomplice who participates in the poet's vision. In specifying conceptual words like "paradise," "legend," and "phantom," Rimbaud naturalizes the poem's dream logic. Thus we come to accept without question the presence of copper palm trees and castles built of bone as if all cities contained such phenomena.

The position of the "I" in the *Illuminations* presents a special anomaly. Like most of Rimbaud's prose poems, "Villes I" is written in the third person. After the initial exclamation, "Ce sont des villes!" we are given a series of descriptive and seemingly objective statements: this happens, and then this, and then the following. Not until the twenty-second sentence when the "je" makes its first appearance does this movement break. But in Rimbaud, the Romantic distinction between subject and object, a distinction that persists in the poetry of Yeats and Eliot, collapses. The Rimbaud of the *Illuminations* could never have written lines like "And therefore I have sailed the seas and come / To the holy city of Byzantium,"[24] or "Here I am, an old man in a dry month / Being read to by a boy, waiting for

[24] "Sailing to Byzantium," *The Collected Poems of W. B. Yeats* (New York: Macmillan, 1956), p. 191.

rain,"[25] or "I found a dimpled spider, fat and white,"[26] or even his own early poem "Sensation," which begins: "Par les soirs bleus d'été, j'irai dans les sentiers" ("On blue summer evenings, I will go along the paths").

In his so-called *Lettres du Voyant* (to Charles Izambard, 13 May 1871 and to Paul Demeny, 15 May 1871), Rimbaud declares that the Romantics "n'avaient pas trouvé du Moi que la signification fausse" ("had found only the false meaning of the Self"). A poet like Lamartine "est quelquefois voyant, mais etranglé par la forme vieille" ("is sometimes a seer, but strangled by the old form"). As for Musset, "il y avait des visions derrière la gaze des rideaux: il a fermé les yeux" ("there were visions behind the gauze of the curtains: he closed his eyes").[27] For poetry must not be confessional:

> C'est faux de dire: Je pense. On devrait dire: On me pense.
> *Je* est un autre. Si le cuivre s'éveille clairon, il n'y a rien de sa faute.
>
> (pp. 344-345)
>
> (It is wrong to say: I think. One ought to say: I am being thought.
> I is Another. If brass wakes up a trumpet, it is not its fault.)

What do these fighting words really mean? The formula "On me pense" suggests, as Northrop Frye has observed, that the poet becomes the medium of an oracle, that autonomous voices speak through him, and that he is concerned to utter rather to address, his back turned on his audience.[28] Yet—and this is perhaps the key point—in Rimbaud's case, the "voices" are not those of divine oracles;

[25] "Gerontion," Eliot, *Collected Poems*, p. 29.

[26] "Design," *The Complete Poems of Robert Frost* (New York: Holt, Rinehart and Winston, 1967), p. 296.

[27] Rimbaud, pp. 348-349.

[28] "Towards Defining an Age of Sensibility," in *Fables of Identity: Studies in Poetic Mythology* (New York: Harcourt, Brace & World, 1963), p. 136.

they come not from *outside* and *above* but, like the magic flood that wells up underground in so many of his poems, from *inside* and *below*, from the poet's own subconscious. As Jean-Pierre Richard puts it, "Car si JE est un AUTRE, c'est bien je qui a produit cet autre." ("For If I is ANOTHER, it is still the "I" that produces that other.")[29] Therefore the poet can say: "J'assiste à l'éclosion de ma pensée: je la regarde, je l'écoute" ("I am present at the birth of my thought: I look at it and listen to it"). Like Laing's "Divided Self," the "schizoid" poet stands back and inspects his "moi" as if it belonged to somebody else. Indeed, the poet is no more able than is his reader to explain the content of his visions: "Il arrive à l'*inconnu*, et quand, affolé, il finirait par perdre l'intelligence de ses visions, il les a vues!" ("He reaches the *unknown*, and when, crazed, he ends by losing the understanding of his visions, he has seen them!")

If the "I" becomes "another," the Romantic dualism of subject and object is resolved; the self no longer contemplates nature but becomes part of its operational processes. "[Le poète]," says Rimbaud, "est chargé de l'humanité, *des animaux même*; il devra faire sentir, palper, écouter ses inventions." ("[The poet] is responsible for humanity, *even for the animals*; he must make his inventions feel, smell, and hear.") Thus the poet of "Villes," seemingly offstage, has already entered the objects of his field of vision. From the very beginning, the Alleghenies and Lebanons of dream rise up as if they were human. The sea, "troubled by the eternal birth of Venus" and "heavy with Orpheonic fleets and the murmur of precious shells," is viewed, not from the outside of a perceiving mind, but rather from the inside, as if the poet wanted to convey how it feels to be a troubled ocean, capable of bringing forth strange music. Again, the "harvests of flowers, large as our weapons and our vessels" are seen from within: the poet identifies with their sexuality, their power, their noise. The following sentence is especially interesting: "Là-haut, les pieds dans la

[29] *Poésie et profondeur*, p. 193.

cascade et les ronces, les cerfs tettent Diane." ("Up there, their feet in the waterfall and the brambles, stags suckle at Diana's breast.") The image has a peculiar, somewhat unpleasant immediacy, but it is difficult at first to say why. The key, I think, lies in the word "Là-haut," which implies that the narrator is somewhere below, observing the mountain scene of Diana suckling the stags above him. But the notion of distance is negated by the reference to "les pieds dans la cascade et les ronces"—a detail one could hardly perceive from far away. Perspective is, in other words, distorted, and one has the sense that the poet is himself "Là-haut," participating in the suckling process.

What Rimbaud calls "le dédoublement du moi"—the notion of "On me pense"—was to become a cornerstone of the new poetic of indeterminacy. For Rimbaud's is not just a new version of the concept of the Double—a familiar enough Romantic topos—it is, rather, the creation of a verbal field where the identity of the "I" is dissolved. In "Enfance," for example, the poet alternately appears as "I" ("Je suis le piéton de la grande route par les bois nains") ("I am the pedestrian on the main road through the dwarf forests"), and as "you" ("Au bois il y a un oiseau, son chant vous arrête et vous fait rougir") ("In the forest there is a bird, his song stops you and makes you blush"). But the narrator can just as easily disappear into the world of objects, which nevertheless bears the imprint of his presence: "Les nuées s'amaissaient sur la haute mer faite d'une éternité de chaudes larmes" ("Clouds gathered over the high sea, made of an eternity of hot tears").

Such participation in the life of external phenomena is found, in somewhat different form, in Pound's *Cantos*. For although the *Cantos* are, in one sense, profoundly autobiographical—they contain countless references to Pound's own life, to personal friends, fellow artists, former professors, particular incidents in particular hotels or restaurants, dialogue with priests or politicians—they reveal remarkably little about Pound's inner life. Indeed, Pound distances what would otherwise be personal by the force of his montage: images, insistently illusionistic in themselves, jostle one another on a kind of shallow screen or flat documentary surface so that their possible psychological import is subordinated to the linguistic play of surfaces.

Or consider the case of Beckett. In *How It Is*, the narrator, ostensibly recounting "how it was . . . before Pim with Pim after Pim," increasingly disavows the existence of a separate person named Pim or Bom or Pam Prim:

> I talk like him Bom will talk like me only one kind of talk here one after another the voice said so it talks like us the voice of us all quaqua on all sides then in us when the panting stops bits and scraps that's where we get it our old talk each his own way each his needs the best he can it stops ours starts starts again no knowing.[30]

Here the difference between subject and object, indeed between the speaker and his own words, disappears. Beckett's mode provides a context for a statement John Ashbery made in 1972, when he was asked why his poems utilize such confusing pronouns:

> The personal pronouns in my work very often seem to be like variables in an equation. "You" can be myself or it can be another person, someone whom I'm addressing, and so can "he" and "she" for that matter and "we"; sometimes one has to deduce from the rest of the sentence what is being meant and my point is also that it doesn't really matter very much, that we are somehow all aspects of a consciousness giving rise to the poem and the fact of addressing someone, myself or someone else, is what's the important thing at that particular moment rather than the particular person involved. I guess I don't have a very strong sense of my own identity and I find it very easy to move from one person in the sense of a pronoun to another and this again helps to produce a kind of polyphony in my poetry which I again feel is a means toward greater naturalism.[31]

[30] (New York: Grove Press, 1964), p. 76.

[31] Janet Bloom and Robert Losada, "Craft Interview with John Ashbery," *New York Quarterly*, 9 (Winter 1972), 224-225.

Such dissolution of identity—the notion that "*Je* est un Autre"—has troubled many readers, accustomed as we are to the consistency of voice that we find in Eliot's "Ash Wednesday" or Stevens' "Auroras of Autumn," or Theodore Roethke's "Lost Son" or Robert Lowell's *Life Studies*. Even *The Waste Land*, with its dramatic interplay of voices, does not prepare us for the kind of situation we find in a poem like "These Lacustrine Cities," where it is impossible to determine who is doing what to whom.

We are now in a better position to understand Charles Tomlinson's remark, cited in Chapter One, that "In the reaction of Rimbaud to Baudelaire, lies the germ of half the subsequent history of French poetry."[32] This is not meant to be a criticism of Baudelaire, whom Rimbaud himself called "le premier voyant, roi des poètes, *un vrai Dieu*" ("the first seer, king of poets, *a real God*").[33] "Le premier voyant" in the sense that Baudelaire was the first to articulate the vision of the modern city (and, by extension the modern world), in which, as Walter Benjamin says, "shock experience has become the norm,"[34] the city of the jostling, amorphous crowd, redeemed only in dreams and fantasies when desire is momentarily liberated, which reappears in Rimbaud's own "Parade" as it does in *The Waste Land* and in dozens of other classics of Early Modernism.

But Rimbaud's reservations are also telling. After praising Baudelaire as "a true God," he adds, as a kind of afterthought, "Encore a-t-il vécu dans un milieu trop artiste; et la forme si vantée en lui est mesquine. Les inventions d'inconnu réclament des formes nouvelles" ("And yet he lived in too artistic a milieu; and the form so highly praised in him is trivial. Inventions of the unknown call for new forms"). Too "artistic," perhaps, in that Baudelaire still longed for a coherent verbal universe, an organic poetry that would reflect, however obliquely, the external reality beyond its parameters. His great poem "Le Voyage," for

[32] "Rimbaud Today," *Essays in Criticism*, 9 (1959), 94.

[33] Rimbaud, p. 349.

[34] "On Some Motifs in Baudelaire" (1939), in *Illuminations*, trans. Harry Zohn and ed. Hannah Arendt (New York: Schocken Books, 1969), p. 162.

example, explores the bitter staleness and profound boredom of the human "voyage," whereas Rimbaud's "Bateau ivre" provides no such larger view, presenting the reader not with what it *means* to "voyage," both literally and imaginatively, in the modern world, but rather with the *how*, the process whereby the boat-poet enters "le Poème de la Mer" and his gradual surfeit.

Or again, consider Baudelaire's dream city, as presented in a poem like "Rêve parisien."[35] The ruling concept here is that of *artifice*. In his longing to escape "l'horreur de mon taudis" ("the horror of my miserable slum room") and the realities of a day-to-day life where "le ciel versait des ténèbres / Sur le triste monde engourdi" ("the sky rained down darkness / On a sad, lethargic world"), the poet invents a pleasure dome in which there is no human life, no sound, no natural light, whether of sun or moon. In this mysterious otherworldly realm, there are diamond abysses and tunnels of precious stones, groves made not of trees but of colonnades, statues of gorgeous nymphs reflected in endless mirrors and in the iridescent waters of subterranean fountains and cataracts. Every image contributes to the sense of mystery and artifice, thus pointing to a stable and coherent symbolic center. It is this stability, this grounding of images that Rimbaud was to deny in his own dream cities, as we have seen in the case of "Villes."

For Rimbaud no longer believed in the efficacy of the symbol. Jean-Pierre Richard writes:

> Rimbaud refuse toutes les formes sensibles du profond, et c'est là ce qui marque son vrai divorce avec Baudelaire. Ses visions s'étalent sur un écran sans épaisseur; pellicules suprêmement minces, et pourtant increvables, car il n'y a rien derrière, ni épaisseur, ni abîme, ni être, ni néant, ni dieu, ni infini. . . .[36]

> (Rimbaud rejects all manifestations of depth, and it is this which marks his real divorce from Baudelaire. His

[35] *Oeuvres Complètes*, ed. Y. G. Le Dantec et révisée Claude Pichois (Paris: Bibliothèque de la Pléiade, 1961), pp. 96-98.

[36] *Poésie et profondeur*, p. 240.

visions display themselves on a shallow screen; film-strips supremely thin and yet unbreakable for there is nothing behind them, neither volume nor abyss nor being nor nothingness nor god nor the infinite. . . .)

Having renounced Baudelairean *depth,* Rimbaud could only turn to less "artistic" sources for his "formes nouvelles." In the section of *Une Saison en enfer* called "Alchimie du verbe," he defines these new art forms:

> J'aimais les peintures idiotes, dessus de portes, décors, toiles de saltimbanques, enseignes, enluminures populaires; la littérature démodée, latin d'église, livres érotiques sans orthographe, romans de nos aïeules, contes de fées, petits livres de l'enfance, opéras vieux, refrains niais, rhythmes naïfs.
>
> (p. 228)
>
> (I loved absurd paintings, door panels, stage sets, back-drops for acrobats, sign-boards, popular engravings; literature that is out of fashion, Church Latin, erotic books with bad spelling, novels of our grandmothers, fairy tales, little books of childhood, old operas, silly refrains, artless rhythms.)

Absurd paintings, door panels, popular engravings, erotic books with bad spelling, silly refrains—from Dada to the present, French poetry has, as Tomlinson says, been drawn to these hybrid "anti-Art" genres rather than to the beautifully made lyrics of Baudelaire. And although our own early Modernist poets generally resisted the indeterminacy model of the *Illuminations*, the notion of enigma, of the poem as language construction in which the free play of possible significations replaces iconic representation, began to gain adherence among avant-garde writers. For some, like Gertrude Stein, the immediate impetus came, not directly from Rimbaud and his poetic heirs, but from the visual arts: from the great Cubist and Dada painters who were her contemporaries. How this process of assimilation took place is the subject of my next chapter.

CHAPTER THREE

Poetry as Word-System: The Art of Gertrude Stein

Act so that there is no use in a centre.
—Gertrude Stein, *Tender Buttons*

I

IN 1915, the most popular book of poems in America was Edgar Lee Masters' collection of imaginary epitaphs called *Spoon River Anthology*. Here is a typical Masters portrait:

Elsa Wertman

I was a peasant girl from Germany,
Blue-eyed, rosy, happy and strong.
And the first place I worked was at Thomas Greene's.
On a summer's day when she was away
He stole into the kitchen and took me
Right in his arms and kissed me on my throat,
I turning my head. Then neither of us
Seemed to know what happened.
And I cried and cried as my secret began to show.
One day Mrs. Greene said she understood,
And would make no trouble for me,
And, being childless, would adopt it.
(He had given her a farm to be still.)
So she hid in the house and sent out rumors,
As if it were going to happen to her.
And all went well and the child was born—They were so kind to me.
Later I married Gus Wertman, and years passed.
But—at political rallies when sitters-by thought I was crying

At the eloquence of Hamilton Greene—
That was not it.
No! I wanted to say:
That's my son! That's my son![1]

The appeal of such a poem was entirely dependent on its subject matter; Masters' graveyard poems promised major revelations about the hypocrisy of small-town Puritan America with its face-saving ruses, the disparity between genteel appearance and harsh reality, the sufferings of the little people at the expense of the smug rich. "Elsa Wertman" is a poem rather than a "True Confession" for no better reason than that Masters has chopped up his referential narrative into line units, although it is never clear why a line begins or ends where it does. Transpose the lines any way you like and nothing much happens, for instance:

When she was away he stole into the kitchen
And took me right in his arms
And kissed me on my throat, I turning my head.

How to compose a literary portrait that might avoid such dreary literalness—this was a problem that preoccupied Gertrude Stein in the years preceding the War. Of course there were plenty of models more interesting than *Spoon River Anthology*, for example, Yeats's mythologizing portraits of Maud Gonne in *The Green Helmet* (1910), Pound's Browningesque "Portrait d'une Femme" (1912), or Eliot's "Prufrock" and "Portrait of a Lady."[2] But in these poems, the movement is from the particular to the generic or archetypal, from Maud Gonne as a real woman, tall and strikingly handsome with her flaming red hair, who devoted herself to the cause of Irish Nationalism, to Maud as the embodiment of "beauty like a tightened bow," the

[1] *Spoon River Anthology* (New York: Macmillan, 1916), p. 114.

[2] Both written between 1910 and 1911 although not published until 1917 in *The Love Song of J. Alfred Prufrock and Other Observations*.

"terrible beauty" that erupted in the Easter Rising and that Yeats associated with Helen of Troy.

The creation of such symbolic figures as Maud-Helen was alien to Gertrude Stein, whose portraits of real people—Matisse, Picasso, Mabel Dodge, Ada (Alice B. Toklas)—were attempts to render in words what she called "the rhythm of anybody's personality":

> I wrote portraits knowing that each one is themselves inside them and something about them perhaps everything about them will tell some one all about them that thing. . . . I was doing what the cinema was doing, I was making a continuous succession of the statement of what that person was until I had not many things but one thing.[3]

The "continuous succession of the statement of what that person was" is necessary because "after all the human being essentially is not paintable."[4] One can describe a person by recording a sequence of actions, words, or gestures, but one cannot perceive another person in his or her totality. This is a lesson Gertrude Stein learned from Picasso:

> Really most of the time one sees only a feature of a person with whom one really is, the other features are covered by a hat, by the light, by clothes for sport and everybody is accustomed to complete the whole entirely from their knowledge, but Picasso when he saw an eye, the other one did not exist for him and only the one he saw did exist for him.[5]

Such "Cubist" deconstruction of the forms of women

[3] "Portraits and Repetition," *Lectures in America* (New York: Random House, 1935), rpt. in Gertrude Stein, *Writing and Lectures 1919-1945*, ed. Patricia Meyerowitz (Baltimore: Penguin Books, 1974), pp. 103-106. This text is subsequently cited as *W & L*.

[4] *The Autobiography of Alice B. Toklas* (New York: Harcourt Brace, 1933), rpt. in *Selected Writings of Gertrude Stein*, ed. Carl Van Vechten (New York: Vintage Books, 1962), p. 112. Subsequently cited as ABT.

[5] *Picasso* (London: B. T. Batsford, 1938), p. 15.

resulted in a series of portrait-poems like *Susie Asado* (1913)[6]:

Sweet sweet sweet sweet sweet tea.
        Susie Asado.
Sweet sweet sweet sweet sweet tea.
        Susie Asado.
Susie Asado which is a told tray sure.
A lean on the shoe this means slips slips hers.
When the ancient light grey is clean it is yellow, it is a silver seller.
This is a please this is a please there are the saids of jelly. These are the wets these say the sets to leave a crown to Incy.
Incy is short for incubus.
A pot. A pot is a beginning of a rare bit of trees. Trees tremble, the old vats are in bobbles, bobbles which shade and shove and render clean, render clean must.
          Drink pups.
Drink pups drink pups lease a sash hold, see it shine and a bobolink has pins. It shows a nail.
What is a nail. A nail is a unison.
Sweet sweet sweet sweet sweet tea.

The comparison of Gertrude Stein's verbal art to Cubist painting has been made again and again but not, I think, correctly.[7] It will not do, for instance, to say that *Susie Asado* is an abstract portrait compared to such "concrete" and

[6] *Susie Asado* was first published in *Geography and Plays* (New York: Four Seasons, 1922). Reprinted in *Selected Writings*, p. 549.

[7] See, for example, L. T. Fitz, "Gertrude Stein and Picasso: The Language of Surfaces," *American Literature*, 45 (1973), 228-237; Marilyn Gaddis Rose, "Gertrude Stein and Cubist Narrative," *Modern Fiction Studies*, 22, no. 4 (Winter 1976-77), 543-555; Michael J. Hoffman, *The Development of Abstractionism in the Writings of Gertrude Stein* (Philadelphia: Univ. of Pennsylvania Press, 1965), pp. 161-174, 176-181. Much more useful than these is Wendy Steiner's chapter, "Literary Cubism: The Limits of an Analogy," in her *Exact Resemblance to Exact Resemblance, The Literary Portraiture of Gertrude Stein* (New Haven: Yale University Press, 1978), pp. 131-160. Because Steiner's emphasis is on the way portraits refer to their subjects, she tends, I think, to overstress the difference between the verbal

"realistic" ones as Masters' "Elsa Wurtman." In discussing Stein's Cubism, critics repeatedly speak of "non-representational" or "abstract" art, of "flat surface," "shifting perspective" and "interacting planes." All these are slippery terms: Kandinsky was one of the first non-representational painters of the twentieth century but he was hardly a Cubist. "Flat surface" is one of the central features of Oriental art which is nonetheless illusionist. "Shifts in perspective" are a hallmark of the Baroque, and so on. The paintings of Picasso and Braque are, in fact, "abstractions" only in a very special sense. Take the case of Picasso's *Ma Jolie* (*Woman with Guitar*) painted in 1911-12 (Figure 1).

Ma Jolie carries the distortions of Analytic Cubism very far indeed. There is, to begin with, no distinction between solid forms (arms, knees, elbows, guitar, table) and the space around them. Mass and void are fused and the precise location of discrete objects in some kind of illusory depth gives way to a volatile structure of dismembered planes whose spatial positions are ambiguous. Thus the beige triangular plane near the lower left seems to be at once in front of and behind the grayish cup shape (possibly the well of a pipe) that intersects it. Objects seen in outline like the lamp on the lower right dissolve into opaque textured planes. The overlapping triangle-shapes, moving from top to bottom, originate in what may be the abstracted image of a face but then again it may be only an opaque cube with a transparent top. Light and shadow create a fantastic geometry of surfaces, a geometry that implies relationships in an illusory depth at the same time that it insists on the flatness of the surface.

But despite Picasso's decomposition of the human figure and its environment, *Ma Jolie* retains a network of what we may call "representational traces"[8]—the words "Ma Jolie"

---

and the visual, and hence she insists on the limits of what she calls the Cubist analogy.

[8] See E. H. Gombrich, *Art and Illusion, A Study in the Psychology of Pictorial Representation*, the A. W. Mellon Lectures in the Fine Arts, 1956 (New York: Pantheon Books, Bollingen Series 35, 1960), pp. 281-286.

in big block letters, the musical clef, the four-lined staff. Robert Rosenblum points out that the title "Ma Jolie" is a *double-entendre*, referring both to the refrain of a popular tune of the time ("O Manon, ma jolie, mon coeur te dit bonjour") and to Picasso's affectionate name for his mistress Eva.[9] The conjunction of such referential features with the fragmented, abstracted items depicted on the canvas creates an odd uncertainty. Which is "real"—the letters and musical symbols or the shifting and partial appearances of human forms and objects?

Cubist painting is thus characterized by a peculiar tension between conventional symbols (letters, musical notes, numbers, or such *trompe l'oeil* devices as real nails or scraps of newspaper) and stylized images of reality. In *Ma Jolie*, the printed letters appear to shift and fade in space and yet they rest flatly upon the opaque plane of the canvas as if they were printed letters on a page. The painting invites us to identify familiar forms and objects (a guitar string? an elbow? a knee? a lamp?) at the same time as it prevents us from applying the test of consistency. It is impossible to "read" such a painting as a coherent image of reality. Whatever interpretation we advance is put into question by the appearance of contradictory clues. The ambiguity of the image is thus impossible to resolve.

It is this tension between reference and compositional game, between a pointing system and a self-ordering system that we find in *Susie Asado*.[10] Unlike, say, "Prufrock," *Susie Asado* requires no special knowledge on the part of the reader. With the exception of "incubus," which has a special place in the poem, its vocabulary is perfectly or-

[9] *Cubism and Twentieth-Century Art*, rev. ed. (New York: Harry N. Abrams, 1976), p. 65. Rosenblum's excellent study, to which I am indebted throughout, makes clear that (1) Cubism is part of a larger continuum which includes Vorticism and Futurism, Dada and Surrealism, and (2) that, far from being equivalent to "Abstract" painting, Cubist art "always has an ultimate reference to external reality" (p. 45).

[10] These terms are David Antin's: see "Some Questions about Modernism," *Occident*, 8 (Spring 1974), 13. The whole essay-interview (pp. 7-38), is central to our understanding of Stein's impact on contemporary poetry.

dinary—*sweet, tea, tray, lean, shoe, grey, clean, yellow, please, jelly.* But whereas "Prufrock" is essentially "about" a particular kind of mental state—the spiritual anemia and emotional paralysis of a self-conscious and yearning modern man—Stein's portrait is not at all "about" the Flamenco dancer whose performance she and Alice Toklas admired on their trip to Spain and whose dance, so Stein tells us, inspired the portrait.[11] We know Prufrock by his morning coat, his collar mounting firmly to his chin, his bald spot. We know nothing about the appearance of Susie Asado. Like Picasso's *Ma Jolie,* Susie is never distinguished from the space in which she moves; we "see" neither her nor the Spanish dance she performs. Rather, a number of "verbal planes" are superimposed so as to create the kind of geometric fantasy found in the Picasso painting.

One such verbal plane is created by the poem's sound. *Susie Asado* does present approximations of dance rhythms. It begins with six emphatic beats:

> Swéet swéet swéet swéet swéet teâ

followed by the tripping rhythm, a kind of counterturn of

> ´ ˘ // ˘ ´ ˘
> Susie Asado

The assonance of high front dipthongs (iy) embedded in hard stops and spirants, leads up to the contrasting low

[11] In "Portraits and Repetition," Stein refers to her "early Spanish period [which] finally resulted in things like *Susie Asado* and *Preciosilla,*" *W & L,* p. 118. Carl Van Vechten concludes that both these compositions "make an attempt to recapture the rhythm of the same flamenco dancer" (*Selected Writings,* p. 548). But in *Charmed Circle: Gertrude Stein & Company* (New York: Praeger, 1974), James Mellow notes that whereas *Susie Asado* was inspired by a dancer named La Argentina, Preciosilla was a different performer, whose brilliant flashing eyes Alice B. Toklas compared to the diamond earrings she wore. Mellow writes: "Under the influence of the flamenco rhythms of the Spanish songs, Gertrude explored a new mode of syntax in which there were barely any associative meanings to the words she chose, only an insistent rhythm that ended in an astonishing burst of abstract language" (pp. 162-163). This insistence on the "abstract" style of the Spanish portraits is characteristic of Stein criticism but, as I shall argue, not quite accurate.

back diphthong of "Súsie" and then falls off in a series of diminishing vowel sounds: "ə̀ sáHd ə̀." When the phrase is repeated, the sound is not unlike that of stamping feet accompanied by castanets.[12]

In the course of the composition, the rhythm accelerates: "This is a please this is a please there are the saids of jelly. These are the wets these say the sets to leave a crown to Incy," which can be scanned:

/ ˘ ˘ / // / ˘ ˘ / // / ˘ ˘ / ˘ / ˘
/ ˘ ˘ / // / ˘ ˘ / // ˘ / ˘ / ˘ /

Rhyme and repetition underscore this movement. With the mention of the incubus, a sense of the demonic, the erotic is introduced, but only gently, playfully: it is, after all, a mere "Incy." After this reference, the rhythm slows down:

˘ / // ˘ / // ˘ ˘ ˘ / ˘ // ˘ ˘ ^ / ˘ /
A pot. A pot is a beginning of a rare bit of trees.

The slow movement then gives way to what sounds like emphatic stamping:

/ / // / / // / ˘ / ^
Drink pups // drink pups // lease a sash hold

The sentence "A nail is a unison" (˘ / // ˘ ˘ / ˘ /) enacts the resolution of sounds in a harmonic concordance as we move, full circle, from iamb to iamb, from "n" to "n." Finally, we have the recapitulation of the opening dance movement:

/ / / / / ^
Sweet sweet sweet sweet sweet tea.

[12] For the sake of convenience, I adopt the simplified notation used by George Trager and Henry Lee Smith Jr. in *An Outline of English Structure* (Washington: American Council of Learned Societies, 1957). There are four degrees of stress: primary (´), secondary (^), tertiary (`), and weak (˘). A double bar (//) indicates a caesura. It is interesting to note that *Susie Asado* was the first Stein text set to music by Virgil Thompson. In his autobiography, Thompson writes: "With meanings already abstracted, or absent, or so multiplied that choice among them was impossible, there was no temptation toward tonal illustration, say, of birdie babbling by the brook or heavy hangs my heart" (*Virgil Thompson* [New York: Alfred A. Knopf, 1966], p. 90).

If this were all, *Susie Asado* would be an interesting exercise in sound imitation and no more. But words, as even Gertrude Stein recognized, have meanings, and the only way to MAKE IT NEW is not to pretend that meaning doesn't exist but to take words out of their usual contexts and create new relationships among them. The phonemic or what we might call the "Flamenco dance" plane interacts with a variety of other "planes" or, more accurately, semantic codes. The title, for example, has erotic overtones. "Asado" means "roasted" in Spanish, and the notion of a "roasted susie" associated with "sweet tea" (with a pun on "sweetie") is obviously a sexual one. In the companion portrait, *Preciosilla*, we have the line, "Toasted susie is my icecream."[13] If we follow this lead, we can trace a chain of metonymic associations: "tray sure" (pun on "treasure")—"slips slips hers"—"yellow"—"This is a please"—"These are the wets"—"Incy"—"see it shine."

But, and this is where the Cubist connection comes in, the "roasted susie" erotic code can be just as easily construed as a pretty Japanese tea ceremony. The name "Susie Asado" sounds, for that matter, much more Japanese than Spanish. We can, accordingly, take the opening lines with their pun or "sweet tea" as an image of a Japanese geisha girl, gliding back and forth gracefully as she serves tea on what seems to be a garden terrace. A series of contiguous images supports this reading: "sweet tea"—"Susie Asado"—"told tray"—"silver seller" (pun on "silver cellar")—"jelly"—"pot"—"rare bit of trees" (pun on "rarebit of cheese")—"Trees tremble"—"shade"—"sash"—"shine." If we concentrate on this code, we can observe that the poem moves from agent to act (the carrying of the tray), to that which is on the tray (silver cellars, jelly), to the "pot" the tea comes out of, and then, in turn, to a larger receptacle like a vat, just as in Cubist painting, carafe shapes will repeat, with some variation, the shapes of glass bottles, and so on. As we move from "pot" to "vats," we move by analogy from

[13] *Composition as Explanation* (London: Hogarth Press, 1926), rpt. in *Selected Writings*, pp. 550-551.

those who drink tea in the garden to the pups who drink from the water bobbles in vats. The "bobolink" which "has pins" is another "link" or analogue for Susie Asado herself, whose movements recall a chirping bird: "Sweet sweet sweet. . . ." Finally, the nail, introduced near the end of the text, functions rather like the *trompe l'oeil* nail used by Cubist painters. It holds the portrait together and thus provides a "unison," that is, the agreement or consonance of concordant sounds. As the initial musical note from which intervals are reckoned, this "unison" takes us full circle to the beginning of the poem and so, appropriately, the last line repeats the first.

But of course *Susie Asado* is not really "about" a Japanese tea ceremony either. Contradictions evolve: for example, in the second half of the poem, the Oriental scene seems to have dissolved into a Western one, with its pots, vats, bobbles, pups, and nails. And the metonymic sequence cited above is offset by the embedding of individual words in seemingly irrelevant contexts. What is "a said of jelly"? A "told tray sure"? Syntax is repeatedly called into question, for here adjectives and verbs function as nouns ("A lean on the shoe"; "This is a please"), auxiliaries follow main verbs ("render clean must"), and predication becomes meaningless ("When the ancient light grey is clean it is yellow"). A equals B or modifies C or is in apposition to D, but how and why?

These are questions Gertrude Stein would want us to ask. For her verbal configurations are set up precisely to manifest the arbitrariness of discourse, the impossibility of arriving at "the meaning" even as countless possible meanings present themselves to our attention. We can, if we choose, focus on the homoerotic theme of *Susie Asado*, ignoring the other codes I have been discussing. But it all depends on our angle of vision. If the Japanese configuration strikes our attention, we are likely to subordinate the sexual note, relating "Asado" to the "told tray" and "Trees that tremble" rather than to "These are the wets." In this sense, Gertrude Stein's style does parallel, as much as the style of any one art can parallel that of another, the instability, indeterminacy, and acoherence of Cubism. In Stein's portrait, the figure of the woman is not to be found; her presence simply generates a variety of possible plots or images that don't mesh. Consider what titles we might give the poem: "Watching the Flamenco Dance," "A Valentine from Gertrude to Alice," "The Japanese Tea House," "Afternoons in Saint-Rémy," and so on. Just as Picasso's structure of dismembered planes has no vanishing-point, so *Susie Asado* has no fixed center; it becomes, in John Ashbery's words, a "hymn to possibility."[14]

Skeptical readers will object at this point, arguing that texts like *Susie Asado* are unnecessarily obscure, unreadable, and boring, that Stein fails to communicate a coherent meaning to the reader. The line between sense and nonsense is, of course, a narrow one. Remove all vestiges of reference and the text collapses into a series of empty sounds. To illustrate the difference between the "sense" of a Stein composition and nonsense verse, between *play* and *game*, it might be interesting to compare Edith Sitwell's "Jodelling Song" (1922) to its named source, which is Gertrude Stein's "Accents in Alsace" (1919):

From *Accents in Alsace*[15]

Sweeter than water or cream or ice. Sweeter than bells
of roses. Sweeter than winter or summer or spring.
Sweeter than pretty posies. Sweeter than anything is
my queen and loving is her nature.
 Loving and good and delighted and best is her little
King and Sire whose devotion is entire who has but
one desire to express the love which is hers to inspire.
 In the photograph the Rhine hardly showed.
 In what way do chimes remind you of singing. In

[14] "The Impossible" (review of Gertrude Stein, *Stanzas in Meditation*), *Poetry*, 90 (July 1957), 251.

[15] *Geography and Plays*, pp. 409-415. In the Notes to her *Collected Poems* (London: Macmillan, 1957), Edith Sitwell says of "Jodelling Song": "This is founded on Gertrude Stein's 'Accents in Alsace,' " and quotes the text (p. 142).

what way do birds sing. In what way are forests black or white.

We saw them blue.

With forget me nots.

In the midst of our happiness we were very pleased.

Jodelling Song[16]

'We bear velvet cream,
Green and babyish
Small leaves seem; each stream
Horses' tails that swish,

And the chimes remind
Us of sweet birds singing,
Like the jangling bells
On rose-trees ringing.

Man must say farewell
To parents now,
And to William Tell,
And Mrs. Cow.

Man must say farewells
To storks and Bettes,
And to roses' bells,
And to statuettes.

Forests white and black
In spring are blue
With forget-me-nots,
And to lovers true.

Still the sweet bird begs
And tries to cozen
Them: "Buy angels' eggs
Sold by the dozen."

Gone are clouds like inns
On the gardens' brinks,

[16] *Collected Poems*, pp. 142-143.

And the mountain djinns,—
Ganymede sells drinks;

While the days seem grey,
And his heart of ice,
Grey as chamois, or
The edelweiss,

And the mountain streams
Like cowbells sound—
Tirra lirra, drowned
In the waiter's dreams

Who has gone beyond
The forest waves,
While his true and fond
Ones seek their graves.'

In composing her "Jodelling Song," Edith Sitwell evidently believed that she was writing in the Gertrude Stein manner. It was Stein's book *Geography and Plays* (1922), in which "Accents in Alsace" appeared, that caused Sitwell to exclaim: "In the future, it is evident that no history of the English literature of our time could be of any worth without a complete survey of the work Miss Gertrude Stein is doing for our language. She is, I am convinced, one of the most important living pioneers."[17]

Gertrude Stein was very pleased with this review. In 1925, when Edith Sitwell visited Paris, a meeting at 27, rue de Fleurus was arranged. In *The Autobiography of Alice B. Toklas* the narrator recalls:

> I remember so well my first impression of her [Edith Sitwell] an impression which indeed has never changed. Very tall, bending slightly, withdrawing and hesitatingly advancing, and beautiful with the most distinguished nose I have ever seen on any human being. At that time and in conversation between Gertrude Stein and herself

[17] See Elizabeth Salter, *The Last Years of a Rebel, a Memoir of Edith Sitwell* (London: Bodley Head, 1967), p. 113.

> afterwards, I delighted in the delicacy and completeness of her understanding of poetry. She and Gertrude Stein became friends at once.
>
> (ABT, pp. 218-219)

Nothing is said of Edith Sitwell's own poetry, and one has the sense that Gertrude Stein's praise was largely a response to Sitwell's admiration for her own work.[18] In any case, the two writers became good friends. Later in 1925, Stein wrote her portrait *Sitwell Edith Sitwell*, which explores the nature of concord and discord, sameness and difference between two friends, ending on this note:

> Absently faces and by and by we agree.
> By and by faces apparently we agree.
> Apparently faces by and by we agree.
> By and by faces apparently we agree.
> Apparently faces by and by we agree.[19]

"Apparently" there was agreement: both poets regarded themselves as revolutionaries, creators of a new language. In her introduction to the translation of Rimbaud's *Illuminations* by her companion and former governess Helen Rootham (1932), Sitwell writes:

> Miss Gertrude Stein has . . . consciously or unconsciously been influenced profoundly by Rimbaud's intense visual activity, and by his powers of dissociation and reassociation—his gift of bringing all the attributes of the world together, irrespective of Time and Place. . . . In that most extraordinary and, to me, exceedingly beautiful book, *Geography and Plays* . . . we find many passages which, whilst they are entirely original in phrase, meaning,

[18] In her memoir, Salter tells an amusing anecdote that supports this view. During her stay in Paris, Sitwell was invited by Sylvia Beach to give a lecture on Gertrude Stein at Shakespeare and Company. Due to some misunderstanding, Sitwell gave a reading of her own poetry instead. Stein was furious and went home in the middle of the reading; Sylvia Beach had to patch things up between the two writers. See p. 114.

[19] *Portraits and Prayers* (New York: Random House, 1934), pp. 92-95.

> thought, and image, are yet, to my belief, most clearly a development of Rimbaud's habit of creating a newer and more poignant reality by means of association.[20]

For Edith Sitwell, who considered Rimbaud her "closest spiritual relation" and regularly described real persons and places in the vocabulary of the *Illuminations*, this was the highest possible praise.[21] Whether Gertrude Stein was in fact influenced by Rimbaud is another matter. Certainly it was not a conscious influence, for Stein never mentions his name. On the other hand, she was closely associated with Apollinaire and Jacob, both of whom were devoted followers of Rimbaud, so there may well have been what Sitwell calls an "unconscious" connection.

In any case, Sitwell repeatedly praises Stein's ability "to deprive words of their old smothering associations"; the "anarchic breaking up and rebuilding of sleepy families of words and phrases, for which Miss Stein is responsible" becomes her own goal.[22] Oddly, this aesthetic does not pre-

[20] "Introductory Essay," *Prose Poems from Les Illuminations of Arthur Rimbaud*, put into English by Helen Rootham (London: Faber and Faber, 1932), pp. 39-40.

[21] See Sitwell, *Taken Care Of, An Autobiography* (London: Hutchinson, 1965), pp. 4, 7, 32, 216. One of Sitwell's earliest published poems, "Trams," looks like a parody version of Rimbaud's "Villes I":

> Castles of crystal,
> Castles of wood,
> Moving on pulleys,
> Just as you should!
> See the gay people
> Flaunting like flags,
> Bells in the steeple,
> Sky all in rags. . . .
> (*Twentieth-Century Harlequinade* [Oxford: B. H. Blackwell, 1916], p. 9)

Wheels, An Anthology of Verse, whose first volume appeared in 1916 under Sitwell's editorship, is full of Rimbadian echoes: see, for example, Aldous Huxley's "Beauty" and "Gothic" in *Wheels*, Third Cycle (New York: Longmans, Green & Co., 1918), pp. 20-31.

[22] *Aspects of Modern Poetry* (London: Duckworth, 1934), pp. 225, 215.

vent Edith Sitwell from trying to naturalize Gertrude Stein's fluid meanings, to "make sense" of Stein's poems and fictions. Thus she writes of *Susie Asado*, "She [Gertrude Stein] produces before our eyes a woman with a canary-like brightness of disposition, a care for household matters, a light high voice, and a rather gay slipshodness, by means of rhythm alone."[23] This is singling out one code at the expense of all the others. Sitwell assumes that Susie Asado must represent a particular kind of woman, an assumption that sheds light on Sitwell's own habits of composition, habits that are really quite unlike those of Gertrude Stein despite the seemingly "experimental" urge of both writers.

Stein's "Accents in Alsace" is a more lyrical, playful composition than the condensed, elliptical *Susie Asado*. The passage in question is part of a longer piece, inspired by Stein's relief mission in Alsace during the winter following the Armistice.[24] It begins with the story of a young German deserter who joins the French Foreign Legion, but the concluding portion, cited by Sitwell in her *Collected Poems*, alludes to the war only obliquely. It is a comic valentine (evidently from Gertrude to Alice) that takes all the stock phrases of sentimental love poetry and points up their absurdity. "Sweeter than water or cream or ice," for example, seems to be built on the analogy of "Sweeter than pretty posies," but it makes no sense since water and ice are not sweet at all. "Sweeter than winter or summer or spring" is similarly playful. In the same vein, the little king who loves his queen is described as "loving and good and delighted and best," as if "best" were an attribute like "loving" or a reference to a specific response like "delighted." In this particular sentence, the rhymes jingle foolishly—"entire" / "desire" / "inspire"—the syntax undergoing all sorts of contortions in order to yield the needed rhyme word.

At this point, the cheerful little love song breaks off and

[23] *Aspects of Modern Poetry*, p. 219.

[24] See Mellow, *Charmed Circle* pp. 235-236; Richard Bridgman, *Gertrude Stein in Pieces* (New York: Oxford, 1970), p. 158.

the narrator says abruptly: "In the photograph the Rhine hardly showed." What does this sentence mean? That the river was hidden by massive troop formations? Dead bodies? That the photographer chose to focus his camera on other items in the landscape? That it is a long-distance shot? We never find out, for the narrator now poses a series of riddling questions: "In what way do chimes remind you of singing? In what way do birds sing? In what way are forests black or white?" These parallel structures are really quite dissimilar. The first question has to do with individual perception, the second is scientific, the third a riddle that has an answer: forests are black-and-white in a photograph. Indeed, Stein remembers that "We saw them blue. / With forget-me-nots," emphasizing the difference between reality and film. The memory of lovely forests, blue with forget-me-nots, leads to the final expression of joy:

In the midst of our happiness we were very pleased.

It is usual to say "In the midst of our happiness, we experienced a sudden sorrow," or "In the midst of our sorrow, we were pleased to hear that. . . ." But the tautology of Stein's statement is playful and charming. "Accents in Alsace" is like a Braque collage in which the fragment of a photograph, possibly showing something ugly or unpleasant, is incorporated into an otherwise bright and sunny still-life, perhaps a plate of fruit next to a guitar on a table covered by a colorful cloth.

By contrast, Edith Sitwell's "Jodelling Song" appears curiously one-dimensional. Its main innovation, and not a particularly remarkable one, is that the stanza form approximates the sound of the jodelling call echoing in the mountains: four truncated trochaic trimeter lines rhyming *abab*. But other than this superficial formal feature, "Jodelling Song" displays no structure at all. It makes a fairly obvious and vague statement: Ganymede, the shepherd boy with whom Zeus fell in love and who became his cupbearer, supplying the ruler of the gods with nectar, has become, in our tawdry modern world, a waiter who "sells drinks." In the course of the poem, he recalls his happy former life in the mountains and mourns for "his true and fond / Ones" who "seek their graves." Since we never know why this modern Ganymede had to leave his Alpine paradise, it is hard to sympathize with his fate. The Swiss locale is straight out of *Heidi*, with its mountain streams, "sweet bird eggs," "Mrs. Cow," "edelweiss," and cowbells sounding "Tirra lirra." When Edith Sitwell takes over Gertrude Stein's imagery and phrasing, as she does in stanza 5, the result is one of flattening out:

> Forests white and black
> In spring are blue
> With forget-me-nots,
> And to lovers true

Stein's reference was to forests as they are depicted in a photograph and she wonders which is more "real": the film or the mental image "We saw them blue." But in the Sitwell stanza, there is no reason for the forests to be "white and black," especially in the light of what follows: a sort of pop tune in which forests "In spring are blue / With forget-me-nots, / And to lovers true." Such verse hardly succeeds in "depriving words of their old smothering meanings."

Indeterminacy, we should note, is not the same thing as *vagueness*. When Edith Sitwell writes:

> Man must say farewell
> To parents now,
> And to William Tell,
> And Mrs. Cow

we know she is talking about the loss of childhood innocence, but William Tell is there for no better reason than that he fits into the Swiss decor. Presumably he shares the Alpine landscape with Mrs. Cow and the "storks" and "Bettes" and "statuettes" of the next stanza. None of these images has a *raison d'être* other than the appeal of sound (e.g. "Bettes" / "statuettes"; "farewells" / "roses' bells"), Sitwell's problem being that she has so rigidly circumscribed her imagery (mountain streams-chimes-cow bells) that she has no freedom to play with meanings. By contrast, "Accents in Alsace" barely touches on anything Alsatian; rather, it begins with a set of unsituated words and engages these words in a series of syntactic and semantic displacements that generate new meanings. The difference between "Jodelling Song" and "Accents in Alsace" is thus a difference between a text that limits its mobility by following a fixed set of rules, guaranteed to produce "clever" results (rather like a board game), and one that allows for free play, constructing a way of happening rather than an account of what has happened, a way of looking rather than a description of how things look.

II

So far, I have been considering Gertrude Stein's Cubist syntax, as it functions in portraits like *Susie Asado* or brief narratives like "Accents in Alsace." But there are two other styles that she perfected in her early and, to my mind, her most creative period: (1) the "beginning again and again" mode of *Melanctha, The Making of Americans*, and such short stories as *Miss Furr and Miss Skeene*, and (2) the Dada mode of *Tender Buttons, Lucy Church Amiably*, and such plays as *Say It With Flowers*. Let me begin with the first of these, the mode of repetition.

In *Composition as Explanation*, the lecture Gertrude Stein gave at Oxford and Cambridge in 1926 under the sponsorship of Edith Sitwell,[25] "composition" is defined as consisting of three things: "beginning again and again," "a continuous present," and "using everything." As early as 1905 when she wrote what she describes in the lecture as "a negro story called Melanctha," Stein recalls that "There was a groping for using everything and there was a groping

[25] Stein gives an amusing account of the genesis of the lecture and its reception in *ABT*, pp. 219-222.

for a continuous present and there was an inevitable beginning of beginning again and again and again."[26]

What did Gertrude Stein really mean by these terms? The best account of her use of repetition is that of William Gass, whose own fictions bear testimony to a strong Stein influence:

> Life is repetition, and in a dozen different ways Gertrude Stein set out to render it. We have only to think how we pass our days: the doorbell rings, the telephone, sirens in the street, steps on the stairs, the recurrent sound of buzzers, birds, and vacuum cleaners. . . . Everything to the last detail is composed of elements we have already experienced a thousand and a thousand thousand times. Even those once-in-a-lifetime things—overturning a canoe in white water or being shot at, pursuing a squirrel through the attic, sexual excess—are merely unusual combinations of what has been repeatedly around. Our personal habits express it, laws of nature predict it, genes direct it, the edicts of the state encourage or require it, universals sum it up. . . . Life is rearrangement, and in a dozen different ways Gertrude Stein set out to render it. We are not clocks, designed to repeat without remainder, to mean nothing by a tick, not even a coming tock, and so we must distinguish between merely mechanical repetition, in which there is no progress of idea, no advance or piling up of wealth, and that which seriously defines our nature, describes the central rhythms of our lives.
>
> Almost at once she [Stein] realized that language itself is a complete analogue of experience because it, too, is made of a large but finite number of relatively fixed terms which are then allowed to occur in a limited number of clearly specified relations, so that it is not the appearance of a word that matters but *the manner of its reappearance*.[27]

[26] "Composition as Explanation," *W & L*, pp. 25-26.

[27] "Introduction," Gertrude Stein, *The Geographical History of America*

Not the appearance of a word but the manner of its reappearance. This is the lesson Gertrude Stein learned early in her career, between the writing of her first novel *Q. E. D.* and *Melanctha.*[28] Here is the narrator's introduction to Helen Thomas, the heroine of *Q. E. D.*:

> The upright figure was that of Helen Thomas. She was the American version of the English handsome girl. In her ideal completeness she would have been unaggressively determined, a trifle brutal and entirely impersonal; a woman of passions but not emotions, capable of long sustained action, incapable of regrets. In this American edition it amounted at its best to no more than a brave bluff. In the strength of her youth Helen still thought of herself as the unfrustrated ideal; she has as yet no suspicion of her weakness, she had never admitted to herself her defeats.
>
> (*Q. E. D.*, pp. 54-55)

This account of "the American version of the English handsome girl" sounds like a pastiche of Henry James, in whose narratives each clause, each sentence moves the action forward with a little jump, adding important bits of information, qualifying what has gone before, or shedding new light on what has been said and done. Helen's "completeness" is "no more than a brave bluff"; she is "a woman of passions but not of emotions"; "she still thought . . . she had as yet . . . she had never."

Compare the following portrait of Rose Johnson and Melanctha Herbert which appears on the opening page of *Melanctha*:

---

or The Relation of Human Nature to the Human Mind (New York: Vintage, 1973), pp. 24-25.

[28] For the relationship of *Melanctha* to *Q. E. D.*, see Leon Katz, "Introduction," Gertrude Stein, *Fernhurst, Q. E. D. and Other Early Writings* (New York: Liveright, 1971), pp. ix-xlii. This text is subsequently cited as *Q. E. D.* For an interesting discussion of the sexual coding that occurs in *Melanctha*, see Catharine R. Stimpson, "The Mind, the Body, and Gertrude Stein," *Critical Inquiry*, 3 (Spring 1977), 489-506.

> Rose Johnson and Melanctha Herbert had been friends now for some years. Rose had lately married Sam Johnson a decent honest kindly fellow, a deck hand on a coasting steamer.
>
> Melanctha Herbert had not yet been really married.
>
> Rose Johnson was a real black, tall, well built, sullen, stupid, childlike, good looking negress. She laughed when she was happy and grumbled and was sullen with everything that troubled.
>
> Rose Johnson was a real black negress but she had been brought up quite like their own child by white folks.
>
> Rose laughed when she was happy but she had not the wide, abandoned laughter that makes the warm broad glow of negro sunshine. Rose was never joyous with the earth-born, boundless joy of negroes. Hers was just ordinary, any sort of woman laughter.
>
> Rose Johnson was careless and was lazy, but she had been brought up by white folks and she needed decent comfort. Her white training had only made for habits, not for nature. Rose had the simple, promiscuous unmorality of the black people.
>
> Rose Johnson and Melanctha Herbert like many of the twos with women were a curious pair to be such friends.
>
> Melanctha Herbert was a graceful, pale yellow, intelligent, attractive negress. She had not been raised like Rose by white folks but then she had been half made with real white blood.
>
> She and Rose Johnson were both of the better sort of negroes, there in Bridgepoint.[29]

Here the rational, generalizing narrative of *Q. E. D.* gives way to a series of what look like simple repetitions of predicative statements: Rose was this, Melanctha was that. Character traits and typical actions are named over and over again, and yet the most important thing remains unsaid:

[29] *Three Lives* (New York: New Directions, n.d.), p. 85. *Melanctha* is also reprinted separately in *Selected Writings*, pp. 337-457. All page references in the text are to the New Directions edition.

what is the curious bond between these utterly different women?

The novella never provides a meaningful answer to this question. The reader, for that matter, never comes to "know" Melanctha or Rose as particular individuals. It has been argued that Gertrude Stein simply didn't know how to create "character," that perhaps she had a dull mind. Or again, critics have suggested that she moved away from Jamesian psychological realism out of evasiveness, that her reluctance to treat the emotions of her homosexual characters openly resulted in a "protective language" that avoids direct confrontation with its subject. In William Gass's words, "This desire to gain by artifice a safety from the world—to find a way of thinking without the risks of feeling—is the source of the impulse to abstractness and simplicity in Gertrude Stein as it is in much of modern painting, where she felt immediately the similarity of aim."[30]

Evasiveness may well be the source of Gertrude Stein's highly stylized and reductive narratives, but we can also look at her "beginning again and again" mode more positively as born of the conviction that characterization, in the old sense, was no longer meaningful. In a 1946 interview, she said:

> The characters in the novels of the Nineteenth Century lived a queer kind of way. That is to say people lived and died by these characters. They took a violent interest in them: the Dickens characters, the George Eliot characters, the Meredith characters. They were more real to the average human being than the people they knew. . . . At the end of the Nineteenth Century that died out. . . . there really has been no real novel writing in that sense in the Twentieth Century. . . . Take Sherwood Anderson, Hemingway, Fitzgerald, in all these it is the

[30] "Gertrude Stein: Her Escape from Protective Language," *Accent*, 18 (Autumn 1958), 233-244; rpt. in Gass, *Fictions and the Figures of Life* (New York: Alfred A. Knopf, 1971), pp. 79-86. See p. 89.

> title and the form of the book that you remember rather than the characters in the book. . . . Can you imagine any one today weeping over a character? They get excited about the book but not the character.[31]

One might respond to this that Hemingway and Fitzgerald (or Faulkner and Joyce and Lawrence) may not have created "realistic" characters in a nineteenth-century sense, but that Leopold Bloom or Henry Sutpen or Nick Carraway are still more distinct and "real" people than Rose Johnson or Dr. Jeff Campbell or Melanctha Herbert. But if we think of Gertrude Stein as a precursor of our own late twentieth-century fiction, she seems to have been quite right. Take the following comment made in the same interview:

> . . . the novel as a form has not been successful in the Twentieth Century. That is why biographies have been more successful than novels. This is due in part to this enormous publicity business. The Duchess of Windsor was a more real person to the public and while the divorce was going on was a more actual person than anyone could create.
>
> (*Primer*, p. 22)

A visit to any large bookshop will confirm the truth of Gertrude Stein's statement. The public cannot be supplied with enough biographies: political figures, rock stars, writers like Delmore Schwartz (whose work most people have never read but whose life reads like a novel)—anyone whose life contains the slightest bit of drama becomes potentially interesting. *People* magazine is sold at every supermarket counter in America. And meanwhile serious fiction has turned inward, examining its own modes of existence, the power of its language as language, of "composition as explanation."

[31] "A Transatlantic Interview 1946," in Robert Haas (ed.), *A Primer for the Gradual Understanding of Gertrude Stein* (Santa Barbara: Black Sparrow Press, 1976), pp. 21-22. Subsequently cited as *Primer*.

Gertrude Stein's rejection of realistic fiction at such an early date (*Melanctha*, after all, predates Galsworthy's *A Man of Property*) must also be understood as a reflection of the Paris art world in which she moved. Her delight in artifice and abstraction makes more sense when we remember that her primary contact, during her formative years, was with the painters rather than the writers. Of *Melanctha*, she says in the 1946 interview:

> Everything I have done has been influenced by Flaubert and Cézanne, and this gave me a new feeling about composition. Up to that time composition had consisted of a central idea, to which everything else was an accompaniment and separate but which was not an end in itself, and Cézanne conceived the idea that in composition one thing was as important as another thing. Each part is as important as the whole, and that impressed me enormously, and it impressed me so much that I began to write *Three Lives* under this influence and this idea of composition and I was more interested in composition at that moment, this background of word-system . . . and the Negro story [*Melanctha* in *Three Lives*] was a quintessence of it.
>
> (*Primer*, p. 15)

What Stein means here, I think, is that the objects of Cézanne's representation—whether an apple, a bottle, or a human figure—revert intermittently to what Leo Steinberg has called "un-definition." "At certain expendable points, the demarcation of planes is checked so that, whatever their place in depth, they may be retrieved by the neutral substrate of the canvas . . . with the result that the layers of depth predicated by the representation relapse continually into unpredication, and remain mysteriously interwoven on—and reclaimed by—the immanent picture plane."[32] In this case, "one thing" is, of course, "as important as another thing." A similar "intermittency principle" governs the composition of *Melanctha*.

[32] "Resisting Cézanne: The Polemical Part," *Art in America*, 67 (March-April, 1979), 121.

The novella is usually read as a tale of conflict between rival values. As Richard Bridgman puts it:

> The frustrated trio [of the earlier *Q. E. D.*] is reduced to two persons in a standoff. This permitted Gertrude Stein to show in greater schematic detail how people in love are inevitably attracted to one another, then equally inevitably, separated. Calm seeks passion, conventionality seeks liberation, while conversely turmoil seeks peace and looseness yearns for control. But having located their opposites, these forces are then repelled. . . . Provided names, the forces are Jeff Campbell, a Negro physician who while attending a sick woman, falls in love with that woman's daughter, Melanctha. Their earlier names were Adele and Helen. . . .
>
> (*Gertrude Stein in Pieces*, p. 53)

This is, I think, somewhat misleading. In *Q. E. D.*, Adele and Helen do represent the polar forces Bridgman speaks of, but in the later version of the story, Melanctha and Jeff, the supposed opposites, often seem to coalesce. The blurring that takes place is not coincidental, for essentially, Gertrude Stein implies, people are unknowable and indefinable.

We are told, over and over again, that "Melanctha Herbert was a graceful, pale yellow, intelligent, attractive negress," that she was "patient, submissive, soothing, untiring," but she is also described repeatedly as a woman who "could only find new ways to be in trouble." "Melanctha Herbert was always losing what she had in wanting all the things she saw. Melanctha was always being left when she was not leaving others. . . . She was always full with mystery and subtle movements and denials and vague distrusts and complicated disillusions" (p. 89). And again, "Melanctha Herbert had always had a break neck courage. Melanctha always loved to be with horses; she loved to do wild things" (p. 91).

How do these matter-of-fact statements, made by what seems to be an omniscient third-person narrator, form a coherent image? Melanctha is submissive but wild, graceful but self-destructive, soothing but always getting into trouble, intelligent but never able to get what she wants. A similar indeterminacy is found in the characterization of Jeff Campbell:

> Dr. Jefferson Campbell was a serious, earnest, good young doctor. He liked to take care of everybody and he loved his own colored people. He always found life very easy did Jeff Campbell, and everybody liked to have him with them. He was so good and sympathetic, and he was so earnest and so joyous. He sang when he was happy, and he laughed, and his was the free abandoned laughter that gives the warm broad glow to negro sunshine.
>
> (pp. 110-111)

Jeff is always telling Melanctha to avoid "excitement" and "always know where you were," but he is the one who has the "free abandoned laughter." He is "earnest" but "joyous," "serious" but often laughing; he finds life "very easy" but never really knows what it is he wants.

The core of the narrative is not primarily the portrayal of conflict between opposites. Rather, Gertrude Stein's prose seeks to enact the rhythm of human change, to show how a relationship, any relationship between two people who are at once the same and different, evolves. This is why repetition is essential. The composition must begin over and over again; the same words—*wisdom, excitement, understand, know, certainly, deeply, wander*—and the same sentences are repeated with slight variation, and gradually everything changes.

Consider the meaning of the word "wander" and its cognates. Melanctha's propensity to "wander" has something to do with her mother's nature:

> Mis' Herbert had always been a little wandering and mysterious and uncertain in her ways.
>
> (p. 90)

And a few pages later:

> She was always pleasant, sweet-appearing, mysterious and uncertain, and a little wandering in her ways.
> (p. 92)

"Wandering," in this context, seems to mean "uncertain," "vague"—what we call in current slang, "spacey."

When Melanctha's own "wanderings after wisdom" begin, we take the word in the abstract sense—"wandering" is a search for Experience, an initiation into life, and so on. At other times, the verb is used quite literally: "Melanctha liked to wander, and to stand by the railroad yard, and watch the men and the engines" (p. 97). Or, "Next to the railroad yard it was the shipping docks that Melanctha loved best when she wandered" (p. 101).

But now consider the following successive examples:

1) Jane Harden had many bad habits. She drank a great deal, and she wandered widely (p. 104).
2) Jane grew always fonder of Melanctha. Soon they began to wander, more to be together than to see men and learn their various ways of working. Soon they began not to wander, and Melanctha would spend long hours with Jane in her room . . . (p. 105).
3) Melanctha these days wandered very widely. She was always alone now when she wandered (p. 108).
4) Melanctha now never wandered, unless she was with Jeff Campbell. Sometimes she and he wandered a good deal together (p. 134).
5) They were happy all that day in their wandering (p. 149).
6) Melanctha had begun now once more to wander. Melanctha did not yet always wander (p. 184).
7) And so now in these new spring days, it was with Rose that Melanctha began again to wander. Rose always knew very well in herself what was the right way to do when you wandered. . . . Rose always saw to it that she was engaged to him when she had any one man with whom she ever always wandered. . . . Rose always

was telling the complex and less sure Melanctha, what was the right way she should do when she wandered (p. 200).

8) One day Melanctha had been very busy with the different kinds of ways she wandered (p. 216).

In the first example above, "wander" seems to refer to Jane Harden's promiscuity: we would say today that "she slept around." But example 2 suggests exactly the opposite: Melanctha and Jane stopped "wandering" in order to spend long hours together in Jane's room. In (4) and (5), "wandering" seems to be equivalent to "making love" but, in that case, how can Melanctha "wander" alone (example 3)? "Melanctha did not yet always wander" (6) associates wandering with the wrong kind of sex, with something slightly shady. Yet in (7) the first instance of "wander" means to "explore" or "go out," the second is more or less neutral, and the third means "had an affair with." Finally, in (8), the meaning shifts again: Melanctha was busy, we might say, with different ways of fooling around.

It is Gertrude Stein's procedure, says William Gass, to "treat the elements of the sentence as if they were people at a party, and begin a mental play with all their possible relationships."[33] As we read "Melanctha," we come to know the heroine less and less rather than more and more. From the original certainty that "Melanctha Herbert was a graceful, pale yellow, intelligent, attractive negress," we gradually enter the world of a Melanctha whose behavior is oddly unpredictable. Each repetition of "Melanctha began to wander," or "Melanctha was very good now to Rose Johnson," or "Melanctha began to understand" fragments our sense of the particular person just as a Cubist painting decomposes a given image, accommodating contradictory "readings" of its subject.

Throughout *Melanctha*, Gertrude Stein suggests not only that human beings are essentially inscrutable but also that words are no measure of feeling and that a direct question

[33] "Introduction," *Geographical History of America*, p. 29.

does not necessarily receive a direct answer. The dialogue between Melanctha and Jeff is a case in point. First Melanctha is active and Jeff largely passive; then gradually, very gradually the tables turn: "Jeff did not know how it was that it had happened to him." We never know, any more than does Jeff, what goes wrong between them. The more both use the adverb "certainly" ("I certainly don't rightly understand Jeff Campbell why you ain't all these days been near me, but I certainly do suppose . . . ," p. 145), the less they seem to understand themselves or each other.

In defining the evolving relationship, language does become the analogue of experience. Take, for example, the following paragraph in which Melanctha responds to Jeff's pained question: "Oh Melanctha, darling do you love me? Oh Melanctha please, please, tell me honest, tell me, do you really love me?"

> "Oh you so stupid Jeff boy, of course I always love you. Always and always Jeff and I always just so good to you. Oh you so stupid Jeff and don't know when you got it good with me. Oh dear, Jeff I certainly am so tired Jeff to-night, don't you go be a bother to me. Yes I love you Jeff, how often you want me to tell you. Oh you so stupid Jeff, but yes I love you. Now I won't say it no more now tonight, Jeff, you hear me. You just be good Jeff now to me or else I certainly get awful angry with you. Yes I love you, sure, Jeff, though you don't any way deserve it from me. Yes, yes I love you. Yes Jeff I say it till I certainly am very sleepy. Yes I love you now Jeff, and you certainly must stop asking me to tell you. Oh you great silly boy Jeff Campbell, sure I love you, oh you silly stupid, my own boy Jeff Campbell. Yes I love you and I certainly never won't say it one more time to-night, Jeff, now you hear me."
>
> (p. 177)

What is Jeff—and, more important, what is the reader—

to make of this repetitive speech? In the course of fourteen sentences, Melanctha says "I love you" eight times, but like Mark Antony's repeated insistence that Brutus is an honorable man, each time Melanctha says the words Jeff longs to hear, they sound a little less convincing. For one thing, "I love you" is embedded in a series of qualifying clauses: "you . . . don't know when you got it good with me," "I certainly am so tired," "I certainly am very sleepy," "Now I won't say it no more tonight, you hear me." Melanctha also makes repeated disclaimers: "I always just so good to you," "you don't any way deserve it," "You certainly must stop asking me to tell you." And the text contains some telling substitutions: "of course I always love you" becomes "but yes I always love you" and then "Yes I love you now Jeff," where "now" can be taken in a number of ways.

What can Jeff make of Melanctha's words? "Yes Jeff Campbell heard her but somehow it was wrong now, the way Melanctha said it. Jeff always now felt baffled with Melanctha" (p. 177). It is a bafflement the reader shares. For Stein's mode of repetition does not intensify or heighten meaning. On the contrary, the reappearance of the word creates a peculiar gap in the text. The relation of word to feeling which is still present in, say, Molly Bloom's final triumphant "Yes," is subverted in *Melanctha*. "Yes I love you" becomes a way of speaking that has lost its relational force. Gertrude Stein can, in other words, tell us what her characters say and do but not what that speech or action *means*. What engages our attention as readers, then, is that, like Jeff Campbell, we are made to feel that the truth is just about to be disclosed only to learn—in the course of "beginning again and again"—that such "truth" can never be accessible.

In this context, the ending of *Melanctha* seems curiously out of key. After Melanctha and Jeff break up, she finds new ways of "getting into trouble," first with Rose Johnson, then with Jem Richards, and finally by herself. Then she becomes ill:

> Melanctha went back to the hospital, and there the Doctor told her she had the consumption, and before long she would surely die. They sent her where she would be taken care of, a home for poor consumptives, and there Melanctha stayed until she died.
>
> (p. 236)

Such emphatic closure seems inappropriate for a composition based on the principle of "beginning again and again" and "a continuous present." It is an interesting example of *not* "using everything." In a narrative that has begun with a limited number of verbal elements, and that has repeated those elements so as to create configurations that make us see more and more ways of looking at the nature of "love" between two people, the sudden introduction of "hospital," "doctor," "consumption," and "died" is oddly out of key. Two years later, when she wrote *Miss Furr and Miss Skeene,* Gertrude Stein had resolved this problem, the central motif, "they were very gay there," being repeated with the most subtle gradations and variations, culminating in the moment when, no longer living with Miss Skeene, Miss Furr "was regular in being gay, she always was living very well and was gay very well and was telling about little ways one could be learning to use in being gay, and later was telling them quite often, telling them again and again."[34]

Melanctha, Miss Furr and Miss Skeene, The Making of Americans, the Picasso portrait of 1909—all these are examples of verbal compositions in which indeterminacy is created by repetition and variation, sameness and difference, a rhetorical pattern of great intricacy, which is set up so as to create semantic gaps. Gertrude Stein's syntax enacts the gradually changing present of human consciousness, the instability of emotion and thought. The gap between signifier and signified is repeatedly emphasized, a gap that

[34] According to Richard Bridgman, *Miss Furr and Miss Skeene* was written between 1908 and 1912. It first appeared in *Geography and Plays* (1922). Rpt. in *Selected Writings,* pp. 561-568.

leaves room for continuous verbal play. *Melanctha* has been compared to film in its near-repetition of similar frames creating a continuous present,[35] but perhaps it is closer to Picasso's series of portrait-sketches of particular women, series in which each sketch reflects just a slight change in tone.

If *Melanctha* displays a structure of accumulation, *Tender Buttons* (1914) is a composition based on what Duchamp called, with reference to his early Dada paintings of 1912-1913, *reduction*.[36] The very title *Tender Buttons* is a kind of Dada joke for, by definition, buttons are not tender. It has been suggested that Gertrude Stein is referring to buds (the French *tendres boutons*) or to nipples,[37] but perhaps the best way to take the title is simply as an indication that the text itself will emphasize metamorphosis: hard objects become soft, wet substances dry up, persons turn into objects, buttons sprout before our eyes. In this sense, Gertrude Stein's series of verbal still-lifes (its three sections are entitled "Objects," "Food," and "Rooms") anticipates Surrealist art.[38]

The Dada matrix is important for in 1911, when Gertrude Stein was writing *Tender Buttons*, Duchamp was painting the first version of *Nude Descending a Staircase*, a painting

[35] See Bruce Kawin, *Telling it Again and Again, Repetition in Literature and Film* (Ithaca: Cornell University Press, 1972), p. 125.

[36] In an interview with James Johnson Sweeney (1946), Duchamp says: "The reduction of a head in movement to a bare line seemed to me defensible. A form passing through space would traverse a line; and as the form moved the line it traversed would be replaced by another line—and another and another. Therefore I felt justified in reducing a figure in movement to a line rather than to a skeleton. Reduce, reduce, reduce was my thought,—but at the same time my aim was turning inward, rather than toward externals" (*Theories of Modern Art*, ed. Herschel B. Chipp [Berkeley and Los Angeles: University of California Press, 1968], p. 393).

[37] See David Lodge, *The Modes of Modern Writing: Metaphor, Metonymy, and The Typology of Literature* (London: Edward Arnold, 1977), p. 153.

[38] See Lodge, *Modes of Modern Writing*, p. 152; William Wasserstrom, "The Sursymamericubealism of Gertrude Stein," *Twentieth-Century Literature*, 21 (February 1975), 90-106.

that uses Cubist means for new ends (see Figure 2). Duchamp's colors—tans and browns—are still those of Picasso or Braque, and the dismemberment of planes and multiple perspectives recall Analytic Cubism, but Duchamp's painting is less formalist and objective, more bizarre and erotic than, say, *Ma Jolie*. Duchamp dissects the nude's motion on the staircase as one might analyze the moving parts of a machine, a kind of fantastic dream machine whose mechanical parts are indeterminate in shape and behavior, challenging the viewer, stationed somewhere below the staircase, to make of the "nude" coming toward him whatever he likes. In *The Cubist Painters* (1913), Apollinaire called the art of Duchamp and Picabia (who was to become a close friend of Gertrude Stein's), "Orphic Cubism," which he defined as "the art of painting new structures out of elements which have not been borrowed from the visual sphere, but have been created by the artist himself."[39] What Apollinaire means here is that in the painting of Duchamp and Picabia, the relation between signifier and signified becomes even more tenuous than in the Cubist art of Braque and Picasso, which always insists on retaining at least some reference to external reality. Such "representational traces" as the *trompe l'oeil* nails, letters, numbers, and musical notes found in Cubist painting now disappear only to come in by the back door, a few years later, in Duchamp's Readymades—bottle rack, bicycle wheel, urinal—which take *real* objects of the most ordinary kind and transplant them into "artistic" contexts by means of placement and title.

Elaborate attempts have been made to decipher the individual still-lifes of *Tender Buttons*, but the text has remained peculiarly resistant to interpretation.[40] In a very suggestive essay, Neil Schmitz argues that Gertrude Stein's

[39] "The Cubist Painters: Aesthetic Meditations," trans. Lionel Abel, in *Theories of Modern Art*, ed. Chipp, p. 228. For Stein's reaction to the early Duchamp and Picabia, see *ABT*, pp. 125-126, 198.

[40] The most valiant attempt to "crack the code" is that of Allegra Stewart in *Gertrude Stein and the Present* (Cambridge: Harvard University Press,

central purpose is to challenge the primacy of the text itself, to manifest the arbitrariness of its discourse:

> *Tender Buttons* records, moment by moment, the play of the mind with the world before her [Stein]. But since the writer is not fixed, writing from a position, from a clarifying knowledge of the nature of things, and since the world (carafes, cushions, umbrellas, mutton, celery) is also in process, presenting only phases and attributes in their time and place of existing, nothing can be named and then classified, given as real. Everything is contingent, changing as it moves and the mind moves . . . the denotated world collapses. . . . Words as buttons, fastening side to side, signifier to signified, become tender, pliable, alive in the quick of consciousness.[41]

Schmitz's emphasis on writing as play and on structure as "momentary *con*-struction, made and unmade by the writer pushing into the silence of the literary moment,"[42] strikes me as entirely right, but since the thrust of his argument is essentially negative ("the ground of identification is destroyed"; "commonplace objects are no longer in their common places"), it remains to show how the enigmatic texts that comprise *Tender Buttons* work as poetic

---

1967). Stewart argues that *Tender Buttons* is an extended meditation in the form of a mandala, a "magic circle" or enclosure for the unconscious mind, originating in its maker's unconscious but elaborated with more or less conscious purpose, as an act of self-creation. Stewart's Jungian interpretations are so ingenious that what Stein has actually written becomes all but unrecognizable. Even Richard Bridgman, in his otherwise excellent study of Gertrude Stein, seems to try too hard to explicate the poems in *Tender Buttons*; see pp. 124-136. Cf. Michael J. Hoffman, *Abstractionism in Gertrude Stein*, pp. 175-197.

[41] "Gertrude Stein as Post-Modernist: The Rhetoric of *Tender Buttons*," *Journal of Modern Literature*, 3 (July 1975), 1206-1207. See also Schmitz's excellent discussion of language and identity in Stein's portraits and autobiography in "Portrait, Patriarchy, and Mythos: The Revenge of Gertrude Stein," *Salmagundi*, 40 (Winter 1978), 69-91.

[42] Schmitz, "The Rhetoric of *Tender Buttons*," 1214.

fictions. If the denotated world does collapse, as Schmitz suggests, what sort of world takes its place?

In *Tender Buttons*, objects—a carafe, an umbrella, a red stamp, a handkerchief—not only are fragmented and decomposed as they are in Cubist still-life; they also serve as false leads, forcing the reader to consider the very nature of naming. Here the Dada analogy can be helpful. Consider Duchamp's *The Bride* of 1912 (Figure 3). The title, like the titles of Gertrude Stein's "Objects," is enigmatic: what do these rotating disks, diagrammatically dotted paths of motion and fractured planes have to do with a bride? Duchamp's mechanical apparatus, made of tubular, bulbous forms connected by curious pipes and tendons, is neither fully "human" nor a fully man-made machine. It exists in a space somewhere in between, a mysterious being in a dream landscape, wired up, connected, and ready to make love—or simply to manufacture an unnamable product.

A similar type of enigma is found in "A Substance in a Cushion," which is the third entry under "Objects":

A SUBSTANCE IN A CUSHION

> The change of color is likely and a difference a very little difference is prepared. Sugar is not a vegetable.
>
> Callous is something that hardening leaves behind what will be soft if there is a genuine interest in there being present as many girls as men. Does this change. It shows that dirt is clean when there is a volume.
>
> A cushion has that cover. Supposing you do not like to change, supposing it is very clean that there is no change in appearance, supposing that there is regularity and a costume is that any the worse than an oyster and an exchange. Come to season that is there any extreme use in feather and cotton. Is there not much more joy in a table and more chairs and very likely roundness and a place to put them.
>
> A circle of fine card board and a chance to see a tassel.
>
> What is the use of a violent kind of delightfulness if

there is no pleasure in not getting tired of it. The question does not come before there is a quotation. In any kind of place there is a top to covering and it is a pleasure at any rate there is some venturing in refusing to believe nonsense. It shows what use there is in a whole piece if one uses it and it is extreme and very likely the little things could be dearer but in any case there is a bargain and if there is the best thing to do is to take it away and wear it and then be reckless be reckless and resolved on returning gratitude.

Light blue and the same red with purple makes a change. It shows that there is no mistake. Any pink shows that and very likely it is reasonable. Very likely there should not be a finer fancy present. Some increase means a calamity and this is the best preparation for three and more being together. A little calm is so ordinary and in any case there is sweetness and some of that.

A seal and matches and a swan and ivy and a suit.

A closet, a closet does not connect under the bed. The band if it is white and black, the band has a green string. A sight a whole sight and a little groan grinding makes a trimming such a sweet singing trimming and a red thing not a round thing but a white thing, a red thing and a white thing.

The disgrace is not in carelessness nor even in sewing it comes out of the way.

What is the sash like. The sash is not like anything mustard it is not like a same thing that has stripes, it is not even more hurt than that, it has a little top.[43]

Where, one wonders, is the cushion of the title? It is mentioned in the third paragraph: "A cushion has that cover," and again, more elliptically, in the fifth: "In any kind of place there is a top to covering." The "feather and cotton" mentioned in line 10 may refer to the substance

[43] *Tender Buttons* (New York: Claire Marie Press, 1914); rpt. in *Selected Writings*, pp. 459-509. All subsequent references are to this text. *Tender Buttons* is also reprinted in *W & L*, pp. 161-206.

inside the cushion, and perhaps the "tassel," "string," "sash," and "band" mentioned in the course of the text have something to do with cushion covers. But the fact is that the cushion of the title is not at the center of this prose poem. Rather, Gertrude Stein gives us a sequence of synecdochic images which refer to the making of a new "costume," evidently a fashionable ladies' suit and hat, on the sewing machine. In this context, the cushion appears as a possible pin-cushion. The invisible "pins" are hidden in such sentences as "Sugar is not a vegetable" and "Callous is something that hardening leaves behind what will be soft if there is a genuine interest in there being present as many girls as men."

I do not wish to imply that "A Substance in a Cushion" contains a literal description of the sewing process. Someone—we cannot say who—is considering the desirability of investing in a new fashionable outfit. She may be discussing it with someone else (Gertrude talking to Alice as the latter sews?) or simply talking to herself. In any case, the "costume" represents a "change." "The change of color is likely and a difference a very little difference is prepared." It will be something new: "Sugar is not a vegetable." Perhaps the color is not immediately appealing when seen on a small swatch of fabric, but when one steps back, it looks different: "dirt is clean when there is volume."

There is tension throughout between change and no-change, difference and sameness. "Supposing you do not like to change . . . supposing that there is regularity." And again, "What is the use of a violent kind of delightfulness if there is no pleasure in not getting tired of it." All this time, the unnamed project, evidently having to do with the creation of a new wardrobe, seems to be going on, entrancing the speaker. "A circle of fine card board and a chance to see a tassel." A new hat maybe. She tells herself that there is pleasure in "venturing in refusing to believe nonsense," but after all "the little things" (what little things?) "could be dearer." "In any case there is a bargain" and so "the best thing to do is to take it away and wear it and then be reckless be reckless."

Gertrude Stein never allows her reader to visualize the imaginary costume that is being created; its parts remain parts of an unspecified whole. Possibly the suit is made of "feather and cotton," but later we read:

A seal and matches and a swan and ivy and a suit.

which suggests a suit made of sealskin, something that matches something else, a swan boa or swan feather, and ivy trim. The emergent dream suit can be pictured in all sorts of ways: is it "Light blue and the same red with purple" and, if so, why does Gertrude Stein say "Any pink shows that"? Is the fabric hard or soft? And the hat is an even greater mystery. Perhaps it is "A circle of fine card board and a chance to see a tassel," although in the context, this reference could point to the "still-life" of "a table and more chairs and very likely roundness and a place to put them" as well. Out of a strange little closet that, we are told, "does not connect under the bed," a black and white band emerges, boasting a green string. One thinks of a little lizard coming out from under the bed. And now the machine goes to work: "A sight a whole sight and a little groan grinding makes a trimming such a sweet singing trimming and a red thing not a round thing but a white thing, a red thing and a white thing." The text refers to an "it" that is being made but we never know what "it" is any more than we can specify the "you" of the third paragraph or the "this" in the phrase, "This is the best preparation for three and more being together." What does "three" refer to here and how are they "together"?

Gertrude Stein's fluidity of reference creates what John Ashbery, whose pronouns are similarly indeterminate, has called "An all-purpose model which each reader can adapt to fit his own set of particulars."[44] The poet wants us to be

[44] "The Impossible," *Poetry*, 90 (July 1957), 251.

able to fill in the gaps in whatever way suits us. Thus we can picture a delicate little hat with a tassel and purple sash, but we can just as easily think of a squishy substance inside a "cover," just as there is "an oyster and an exchange." The chief rhetorical device used in the poem, x is not y, is thus ironic, promising, as it does, certainties that don't exist:

Sugar is not a vegetable
A red thing is not a round thing
A closet does not connect under the bed
The disgrace is not in carelessness nor even in sewing
The sash is not like anything mustard

Substances are defined by what they are not, but what they *are* remains open to question. And Gertrude Stein wants it that way because her real subject is change. "Come to season that," she remarks, building her phrase on the analogy of "Come to think of that." Buttons can be tender. Light blue can be pink. Dirt is clean when there is a volume. Nothing is what it seems to be. Closets don't connect under beds—did anyone ever think they should? Pronouns have no referents. Prepositional and adverbial modifiers are used misleadingly ("In any case there is a bargain"; "Very likely there should not be a finer fancy present"); aphorisms are created out of elements that don't cohere ("The question does not come before there is a quotation"); parts refer back to no wholes ("It shows what use there is in a whole piece"; "there is sweetness and some of that"). Nor can we define conceptual words like "delightfulness," "pleasure," and "nonsense," because the context provides no specifying limits that allow us to place these abstractions.

A text like "A Substance in a Cushion" marks a move toward Surrealism. It takes words designating the most ordinary objects—pincushions, fabric, closets, beds, a sash, a tassel—and puts them in extraordinary situations, treating these things as if they had a life and volition of their own. Like Duchamp's "bride," inanimate objects thus assume an erotic energy. The "substance in a cushion" can refer to a woman's genitalia, and "a violent kind of delightfulness" then turns out to be sexual pleasure. "Any pink shows that," as Stein remarks in the next paragraph.

But it would be just as wrong to read the text as being "about" sexual play as it is to assume that it is only "about" cushions or "about" the purchase of beautiful fabric and the sewing of a dress. The meaning of "A Substance in a Cushion," like that of the title *Tender Buttons*, remains latent, impossible to translate into something else. And indeed the important thing is not to establish a fixed meaning for any one item here (e.g. tender buttons as nipples), but to see how carefully Gertrude Stein has structured the whole sequence. The implications of "A Substance in a Cushion" are picked up in poem after poem: "Mildred's Umbrella," "A Method in a Cloak," "A Long Dress," "A Red Hat," "A Blue Coat," and so on. At the end of the sections called "Objects," Stein places the following poem:

THIS IS THE DRESS, AIDER

> Aider, why aider why whow, whow stop touch, aider whow, aider stop the muncher, muncher, munchers.
>
> A jack in kill her, a jack in, makes a meadowed king, makes a to let.
>
> (p. 476)

Here "Aider" is a pun on "Ada" (Gertrude's pet name for Alice), and the allusions are to the sex act and orgasm.[45] In the following section, "Food," sexual dress images continue to appear, as in "Eggs," which has the sentence, "Cunning shawl, cunning shawl to be steady" (p. 487). And even in the third section, "Rooms," where we have a mysterious space that has no "centre," we find "A cape is a cover, a cape is not a cover in summer" as well as an "elastic tumbler" and a "celebrating hat." Indeed, the whole of *Tender Buttons* may be said to take place in an indeterminate room without "centre," in which food and dressing and love rituals are occurring interchangeably. The public life of Ger-

[45] See Schmitz, "The Rhetoric of *Tender Buttons*," 1211.

trude and Alice—their dinners with Picasso and Fernande, their journey to Spain, Gertrude's quarrel with Hemingway—these are appropriate subjects for *The Autobiography of Alice B. Toklas*. But private life is different and demands a different language:

> The author of all that is in there behind the door and that is entering in the morning. Explaining darkening and expecting relating is all of a piece.
>
> (p. 499)

"*Tender Buttons*," says David Lodge, "is a feat of *de*creation: the familiar tired habits of ordinary discourse are shaken off by 'jolting words and phrases out of their expected contexts' and this is certainly exhilarating, but the treatment is so drastic that it kills the patient."[46]

This seems to me not quite fair to Gertrude Stein, at least not the Gertrude Stein of *Tender Buttons*. Perhaps the best way to think of a text like this one is to compare it to an X-ray. Words are related so as to show what is there beneath the skin, what is *behind* the social and artistic surface presented with such wit and drama in Stein's more traditional works like *The Autobiography of Alice B. Toklas* and *Everybody's Autobiography*.

To read a text like *Tender Buttons* can be exasperating and boring if one expects to find actual descriptions of the objects denoted by the titles—a carafe, a cloak, eyeglasses, a cutlet, cranberries. But Stein's are by no means Imagist poems. Rather, the author offers us certain threads that take us into her verbal labyrinth, threads that never quite lead us out on the other side but that recreate what Ashbery calls "a way of happening." Gertrude Stein's linguistic codes are tentative and buried; her Surrealist transformations of events must be taken literally as vivid if indefinable presences. As she says in "Roastbeef," "Any time there is a surface there is a surface and every time there is a suggestion there is a suggestion."

[46] *Modes of Modern Writing*, p. 154.

CHAPTER FOUR

"Lines Converging and Crossing" The "French" Decade of William Carlos Williams

—By form is meant everything in a work which relates to structural unity rather than to "meanings" dragged over from former associations.

—*Contact*, June 1923

—There is no need to explain or compare. Make it, and it *is* a poem.

—*The Descent of Winter*, 1928[1]

IN THE SPRING of 1922, the *Little Review* published a special number devoted to Francis Picabia. Aside from Picabia's own Dada compositions (poems, paintings, the man-

[1] The following abbreviations for Williams' works are used throughout:

SAA	*Spring and All*, in *Imaginations*, ed. Webster Schott. (New York: New Directions, 1970).
KH	*Kora in Hell*, in *Imaginations*.
DW	*The Descent of Winter*, in *Imaginations*.
IMAG	All other shorter prose pieces in *Imaginations*.
CEP	*The Collected Earlier Poems of William Carlos Williams* (Norfolk, Conn.: New Directions, 1951).
CLP	*The Collected Later Poems of William Carlos Williams* (New York: New Directions, 1963).
P	*Paterson* (New York: New Directions, 1963).
PB	*Pictures from Brueghel and Other Poems* (New York: New Directions, 1962).
A	*The Autobiography of William Carlos Williams* (New York: New Directions, 1951).
SE	*Selected Essays of William Carlos Williams* (New York: Random House, 1954; rpt. New Directions, 1959).
IWWP	*I Wanted to Write a Poem: The Autobiography of the Works of A Poet*, ed. Edith Heal (Boston: Beacon Press, 1958).

ifesto "Anticoq"), the issue included such items as two Cocteau poems ("Saluant Picabia" and "Saluant Tzara"), Gertrude Stein's "Vacation in Brittany," Sherwood Anderson's essay, "The Work of Gertrude Stein," and the first installment of a translation of Apollinaire's *Les Peintres cubistes* (1913).

One of the most enthusiastic readers of the Picabia number was William Carlos Williams. "It gives me," he wrote in a letter to the editor, "the sense of being arrived, as of any efficient engine in motion." "I enjoyed thoroughly, absorbedly, Apollinaire's article."[2] Not surprisingly, *Spring and All*, published the following year in Paris by Robert McAlmon's Contact Editions, pays homage to Apollinaire's famous essay. Indeed, *Spring and All*, a book of twenty-seven lyrics dispersed among passages of prose of varying length and tone, is Williams' most "French" composition. It bears the imprint not only of Apollinaire's aesthetic but also of Dada improvisation, of Gertrude Stein's poetry and fiction, and of Rimbaud's *Season in Hell* and *Illuminations*, portions of which had appeared for the first time in English translation in the 1920 *Dial*, side by side with six of Williams' own shorter lyrics.[3] *Spring and All* is, I think, Williams' most remarkable poetic sequence, a work so far ahead of its time that it was safely ignored until the sixties. "Nobody ever saw it," Williams recalled some thirty-five years after

[2] *Little Review*, 7 (Autumn, 1922), 59. Williams' first contact with Picabia, Duchamp, and other Dada painters and poets began in 1913 with the Armory Show. For a good discussion of Williams' ambivalent response to Dada in the decade that followed, see Dickran Tashjian, *Skyscraper Primitives, Dada and the American Avant-Garde, 1910-1925* (Middletown: Wesleyan University Press, 1975), pp. 86-90, 91-115.

[3] *The Dial*, 69 (July 1920) contains a translation of *A Season in Hell* by J. Sibley Watson (pp. 1-26). The August 1920 issue has Watson's translations of the following prose poems in the *Illuminations*: "Town" ("Ville"), "Childhood" ("Enfance"), "Lives" ("Vies"), and "Departure" ("Depart"). This issue also contains six poems by Williams: "Portrait of a Lady," "To Waken an Old Lady," "The Desolate Field," "Willow Poem," "Blizzard," "Spring Storm." See pp. 162-165.

its publication, "it had no circulation at all—But I had a lot of fun with it."[4]

In assessing Williams' debt to the Apollinaire essay he had read so "absorbedly," we must remember that *The Cubist Painters* was not, despite its title, primarily a defense of Cubism. Indeed, the original title was *Méditations Esthétiques*, with the subtitle *Les Peintres cubistes.* It was the publisher who transposed the two titles, evidently in order to increase sales since Cubism was the fashionable topic of the day.[5] But in the book itself, Apollinaire's aesthetic accommodates a wide variety of painters: Picabia and Duchamp (here called "Orphic Cubists") and the Douanier Rousseau, whose work is sui generis, as well as such "Scientific Cubists" as Braque and Gris. Picasso's painting was considered to be the meeting-ground of these different schools, ranging as it does from the neo-Romanticism of the Blue Period to the severities of Analytic Cubism to Surrealist fantasy. What all these painters had in common—and this is Apollinaire's point about "l'esprit nouveau"—was a rejection of an art that is primarily representational. The modern painters, he insists, "while they still look at nature, no longer imitate it, and carefully avoid any representation of natural scenes which they may have observed. . . . Real resemblance no longer has any importance, since everything is sacrificed by the artist to truth." Or again, "Cubism differs from the old schools of painting in that it aims, not at an art of imitation, but an art of conception, which tends to rise to the height of creation."[6]

In *Spring and All*, Williams echoes Apollinaire in his in-

[4] IWWP, 36. See also Paul L. Mariani, *William Carlos Williams, The Poet and his Critics* (Chicago: American Library Association, 1975), pp. 16-17.

[5] See Herschel B. Chipp (ed.), *Theories of Modern Art, A Source Book By Artists and Critics* (Berkeley: University of California Press, 1968), p. 220; Paul Waldo Schwartz, *Cubism* (New York: Praeger, 1971), pp. 59-65.

[6] The text, translated and slightly abridged by Lionel Abel, is found in Chipp, *Theories of Modern Art*, pp. 221-248; see pp. 222, 227. All subsequent references to Apollinaire's *Les Peintres cubistes* are to this text.

sistence on "the falseness of attempting to 'copy' nature" (SAA, 107):

> Such painting as that of Juan Gris, coming after the impressionists, the expressionists, Cezanne . . . points forward to what will prove the greatest painting yet produced.
>
> —the illusion once dispensed with, painting has this problem before it: to replace not the forms but the reality of experience with its own—
>
> up to now shapes and meanings but always the illusion relying on composition to give likeness to "nature". . . .
>
> —It is not a matter of "representation"—which may be represented actually, but of separate existence.
>
> enlargment—revivification of values
>
> (SAA, 117)

For Apollinaire, the rejection of mimesis meant the move toward "an entirely new art," "pure painting," as abstract as possible and relying "a good deal on mathematics" (p. 222):

> The new painters do not propose, any more than did their predecessors, to be geometers. But it may be said that geometry is to the plastic arts what grammar is to the art of the writer. Today, scientists no longer limit themselves to the three dimensions of Euclid. The painters have been led quite naturally . . . to preoccupy themselves with new possibilities of spatial measurement which, in the language of the modern studios, are designated by the term *the fourth dimension*.
>
> (p. 223)

This notion evidently appealed to the Williams of *Spring and All*:

> And what is the fourth dimension? It is the endlessness of knowledge—
>
> It is the imagination on which reality rides. . . . It is

> a cleavage through everything by a force that does not exist in the mass and therefore can never be discovered by its anatomization.
>
> (SAA, 139)

And in a 1925 essay on Marianne Moore, Williams notes: "A course in mathematics would not be wasted on a poet, or a reader of poetry, if he remember no more from it than the geometric principle of the intersection of loci: from all angles lines converging and crossing establish points."[7]

These were lessons learned not only from the painters, as transmitted by Apollinaire, but also from certain writers, most notably Gertrude Stein. "The poem being an object (like a symphony or cubist painting)," says Williams in his *Autobiography*, recalling his role in the Objectivist movement of the early thirties, "it must be the purpose of the poet to make of his words a new form. . . . it was Gertrude Stein, for her formal insistence on words in their literal, structural quality of being words, who had strongly influenced us. . . . It all went with the newer appreciation, the matter of paint upon canvas as being of more importance than the literal appearance of the image depicted" (A, 265).

But Williams also understood that, in the case of poetry, and, for that matter, in the case of Cubist painting as well, pure abstraction was not the goal. As he observes in *Spring and All*:

> . . . the writer of imagination would attain closest to the conditions of music not when his words are dissociated from natural objects and specified meanings but when they are liberated from the usual quality of that meaning by transposition into another medium, the imagination.
>
> (SAA, 150)

[7] This essay first appeared in *The Dial*, 78 (May 1925), 393-401. Reprinted in IMAG, 308-318. For this and all other bibliographical information, the reader should consult Emily Mitchell Wallace, *A Bibliography of William Carlos Williams* (Middletown: Wesleyan University Press, 1968).

Thus the Gertrude Stein of *Tender Buttons* (1914) "has completely unlinked [words] . . . from their former relationships in the sentence"; she "has gone systematically to work smashing every connotation that words have ever had, in order to get them back clean."[8] Such decomposition is essential, for poetry, as Williams says in the Marianne Moore essay, is a matter of "wiping soiled words or cutting them clean out, removing the aureoles that have been pasted about them or taking them bodily from greasy contexts" (IMAG, 315-316).

"Removing the aureoles" is equivalent to removing the metaphoric or symbolic associations words have. So the poet of *Spring and All* declares: "Crude symbolism is to associate emotions with natural phenomena such as anger with lightning, flowers with love it goes further and associates certain textures with" (SAA, 100). The preposition here and elsewhere (the next paragraph contains a sentence that ends with the phrase "such a paper as") is not followed by an object because Williams repudiates analogy. "Empty" writing is "typified by use of the word 'like' " (SAA, 100), and he declares:

> What I put down of value will have this value: an escape from crude symbolism, the annihilation of strained associations, complicated ritualistic forms designed to separate the work from "reality". . . . The word must be put down for itself, not as a symbol of nature but a part, cognizant of the whole. . . .
>
> (SAA, 102)

"Not as a symbol of nature but a part." The implication of this distinction is that words will be related metonymically rather than metaphorically, that the poetic effect will depend less upon polyvalence (vertical relationships along the axis of similarity) than upon the "horizontal" arrangement of contiguous word groups. Just as the "Cubist"

[8] "The Work of Gertrude Stein," *Pagany*, 1 (Winter 1930), 41-46; rpt. IMAG, 341-351; see 347; "A 1 Pound Stein," *The Rocking Horse*, II, 3 (1935), 3-5; rpt. SE, 162-166; see 163.

painter recognizes that, in Apollinaire's words, "You may paint with whatever material you please, with pipes, postage stamps, postcards or playing cards, candelabra, pieces of oil cloth, collars, painted paper, newspapers" (p. 232), so the verbal artist like Gertrude Stein takes words and *unlinks* them "from their former relationships in the sentence." One is reminded of Viktor Shklovsky's famed definition of art as *defamiliarization*, especially the idea that "An image is not a permanent referent for those mutable complexities of life which are revealed through it; its purpose is not to make us perceive meaning, but to create a special perception of the object."[9]

Williams' anti-Symbolist stance, his longing to annihilate "strained associations" can be understood by comparing a sample passage from *Kora in Hell*, his first experiment in improvisation, to the opening of Eliot's "Love Song of J. Alfred Prufrock," published in 1917 when Williams was half-way through the Prologue to *Kora*, and dismissed by him, with characteristically vehement exaggeration, as the work of a "subtle conformist," a mere "rehash" of Verlaine, Baudelaire, and Maeterlinck (*Kora*, 24).

(1) Eliot, "Prufrock," lines 1-12:

Let us go then, you and I,
When the evening is spread out against the sky
Like a patient etherised upon a table;

[9] See Shklovsky, "Art as Technique," in *Russian Formalist Criticism, Four Essays*, trans. and ed. Lee T. Lemon and Marion J. Reis (Lincoln, Nebraska: University of Nebraska Press, 1965), p. 18. The similarity of Shklovsky's concept of defamiliarization to Williams' repeated insistence on "unlinking" the object from its normal relationships is not just coincidental. Early Formalist doctrine was framed as a defense of the new Futurist poetry against the predominant Symbolist aesthetic. Such Symbolist theorists as Aleksandr Potebnja held that "Symbolism in language may be regarded as its poetic value" and codified the notion that "poetry is thinking in verbal images." See Victor Erlich, *Russian Formalism, History—Doctrine* (The Hague: Mouton & Co., 1955), pp. 7-9, 16-24, 145-154.

Thus the reaction of Formalist doctrine to Russian Symbolist poetry (e.g., Aleksandr Blok) prefigures the anti-Symbolism of a later generation of poets and critics of "the Other Tradition" in America.

Let us go, through certain half-deserted streets,
The muttering retreats
Of restless nights in one-night cheap hotels
And sawdust restaurants with oyster-shells:
Streets that follow like a tedious argument
Of insidious intent
To lead you to an overwhelming question . . .
Oh, do not ask, 'What is it?'
Let us go and make our visit.[10]

(2) Williams, *Kora in Hell,* IV, 2 (pp. 36-37):

How smoothly the car runs. And these rows of celery, how they bitter the air—winter's authentic foretaste. Here among these farms how the year has aged, yet here's last year and the year before and all years. One might rest here time without end, watch out his stretch and see no other bending than spring to autumn, winter to summer and earth turning into leaves and leaves into earth and—how restful these long beet rows—the caress of the low clouds—the river lapping at the reeds. Was it ever so high as this, so full? How quickly we've come this far. Which way is north now? North now? why that way I think. Ah there's the house at last, here's April but—the blinds are down! It's all dark here. Scratch a hurried note. Slip it over the sill. Well, some other time.

How smoothly the car runs. This must be the road. Queer how a road juts in. How the dark catches among those trees! How the light clings to the canal! Yes, there's one table taken, we'll not be alone. This place has possibilities. Will you bring *her* here? Perhaps—and when we meet on the stair, shall we speak, say it is some acquaintance—or pass silent? Well, a jest's a jest but how poor this tea is. Think of a life in this place, here in these hills by these truck farms. Whose life? Why there, back of you. If a woman laughs a little loudly one always thinks that way of her. But how she bedizens the country-side.

[10] T. S. Eliot, *Collected Poems 1909-1962* (New York: Harcourt, Brace & World, Inc., 1963), p. 3.

Quite an old world glamour. If it were not for—but one cannot have everything. What poor tea it was. How cold it's grown. Cheering, a light is that way among the trees. That heavy laugh! How it will rattle these branches in six weeks' time.

Prufrock's journey through "half-deserted streets" is not, of course, a mere evening walk. It is the journey of a man who longs for, but has lost, all potency, all capacity to feel and to be. Eliot's carefully chosen images—the empty evening sky, the "patient etherised upon a table," the streets that lead nowhere, the "sawdust restaurants with oyster shells"—create a symbolic complex that defines the anaesthetized consciousness, the life-in-death of the man who speaks these words.

Williams' Improvisation is also "about" a journey, but here the particulars—rows of celery, bitter winter air, the caress of the low clouds, the river lapping at the reeds, the house with its blinds down, the light on the canal, the poor tea, the car rattling down the road—point to nothing *behind* them. The passage seems to be no more than a journal entry in which the poet-doctor describes a drive in the country, evidently after he has made a house-call at a local farm. Driving along, he has an erotic fantasy about a woman who lives nearby, a woman with whom he hopes to have an assignation. Finding her house dark, its blinds down, he decides to leave a note and makes his way back to town, stopping for tea at a roadside inn, the inn he hopes to bring her to at some future time, perhaps "six weeks hence" when he will evidently return to the area.

Prufrock too has his erotic fantasies, dreaming of "arms that are braceleted and white and bare / (But in the lamplight downed with light brown hair!)" But it is implicit from the beginning of his speech that he will never bring these fantasies to life, that the mermaids will not sing to him. Williams' prose poem, on the other hand, remains semantically open. We don't know whether the poet will ever meet "her" or not, whether, for that matter, she has expected his visit or whether he really leaves her a note or only thinks about doing so. Nor does it matter. For Williams' aim here is to capture in *words* the actual process whereby a man, idly driving down a country road, is sexually aroused by the mental image of a desirable woman.

The "defamiliarizing" device in this case is repetition, both verbal and syntactic. Like Gertrude Stein, Williams begins with a seemingly innocuous word or phrase and then repeats that phrase in a series of altered contexts so that meanings are always shifting ground ever so slightly. Thus both paragraphs begin with the sentence, "How smoothly the car runs," but when we meet this sentence the second time around, we read it as an expression of lassitude rather than of eager anticipation; the absence of the expected exclamation point underscores this altered perception. In the first paragraph, the "how" clauses build up momentum, measuring the gradual arousal of the poet:

> How smoothly the car runs
> how they [the rows of celery] bitter the air
> how the year has aged
> how restful these long beet rows
> how quickly we've come this far

These exclamatory utterances are embedded in statements in which the narrator tries to orient himself: he is "*Here* among these farms"; "*here's* last year," "One might rest *here*," "Ah *there's* the house at last, *here's* April but. . . ." He finds assurance among "*these* rows of celery," "*these* farms," "*these* long beet rows." But it is a false assurance for he becomes increasingly disoriented: "Which way is north now? North now?"

Thus the second "How smoothly the car runs" is deflationary, signalling a total change in mood. The poet has not found "her." Under such circumstances, one must be sensible; one must go home again. "This must be the road. Queer how a road juts in." Avoiding the dark that "catches among these trees," he makes a brief stop at "This place," and again his blood pressure seems to rise as he tries to imagine what it would be like to be there with "her." But of course he knows that "a jest's a jest." And so objects in the environment are transformed and now the "how" slots are filled with unpleasant images: "how poor this tea is." The longing of "One might rest here time without end" (paragraph 1) is replaced by a more cynical, "Think of a life in this place, here in these hills by these truck farms. Whose life?" And soon the moment is over: "What poor tea it was. How cold it's grown." Still the light in the trees (like the references to the change of seasons in the first paragraph) brings on a measure of renewed hope and, as the passage ends, the poet is imagining "That heavy laugh" of the desired woman and projects: "How it will rattle these branches in six weeks' time."

"The purpose of art," says Shklovsky, "is not to make us perceive meaning but to create a special perception of the object." Apollinaire made much the same point about Cubist painting: "Representing planes to denote volumes, Picasso gives so complete and so decisive an enumeration of the various elements which make up the object that these do not take the shape of the object. This is largely due to the effort of the viewer, who is forced to see all the elements simultaneously just because of the way they have been arranged" (p. 118). So, in Williams' improvisation, there is no summing up of the protagonist's situation, no final epiphany that "human voices wake us and we drown." Rather we see "plane" after "plane," image after image, separately. In "Prufrock," the "taking of a toast and tea" is a symbolic food ritual, a debasement of the Eucharist; in *Kora*, drinking tea may be either good or bad depending on what has just happened or is about to happen. When the poet finds himself at nightfall alone at the inn without the desired woman, he naturally concludes: "what poor tea it was." The axis of contiguity thus replaces the axis of substitution.

By its very form, an improvisation like "How smoothly the car runs" is designed to emphasize inconsequentiality; Williams himself refers to his bedtime entries as "the reflection of the day's happenings more or less" (IWWP, 27), that is, as bits of automatic writing that allow the unconscious to come into play.[11] Yet there are curious lapses in *Kora in Hell.* In the Prologue, Williams quotes a 1916 letter from his poet friend, H.D., who reproaches him for relying too much on a "hey-ding-ding touch," a "derivative tendency . . . as if you mocked at your own song" (KH, 13). Williams responds indignantly: "H.D. misses the entire intent of what I am doing. . . . It might be said that that touch is the prototype of the Improvisations" (KH, 13). But perhaps H.D. was right. Consider the commentary appended to Improvisation XV, no. 1:

> Bla! Bla! Bla! Heavy talk is talk that waits upon a deed. Talk is servile that is set to inform. Words with the bloom on them run before the imagination like the saeter girls before Peer Gynt. It is talk with the patina of whim upon it makes action a bootlicker. So nowadays poets spit upon rhyme and rhetoric.
>
> (KH, 17)

"The thing that saves your work," wrote Pound to Williams with reference to *Kora*, "is opacity, and don't forget it. Opacity is NOT an American quality. Fizz, swish, gabble, and verbiage, these are *echt* americanish" (KH, 11).[12] But *opacity* is precisely the quality the above passage lacks; it has, on the contrary, too much fizz, swish, gabble, and verbiage. "Bla! Bla! Bla!" is too obvious a way to stress the futility of discourse. The strained comparison of "Words with the bloom on them" to the "saeter girls before Peer Gynt" is excessively cute and oddly violates Williams' own credo, stated on the very next page, that "the coining of

[11] See David Jauss, "The Descent, the Dance, and the Wheel: The Aesthetic Theory of William Carlos Williams' *Kora in Hell*," *Boston University Journal*, (1977), 37; Sherman Paul, "A Sketchbook of the Artist in his 34th Year," in *The Shaken Realist: Essays in Modern Literature in Honor of Frederick J. Hoffman*, ed. Melvin J. Friedman and John B. Vickery (Baton Rouge: Louisiana State University Press, 1970), pp. 36-39.

[12] The letter Williams cites in *Kora* is dated 10 November 1917; see *Selected Letters 1907-1941 of Ezra Pound*, ed. D. D. Paige (New York: New Directions, 1971), pp. 123-125.

similes is a pastime of a very low order" (KH, 18). Again, the metaphorical analogy between "the patina of whim" and a "bootlicker" is hardly an instance of "wiping soiled words" or "removing the aureoles." The "playful" tone of the passage, its air of Dada inconsequentiality, cannot disguise the poet's urge to *say* rather than to *make.* A related example can be found in the two sections that follow IV, 2 ("How smoothly the car runs . . ."):

> The frontispiece is her portrait and further on—the obituary sermon: she held the school upon her shoulders. Did she. Well—turn in here then:—we found money in the blood and some in the room and on the stairs. My God I never knew a man had so much blood in his head! —and thirteen empty whisky bottles. I am sorry but those who come this way meet strange company. This is you see death's canticle.
>
> ---
>
> *A young woman who had excelled at intellectual pursuits, a person of great power in her sphere, died on the same night that a man was murdered in the next street, a fellow of very gross behavior. The poet takes advantage of this to send them on their way side by side without making the usual unhappy moral distinctions.*
>
> (KH, 37-38)

Despite the disclaimer of the last sentence, the poet has in fact made "the usual unhappy distinctions." In showing that rich and poor, educated and uneducated, female and male, meet the same sordid death, he is suggesting that such sex and class labels are meaningless. The lesson of "death's canticle" is, to put it baldly, don't judge a book by its cover. Such expository discourse runs counter to what Williams was to call, some years later, "the disjointing process."[13] One reads much about *Kora* as a process poem, a "field of action in which the reader can read according to

[13] *A Novelette and Other Prose* (Toulon, France: TO Publishers, 1932); rpt. in IMAG, 269-304; see 295.

whatever sequence he wishes," a "sequence of free variations on [the] theme of polarity."[14] But the variations are only partly "free" and the text is not always a "field of action." *Kora in Hell* remains a fascinating experiment in eliminating such traditional features as plot, argument, linear continuity, and connectives. But Williams still hesitates between artistic alternatives, not yet certain how to bring his "Kora" out of her hell.

How can the poet infuse his compositions with the "power TO ESCAPE ILLUSION" (SAA, 112)? A power to be found, so the poet of *Spring and All* believes, in certain Cubist paintings, most notably those of Juan Gris.[15] Williams, who was to remark in later life: "I would rather have been a painter than to bother with these god-damn words" (IWWP, 29), puzzled over this question for years. In the Marianne Moore essay, he observes:

> Unlike the painters the poet has not resorted to distortions or the abstract in form. Miss Moore accomplishes a like result by rapidity of movement. A poem such as "Marriage" is an anthology of transit. It is a pleasure that can be held firm only by moving rapidly from one thing to the next. It gives the impression of a passage through. (IMAG, 311)

Spring and All, published three years after *Kora*, is just such an "anthology of transit": "from all angles lines converging and crossing establish points" (IMAG, 309). One chapter or poem opens up into the next; sentences are left hanging, as in

[14] See respectively, Joseph Riddel, "The Wanderer and the Dance: William Carlos Williams' Early Poetics," in *The Shaken Realist*, p. 63; Bram Djikstra, *The Hieroglyphics of a New Speech: Cubism, Stieglitz, and the Early Poetry of William Carlos Williams* (Princeton: Princeton University Press, 1969), p. 73; J. Hillis Miller, *Poets of Reality: Six Twentieth Century Writers* (New York: Atheneum, 1966), p. 303.

[15] See esp. SAA, 107, 110, 112, 117, and cf. *A Novelette* (1932), whose fourth section is called "Juan Gris" (IMAG, 283-286).

> The farmer and the fisherman who read their own lives there have a practical corrective for—
>
> (SAA, 100)

> It is very typical of almost all that is done by the writers who fill the pages every month of such a paper as
>
> (SAA, 100)

The poems themselves now display a kind of cutting new to Williams. Perhaps the first difference to note between the lyrics collected in *Sour Grapes* (1921) and those of *Spring and All* is that the ubiquitous exclamation point of the former book is now replaced by the dash. Within the space of twenty-seven poems, there is only a single instance of the exclamation point:

> I was your nightgown
> I watched!
>
> (SAA, 115)

An exclamation point implies, of course, a momentary finality, a stop however ecstatic, whereas the dash stresses fluidity, a rapid shift from one thing to another. In *Sour Grapes,* the poetic surface is not yet broken; words are organized into complete sentences:

> The sky has given over
> its bitterness.
> Out of the dark change
> all day long
> rain falls and falls
> as if it would never end.
>
> ("Spring Storm," CEP, 202)

Or

> They call me and I go.
> It is a frozen road
> past midnight, a dust
> of snow caught

in the rigid wheeltracks.
The door opens.
I smile, enter and
shake off the cold.

("Complaint," CEP, 199)

In these poems, Williams has already discovered his characteristic imagery. As James Breslin notes: "he strips objects bare of all acquired associations"; "details do not combine into symbolic clusters but instead create a literal specificity."[16] But between the writing of these sharply etched Imagist poems and the lyrics of *Spring and All*, a marked change has occurred. To call Williams' early poems "Cubist," as does Bram Djikstra, is, I think, to overstress the pictorial component of Cubist art. Djikstra maintains, for example, that "Spring Strains" (1916) "is an elaborate attempt at painting a Cubist picture in words":

> It represents a visual plane, a visual field of action, within which objects are analyzed in a strictly pictorial fashion. They are isolated, intensified through compression, then broken into parts:
>
> two blue-grey birds chasing
> a third struggle in circles, angles
> swift convergings to a point that bursts
> instantly!
>
> Williams shatters the forms in his picture just as a Cubist painter fragments his forms, and in doing so he achieves the "constructive dispersal of these fragments over the canvas" of his poem which Kandinsky mentions in discussing the work of Picasso.[17]

But in fact the structure of the passage cited is still essentially linear; form is not shattered and fragmented. "Spring

[16] *William Carlos Williams, An American Artist* (New York: Oxford, 1970), pp. 78, 52.

[17] *Hieroglyphics of a New Speech*, pp. 64-65.

Strains" is a highly pictorial poem, a sequence of clear visual images. In *Spring and All*, such images are not just "isolated" and "intensified through compression"; they are decomposed:

The red paper box
hinged with cloth

is lined
inside and out
with imitation
leather

It is the sun
the table
with dinner
on it for
these are the same—

Its twoinch trays
have engineers
that convey glue
to airplanes

or for old ladies
that darn socks
paper clips
and red elastics—

What is the end
to insects
that suck gummed
labels?

for this is eternity
through its
dial we discover
transparent tissue
on a spool

But the stars
are round

cardboard
with a tin edge

and a ring
to fasten them
to a trunk
for the vacation—

(SAA, 123-124)

This is not as radical an experiment as Gertrude Stein's "box" poems in *Tender Buttons*,[18] but its Cubist style recalls the fragmentation and superposition of planes, the tension between compositional game and representational reference that characterizes Stein's work. Juan Gris, Williams' "favorite painter" at this time (A, 318), uses geometric analogies to confound the absolute identities of objects and their spatial positions, but he does not submit his objects to the large-scale decomposition we find in, say, Picasso's *Ma Jolie*.

Consider *Still Life Before an Open Window: Place Ravignan*, painted in 1915 (Figure 4). Here we can identify the objects on the table—carafe, bowl of fruit, goblet, newspaper—and the window view—shuttered windows across the street, trees, balcony rails—quite easily. We can also make out the label "MEDOC" and the block letters of "LE JOURNAL." But Gris' "real" objects are seen as through a distorting lens; they are rigidly subordinated to the geometric structure of the painting: a complex set of interlocking triangles and rectangular planes whose spatial positions are ambig-

[18] There are two poems called "A Box" in *Tender Buttons*. Here is the first:

> Out of kindness comes redness and out of rudeness comes rapid same question, out of an eye comes research, out of selection comes painful cattle. So then the order is that a white way of being round is something suggesting a pin and it is disappointing, it is not, it is so rudimentary to be analysed and see a fine substance strangely, it is so earnest to have a green point not to red but to point again.

—"Objects," *Selected Writings of Gertrude Stein*, ed. Carl Van Vechten (New York: Vintage, 1962), p. 463. See also pp. 465-466 for the second "A Box."

uous. Here structure calls attention to itself: carafe, tree trunks, window frames, an apple—all become relational parts of Gris' charged surface.

Just so, Williams' poem is not a "description" of a red paper box in the sense that "Spring Strains" presents the image of "two blue-grey birds" struggling in circles, against the backdrop of a "tissue-thin monotone of blue-grey buds." Like the mysterious boxes of Joseph Cornell, Williams' "box" immediately becomes a kind of open sesame, waiting to be entered:

The red paper box
hinged with cloth

is lined
inside and out
with imitation
leather

Each of the four-line stanzas that follows has the shape of a box, being roughly a small square centered on the wide empty space of the page.[19] The squareness of the stanza is further enhanced by the pervasive presence of consonance at line ends:

or for old ladie*s*
that darn sock*s*
paper clip*s*
and red elastic*s*

On the other hand, syntactic units within a given stanza are regularly broken up by line breaks and internal alliteration as in

through its
dial we discover
transparent tissue
on a spool

[19] Strictly speaking, stanzas 2 and 6 (following the opening couplet) have five rather than four lines, but the analogy to the box still holds.

Here the lineation urges us to take "dial we discover" as a separate semantic unit even though its meaning is totally dependent on the lines in which it is embedded.

The poem's particulars, moreover, refuse to cohere. The red *paper* box turns out to be "hinged with cloth." If it is lined "inside and out" (an odd description for lining usually refers to what is inside) not outside, with "imitation / leather," how can it be made of paper? If its "two-inch trays" have "engineers / that convey glue / to airplanes," it may have large hinges; if, on the other hand, it holds "paper clips / and red elastics" for "old ladies / that darn socks," it must be one of those delicate little boxes with tiny compartments and drawers. "What is the end," the poet asks, "to insects / that suck gummed labels"? But how do insects get at these drawers? And what is the "dial" by means of which "we discover / transparent tissue / on a spool"? Perhaps the combination lock of a jewelry box. But then, would a box that contains airplane glue have a lock? Finally, and most confusing, are the "stars" made of "round / cardboard / with a tin edge" inside the box or do they decorate its surface? How and why would one fasten "them" as opposed to "it" (the box) "to a trunk / for the vacation"?

By the time we reach the end of the poem with its deceptive "boxy" stanzas, we realize that the "box" is purely the poet's construction. We cannot visualize it. "If illusion," writes E. H. Gombrich, "is due to the interaction of clues and the absence of contradictory evidence, the only way to fight its transforming influence is to make the clues contradict each other and to prevent a coherent image of reality from destroying the pattern in the plane."[20] Like a

[20] *Art and Illusion, A Study in the Psychology of Pictorial Representation:* The A. W. Mellon Lectures in the Fine Arts, 1956 (New York: Pantheon Books, 1960), p. 282. In *Skyscraper Primitives*, Dickran Tashjian argues that the lyrics in *Spring and All* are comparable to Duchamp's Readymades: thus the red wheelbarrow is a "readymade transposed into language through accurate, concise description and subtle phrasing. The wheelbarrow on the page gains its reality as an addition to nature because it already exists

Cubist painting, Williams' poem introduces contradictory clues that resist all attempts to apply the test of consistency. Thus the red paper box turns out to be made of cloth or leather; its "dial" may lead us to "eternity," but then again it may just be a ring attaching cardboard stars to a steamer trunk. For that matter, the box is also "the sun" and "the table / with dinner on it," not because there is a metaphoric analogy between these items but by sheer creative fiat. As Williams asserts in the prose section preceding this lyric, "The objects of his world were real to him because he could use them and use them with understanding to make his inventions" (SAA, 122).[21] "The red paper box" begins with an image of a concrete object only to break that image into fragments, making of these fragments a new verbal construct. The form of the poem is one of calculated indeterminacy. One is reminded of the Gris painting in which the house front and trees ostensibly outside the painter's window are rendered as a brightly lit violet-blue plane that seems to be inside the room.

Poem after poem in *Spring and All* is characterized by such Cubist mobility and indeterminacy. No. V is a composition on wind:

Black winds from the north
enter black hearts. Barred from
seclusion in lilies they strike

to destroy—

Beastly humanity
where the wind breaks it—

(SAA, 102)

It is a conventional enough opening: the wind as Shel-

---

as a reality in human experience" (p. 108). I would argue that, on the contrary, Williams' "wheel / barrow" exists nowhere but in the words on the page.

[21] Here Williams is referring to Shakespeare, but he is, of course, also talking about himself as artist.

leyan destroyer and preserver. Williams plays with this notion only to push it aside and replace it with one equally hackneyed—the wind that bloweth where it listeth:

> salt winds—
>
> Sold to them men knock blindly together
> splitting their heads open
>
> That is why boxing matches and
> Chinese poems are the same—That is why
> Hartley praises Miss Wirt.
>
> (SAA, 103)

Vacant shuttles weave the wind. But Williams is not Eliot and he wants to be matter-of-fact, scientific. "There is nothing in the twist / of the wind but—dashes of cold rain."

If the poem ended here—and many Williams poems do end on such a "hard-boiled" note—it would be merely clever. But the poet of *Spring and All* refuses to take this easy way out. He wants to experience wind as fully as possible. In the erotically charged universe of *Spring and All*, the wind cannot remain a symbol, viewed from the outside:

> Black wind, I have poured my heart out
> to you until I am sick of it—
>
> Now I run my hand over you feeling
> the play of your body—the quiver
> of its strength
>
> (SAA, 103)

It is a striking transformation, the poem enacting the rejection of symbolism which has been the subject of the prose section that precedes it, a section that ends with the sentence: "The word must be put down for itself, not as a symbol of nature but a part, cognizant of the whole—aware—civilized" (SAA, 102). All the talk of black winds entering black hearts, of beastly humanity broken by the wind, of day as the time of flower and rocks, and night as the time of hate, gives way to a sense of *living*. How can the black wind be anything but an object of love, a female presence, waiting to be touched so that the "quiver / of its strength" can manifest itself?

"Black winds" also functions within the larger serial structure of *Spring and All.* The orchestration of symbolic images which characterizes a poem like *The Waste Land* gives way, in *Spring and All,* to what David Lodge has called a "field of contiguities."[22] Williams' images—wind, flower, farmer, white, purple—are perfectly transparent; all are nature images, reflecting the sexual energy of the universe, the life force. They are images without depth, but in the shallow space in which they coexist, they create enormously varied configurations. Thus we first meet the word "wind" in the opening pages of *Spring and All*: "Houses crumble to ruin, cities disappear giving place to mounds of soil blown thither by the winds . . ." (SAA, 91). Here the wind is part of the holocaust, but when it next appears, it announces the coming of spring: "By the road to the contagious hospital / under the surge of the blue / mottled clouds driven from the / northeast—a cold wind" (SAA, 95). And again, some fifteen lines further into the poem, we meet "the cold, familiar wind." In poem III about the farmer, "A cold wind ruffles the water / among the browned weeds" (99). In IV, we have, by contrast, "dovetame winds— / stars of tinsel" (99). And so on.

Each time we meet the word *wind,* two things happen. First, we experience the pleasure of recognition, coming, as we do, upon a familiar image we had almost forgotten we knew. Secondly, we distinguish this particular manifestation of the word from all others. As Williams had said in the Prologue to *Kora,* "the coining of similes is a pastime of a very low order. . . . Much more keen is that power which discovers in things those inimitable particles of dissimilarity to all other things which are the peculiar perfections of the thing in question" (*Kora,* 18).

[22] *The Modes of Modern Writing: Metaphor, Metonymy, and the Typology of Literature* (London: Edward Arnold), p. 107.

The final poem in *Spring and All*, which acts as a coda, provides what is perhaps the best clue to the structural dynamics of the serial poem.

XXVII

Black eyed susan
rich orange
round the purple core

the white daisy
is not
enough

Crowds are white
as farmers
who live poorly

But you
are rich
in savagery—

Arab
Indian
dark woman

(SAA, 151)

Read independently, this is no more than an attractive little flower poem in which the black-eyed susan is treated animistically as a "savagely" sensual woman. To compare flowers to women—what could be more hackneyed? Yet a reader who comes across this poem in an anthology and who does not know its context must surely wonder about the third tercet: what do white crowds and poor farmers have to do with the "savagery" of the "Arab / Indian / dark woman"?

Within the confines of poem XXVII, there is no particular connection. But in terms of the larger structure of *Spring and All*, every word has its place. The "Black eyed susan" has not appeared before, but the image brings together all the flower images in the sequence: the "stiff curl of wildcarrot leaf" (5), the "pink confused with white / flower" (96), the "lilacs and azalea trees in flower" (102-103), the metal or porcelain "rose" of VII, the "fields of goldenrod" (133), and the "two horned lilac blossoms" (135).

When the compound noun "Black eyed susan" is taken apart, further connections become visible. "Black" recalls the "long black trees" of the upside-down Chapter XIII (92), the "black orchards" of III, the "black" coronal of IV, the "black winds" and "black fish" of V. "Eyed" relates back to the "new cathedral" of Chapter XIII, which looks down from its towers "with great eyes" (92), the grocery boys who "let their hair grow long / in a curve over one eye" (136), and the "saffron eyeballs" of the "old / jaundiced woman" who "can't die" (130).

In lines 2-12, this deployment of "word echoes" becomes highly refined:

Rich *orange*: Everything
—windows, chairs
obscenely drunk, spinning—
white, blue, orange
—hot with our passion (114)

purple: All along the road the reddish
purplish, forked, upstanding twiggy
stuff of bushes and small trees (95)

It is one with submarine vistas
purple and black fish turning
among undulant seaweed (103)

This is the time of year
when boys fifteen and seventeen
wear two horned lilac blossoms

in their caps—or over one ear. . . .

Horned purple (135-136)

core to solve the core
(pun on *Kore*) of whirling flywheels (109)

the *white* daisy: Pink confused with white
flowers (196)

breasts to see, white and blue—
to hold in the hand, to nozzle (114)

Everything
—windows, chairs
obscenely drunk, spinning—
white, blue, orange
—hot with our passion (224)

beside the white
chickens (138)

the whitish moonlight
tearfully

assumes the attitudes
of the afternoon (141)

crowds: Nightly the crowds
with the closeness and
universality of sand
witness the selfspittle (128)

The crowd at the ball game
is moved uniformly

by a spirit of uselessness
which delights them— (147)

It is summer, it is the solstice
the crowd is

cheering, the crowd is laughing
in detail (149)

farmers: The farmer in deep thought
is pacing through the rain. . . .

the artist figure of
the farmer—composing
antagonist (98-99)

the quality of the farmer's
shoulders (118)

Against this backdrop of familiar images comes the astonishing ending:

Arab
Indian
dark woman

We have been introduced to the notion of "Indian" "savagery" in the reference to the "dash of Indian blood" that characterizes the poor slatternly Elsie of XVIII. "Arab" has not appeared earlier in the poem, but it harks back to the smiling gypsy of XXI and the "Gipsy lips pressed / to my own" of XXIV. "Dark" has, of course, occurred frequently, from the "dark" but "wholly gay" flowerpot of II, with its "darkened" petals, to the light which becomes "darkness and darkness light" of XIV. But although the word "woman" has been used once or twice in the sequence, it is only at the very end of the poem that she is endowed with the attributes, *Arab, Indian, dark.* Furthermore, the conclusion of the lyric points back to its opening line, which contains the only mention of the word "susan" in the whole sequence. By relating these items, Williams thus suddenly opens up the text. For the "Arab / Indian / dark woman" who is also "susan" is verbally a *discovery* even if she has been present all along as a subliminal image. Only as we read the last words of the coda poem, do we suddenly see that this image of "rich . . . savagery" has been at the core of *Spring and All* from the beginning. But at this very moment, Williams abruptly breaks off his narrative, leaving it up to the reader to construct his own flower fantasies.

In retrospect, we find that expressions of sexual desire for a "dark woman" are ubiquitous in Williams' text:

> round flamegreen throats
> petal lays its glow upon petal (96)

> Thither I would carry her
> among the lights . . .
>   a crown for her head with
> castles upon it (99)

> Scheherazade, who lived under the threat (101)

>   some Elsie—
> voluptuous water (132)

> The sea that encloses her young body
> ula lu la lu
> is the sea of many arms

> The blazing secrecy of noon is undone
> and and and
> the broken sand is the sound of love. . . .

> In the sea the young flesh playing
> floats with the cries of far off men
> who rise in the sea

with green arms (136-137)

"Most of my life," says Williams in the prose section preceding poem X, "has been lived in hell—a hell of repression lit by flashes of inspiration" (116). *Spring and All* enacts the difficult process whereby this "hell" is "lit" by flashes of the "dark woman," the Kora who is waiting to be discovered. "Pink," first "confused with white," the "red wheel / barrow / glazed with rain / water / beside the white / chickens," the "rich orange / round the purple core" of the "Black eyed susan," seen in all its vibrancy in contrast to the "white daisy" which "is not / enough"—all these bleeding reds emerge from the dreary landscape of the "Interborough Rapid Transit Co." (147), from "the crowd / at the ball game" (147). The moon emerges from the "oak tree's crotch" (141). Even the "red paper box" with its cloth hinges seems to contain the dark woman in the form of "transparent tissue." Out of the "messy" and unwieldly prose, out of the disorder of language, the bland crowds and "patches of standing water," "dazed spring approaches."

The metonymic model of *Spring and All* looks ahead to the poetic sequences of our own time. Each lyric embedded in Williams' "free prose" sustains rival possibilities: it is at once self-reflexive and open-ended.[23] Thus the "red paper box" means one thing in the context of poem XII, but it is also part of a larger metonymic network which proceeds as follows:

reddish, purplish, forked upstanding, twiggy / stuff of bushes
red where in whorls / petal lays its glow upon petal
red paper box
red elastic

and so on. Or again, the "outline of leaf" in "By the road

[23] On this point, see James E. Breslin, "William Carlos Williams and Charles Demuth: Cross-Fertilization in the Arts," *Journal of Modern Literature*, 6, no. 2 (April 1977), 256-258.

to the contagious hospital" has one function *inside* that poem and another when it is linked to "the round / and pointed leaves" of XXIII or to the "canopy of leaves" of XXIV. *Spring and All* thus fulfills Apollinaire's demand for an anti-illusionist art, for the referentiality of its images is subordinated to their compositional value. The poem enacts the process of coming into being, of flowering, of sexual arousal.

The pre-text of *Spring and All*, Hillis Miller has argued, is Rimbaud's *Illuminations*.[24] This seems at first a surprising statement for, of all Williams' works, it has been *Kora in Hell* that is frequently compared to Rimbaud's prose poems. The connection was first suggested by Pound, and in *The Great American Novel* (1923), Williams wryly comments: "Take the improvisations. What the French reader would say is *Oui, ça, j'ai déjà vu ça; ça c'est de Rimbaud.*"[25] In his study of the influence of French Symbolism on modern American poetry (1929), René Taupin insisted that the Improvisations resembled the *Illuminations* in their purposely random transcriptions of emotions, their imaginative freedom, their conjunction of "voyance" and irony, and their "opacity" as Pound calls it.[26] But Sherman Paul is surely right when he remarks that *Kora* is actually quite unlike Rimbaud's text, that Williams' nervous, casually framed, realistic improvisations have little in common with the highly structured "visionary" compositions of Rimbaud.[27]

Spring and All, on the other hand, does contain interesting echoes of the *Illuminations*. Near the beginning of the book, we read:

[24] "Williams' *Spring and All* and the Progress of Poetry," *Daedalus*, 99 (Spring 1970), 415, 418.

[25] See IMAG, 167. Williams is referring to Pound's letter to him, 12 September 1920; see *Selected Letters of Ezra Pound*, pp. 160-161.

[26] *L'Influence du symbolisme français sur la poésie américaine (De 1910 à 1920)* (Paris: Honoré Champion, 1929), pp. 281-284.

[27] "A Sketchbook of the Artist in his Thirty-Fourth Year," *Shaken Realist*, p. 30.

> Only a day is left, one miserable day, before the world comes into its own. Let us hurry! Why bother for this man or that? In the offices of the great newspapers a mad joy reigns as they prepare the final extras. Rushing about, men bump each other into the whirring presses. How funny it seems. All thought of misery has left us. Why should we care? Children laughingly fling themselves under the wheels of the street cars, airplanes crash gaily to the earth. Someone has written a poem.
>
> (92)

This account of rebirth recalls "Après le déluge," especially the lines:

> Dans la grande rue sale les étals se dressèrent, et l'on tira les barques vers la mer étagée là-haut comme sur les gravures. . . .
>
> Dans la grande maison de vitres encore ruisselante, les enfants en deuil regardèrent les merveilleuses images.
>
> (In the dirty main street, butcher's stalls rose up, and boats were hauled down to the sea, piled high as in engravings. . . .
>
> In the large house, its windowpanes still streaming, children in mourning looked at marvelous pictures.)[28]

In the same chapter, Williams talks of "The new cathedral overlooking the park," which "looked down from its towers today, with great eyes, and saw by the decorative lake a group of people staring curiously at the corpse of a suicide" (92). One immediately thinks of "Enfance, III": "Il y a une cathédrale qui descend et un lac qui monte." ("There is a cathedral that descends and a lake that rises.") And the same image appears in poem XV:

> The decay of cathedrals
> is efflorescent

[28] Rimbaud, *Œuvres*, ed. Suzanne Bernard (Paris: Garnier, 1960), p. 253. Translations are my own.

through the phenomenal
growth of movie houses

whose catholicity is
progress since
destruction and creation
are simultaneous

(127)

This destruction-creation myth is central to *Spring and All* just as it is to the *Illuminations*. In "Conte," as Hillis Miller observes,[29] the bored prince tries to satisfy his superhuman longings by resorting to sadistic acts: he murders all his wives, cuts the throats of his pet animals, hacks his servants to pieces, and sets fire to his palaces, only to discover that "la foule, les toits d'or, les belles bêtes existaient encore." ("The crowds, the gold roofs, the splendid animals were still there.") The imagination is able to destroy everything but can then create only a repetition of what was there before: "Yes, the imagination, drunk with prohibitions, has destroyed and re-created everything afresh in the likeness of that which it was" (SAA, 93). "Like Rimbaud," writes Miller, "Williams must break down all cultural and natural forms, kill everyone, and destroy everything in order to return things to the primal chaos from which a reality without any antecedents may spring. . . . Once this monstrous act of demolition has been satisfactorily completed, the world will be new, and the imagination can turn from acts of destruction to acts of authentic creation."[30]

In accord with this destruction-creation paradigm, Williams' imagery is recognizably Rimbaldian. Flowers, for example, are characterized not by their species—rose, lily, black-eyed susan, goldenrod—but by their genus: they are beings that *flower*, that blossom, that open up. "I expect," says Williams in the prose section that follows poem XXII, "to see values blossom" (140). There are, finally, only two

[29] *Daedalus*, 420.

[30] Miller, *Daedalus*, 421-422.

processes in nature as in art: birth ("the stark dignity of entrance") and death ("the waste of broad, muddy fields / brown with dried weeds"). But because "destruction and creation / are simultaneous," because the "barber" of poem XIV can invent "the newest / ways to grow hair / on bald death" (126), life and death are interdependent. The excitement is, then, to witness the moment of *change*, the movement over the *edge*. "Edge" is one of the key words in *Spring and All*, just as edges exist everywhere in Cubist painting. So,

> The rose is obsolete
> but each petal ends in
> an edge, the double facet
> cementing the grooved
> columns of air—The edge
> cuts without cutting. . . .
>
> The place between the petal's
> edge and the
>
> From the petal's edge a line starts (107-108)
>
> melon flowers that open
> about the edge of refuse (117-118)
>
> But the stars
> are round
> cardboard
> with a tin edge (124)
>
> Underneath the sea where it is dark
> there is no edge (137)

The poet must define this edge, the place where one image or object reaches its terminus and another begins. As Williams says in *Kora*, "The stream of things having composed itself into wiry strands that move in one fixed direction, the poet in desperation turns at right angles and cuts across current with startling results to his hangdog mood" (KH, 17).

But although things have edges and can be placed side by side, there is no center, no "reservoir of eternal models" as Miller puts it.[31] There is only "the ubiquitous life force which gives rise to differences in objects appearing side by side or in sequence from an infinity of centers"—petals, flowers, flamegreen throats, black winds, transparent tissue, banjo jazz, waves of steel. "It is not a matter of 'representation' . . . but of separate existence" (SAA, 117).

Spring and All provides the paradigm for the serial poems Williams wrote throughout the following decade: for example, *The Descent of Winter* (1928) and *A Novelette* (1932). *The Descent of Winter*, begun on board the SS Pennland in the fall of 1927 when Williams was returning to America, having left behind his wife and sons who were to spend the entire year in Europe, was originally projected as a book of love poems to be called *Sacred and Profane*.[32] But in its final form, *The Descent* turned out to be a more hybrid work, a collage of love poems, prose diatribes about American capitalism, anecdotes about the delivery of babies, and so on. Williams never did publish it as a separate book; it appeared in Ezra Pound's *Exile* in the Autumn of 1928.

Like *Spring and All, The Descent* is characterized by a discontinuous structure in which meaning is created by the resonance of contiguous images. But the condensation of the later work is much more radical and most critics have found it excessively obscure.[33] No doubt *The Descent of Winter* is an uneven book; certain prose sections like "A

[31] *Daedalus*, 424.

[32] See *Selected Letters of William Carlos Williams*, ed. John C. Thirwall (New York: McDowell, Obolensky, 1957), p. 85.

[33] See, for example, Rod Townley, *The Early Poetry of William Carlos Williams* (Ithaca: Cornell University Press, 1975, pp. 167-170). The best defense of the sequence is that of Thomas R. Whitaker in his *Williams* (New York: Twayne, 1968), pp. 68-69.

Morning Imagination of Russia" are not so much incoherent as they are boring in their naive didacticism. On the other hand, the sequence contains some of Williams' most brilliant writing. Here is the opening:

9/27

"What are these elations I have
at my own underwear?

I touch it and it is strange
upon a strange thigh."

* * *

9/29

My bed is narrow
in a small room
at sea

The numbers are on
the wall
Arabic I

Berth No. 2
was empty above me
the steward

took it apart
and removed
it

only the number
remains
.2.

on an oval disc
of celluloid
tacked

to the whiteenameled
woodwork
with

two bright nails
like stars
beside

the moon

(DW, 234-235)

The italicized section introduces a note of auto-eroticism that modulates into the bleaker solipsism of the second lyric.[34] "9/29" is like a hard-edged painting, but its general affinities are less with Cubism in its classical phase than with early Surrealism: the collages of Max Ernst, Kurt Schwitters, or René Magritte. Here it is not primarily a matter of breaking up objects and viewing them simultaneously as an organization of flat planes. Rather, the objects themselves undergo surprising transformations. The poem's structure is one of contraction-expansion. First everything contracts: "the narrow bed / in a small room / at sea" gives way to the empty upper berth and then to the arabic number 2 above it, "on an oval disc / of celluloid." The image is minimal and stark, reflecting the emptiness of the observer's consciousness, his total isolation. But as he contemplates this unimportant object silhouetted against "the whiteenameled / woodwork," he suddenly *sees* it freshly; the oval disc, tacked up by "two bright nails," becomes a "moon" supported by stars. In this case, less is more. Having stripped his world of all its trappings, he can once again bring it to life.

In the poems and prose passages that follow, these opposing images—empty berth and moonlight—reappear in a number of altered contexts. We can trace one chain of contiguities from "waves like words all broken" and the "coral island" of "9/30" to the "large rusty can wedged in the crotch" of the locust tree in "10/28," to the woman alone on the "railroad bridge support" of "11/10." At the

[34] Whitaker says: "The entire sequence may be seen as enacting a descent from auto-erotic and barren isolation . . . through expansive and fructifying movements toward a new discovery of community, the past, love, and the writer's vocation" (p. 69).

same time, the countermovement sets in: the "stars / beside / the moon" look ahead to the "orange flames" (237) the "yellow and red grass" (240), and the "leafless beechtree" that "shines like a cloud" (244). And then a few pages further on, we meet:

Dahlias—
    What a red
        and yellow and white
mirror to the sun, round
            and petaled
        is this she holds?

(249)

In the end, it is this "vividness alone" (247) that overcomes the poet's initial despair and solipsism. The sequence ends with the jaunty song of his Creole uncle: "*si j'étais roi de Bayaussi-e, tu serais reine-e par ma foi!*" (265).

The prose poems that alternate with the short lyrics of *The Descent of Winter* exhibit a discontinuity more radical than that of the earlier *Kora in Hell.* Here is "10/27":

> And Coolidge said let there be imitation brass filigree fire fenders behind insured plateglass windows and yellow pine booths with the molasses-candygrain in the wood instead of the oldtime cake-like whitepine boards always cut thick their faces! the white porcelain trough is no doubt made of some certain blanched clay baked and glazed but how they do it, how they shape it soft and have it hold its shape for the oven I don't know nor how the cloth is woven, the grey and the black with the orange and green strips wound together diagonally across the grain artificial pneumothorax their faces! the stripe of shadow along the pavement edge, the brownstone steeple low among the office buildings dark windows with a white wooden cross upon them, lights like fuchsias, lights like bleeding hearts lights like columbines, cherry red danger and applegreen safety. Any hat in this window $2.00 barred windows, wavy opaque glass, a block

> of brownstone at the edge of the sidewalk crudely stippled on top for a footstep to a carriage, lights with sharp bright spikes, stick out round them their faces! STOP in black letters surrounded by a red glow, letters with each bulb a seed in the shaft of the L of the A lights on the river streaking the restless water lights upon pools of rainwater by the roadside a great pool of light full of overhanging sparks into whose lower edge a house looms its center marked by one yellow windowbright their faces!
>
> (DW, 240-241)

In this surreal cityscape, objects in shop windows, seen from what is evidently the window of the poet's moving car, take on strange configurations. The "imitation brass filigree fire fenders," for example, are related syntactically to the "yellow pine booths with the molasses-candygrain in the wood," but whereas the former, placed behind "insured plateglass windows," are items for sale, the latter seem to be part of a candy store or café. Again, the "white porcelain trough" made of baked clay is somehow related to the dark cloth with its orange and green strips, the conjunction suggesting a display case of household goods. But the reference to "artificial pneumothorax" allows us to perceive the white porcelain trough as part of some hospital scene or perhaps a medical supply store. The scene, in any case, dissolves and we next see a "stripe of shadow along the pavement edge, the brownstone steeple low among the office buildings dark windows with a white wooden cross upon them." Seen retrospectively, the yellow pine booths now turn into church pews, and, in this context, the white porcelain trough calls up the image of a baptismal font.

We cannot, in short, locate the items named with any certainty, nor is it possible to define their relationships to one another. The blurring of focus is intentional, for Williams' emphasis is on the mobility and mystery of the city, and the text thus becomes what Charles Olson liked to call an "energy discharge." So the colors of the cloth modulate into city lights—"lights like fuchsias, lights like bleeding hearts lights like columbines." The camera eye then moves farther away from the scene and we get a distance shot of "a great pool of light full of overhanging sparks into whose lower edge a house looms its center marked by one yellow windowbright their faces!"

Williams' modulation of light images is especially interesting. "10/27" begins, of course, as a parody of "And God said, 'Let there be light!' "; here there is only the artificial light of the "imitation brass filigree fire fenders." But such lighting has its pleasures too; in the poet's verbal landscape, it coalesces with the bright neon lights of the city, the traffic lights ("cherry red danger and applegreen safety"), the red glow made by the bulbs around the STOP sign, the moving lights of the elevated train, the "restless water lights upon pools of rainwater," and finally the "great pool of light full of overhanging sparks into whose lower edge a house looms," a house whose "center" is marked by "one yellow windowbright" of faces.

This is perhaps as close as Williams ever came to the language constructions of Gertrude Stein or of her French predecessors. The poet does not give us a realistic or even an impressionist picture of the night-time scene. Rather, he wrenches words from their usual contexts and places them in new relationships. The juxtaposition of light images is one example of such stylization. Another can be found in the patterning of spatial forms. The roundness of the white porcelain trough is repeated in the circular traffic light and the STOP sign. These objects therefore seem to occupy the same space although, literally, some are indoors, some outdoors; some close to the ground, some high up, and so on. Again, the "yellow pine booths" seem to occupy the same space as the white wooden cross, and the "insured plateglass windows" of the storefront dissolve into the dark windows of office buildings, the barred windows of the hat shop, made of "wavy opaque glass," and finally the "yellow" window of the isolated cheery house. The prose poem is a field of contiguities, what John Ashbery was to call a "hymn to possibility."

Read against the background of such verbal compositions, *Paterson*, whose first book appeared in 1946, comes as something of a surprise. *Paterson* is, of course, Williams' major work, the poem that finally made him famous. Paul Mariani calls it "the most radically experimental and successful long poem written in our time";[35] others have hailed it as the great American epic of the twentieth century. Yet the critical success of *Paterson* in the fifties was hardly coincidental. Many who had paid no attention to the shorter poems or to the serial works immediately responded to *Paterson*, no doubt because it satisfied the New Critical demands of the period: for all its seeming openness, it manifested a symbolic superstructure. This is not the place to discuss that network of symbols, which has been frequently explicated,[36] but let me cite just one commentary on the poem, made when Book Two of *Paterson* appeared in 1948. The critic I wish to cite is Robert Lowell, whose own *Lord Weary's Castle* had appeared just two years earlier:

> *Paterson*, Book Two is an interior monologue. A man spends Sunday in the park at Paterson, New Jersey. He thinks and looks about him; his mind contemplates, describes, comments, associates, stops, stutters and shifts

[35] *William Carlos Williams: The Poet and his Critics*, p. 233.

[36] See, for example, Sr. M. Bernetta Quinn, "On *Paterson*, Book One," *The Metamorphic Tradition in Modern Poetry* (New Brunswick: Rutgers University Press, 1955), pp. 89-129; rpt. in *William Carlos Williams, A Collection of Critical Essays*, ed. J. Hillis Miller (Englewood Cliffs: Prentice-Hall, Inc., 1966), pp. 107-120; Glauco Cambon, "William Carlos Williams' *Paterson*," in *The Inclusive Flame* (Bloomington: Indiana University Press, 1963), pp. 183-218; Louis L. Martz, "On the Road to *Paterson*," *Poetry New York*, No. 4 (1951); rpt. in *The Poem of the Mind, Essays on Poetry English and American* (New York: Oxford, 1969), pp. 125-146; Joel Conarroe, *William Carlos Williams' Paterson: Language and Landscape* (Philadelphia: University of Pennsylvania Press, 1970); Walter Scott Peterson, *An Approach to Paterson* (New Haven: Yale University Press, 1967).

like a firefly, bound only by its milieu. The man is Williams, anyone living in Paterson, the American, the masculine principle—a sort of Everyman. . . .

The Park is Everywoman, any woman, the feminine principle, America. The water roaring down the falls from the park to Paterson is the principle of life. The rock is death, negation, the *nul*; carved and given form, it stands for the imagination, "like a red basalt grasshopper, boot-long with window-eyes." The symbols are not allegorical, but loose, intuitive, and Protean.

Paterson, like Hart Crane's *Marriage of Faustus and Helen,* is about marriage. "Rigor of beauty is the quest." Everything in the poem is masculine or feminine, everything strains toward marriage, but the marriages never come off, except in the imagination, and there, attenuated, fragmentary and uncertain. "Divorce is the sign of knowledge in our time." The people "reflect no beauty but gross . . . Unless it is beauty / to be, anywhere, / so flagrant in desire. . . ."

Williams is noted as an imagist, a photographic eye; in Book One he has written "no ideas but in facts." This is misleading. His symbolic man and woman are Hegel's *thesis* and *antithesis*. They struggle toward synthesis—marriage. But fulness, if it exists at all, only exists in simple things, trees and animals; so Williams, like other Platonists, is thrown back on the "idea."[37]

There could hardly be a better account of the meaning of *Paterson* II than Lowell's, and just because his is such an incisive analysis, it gives us pause for thought. The poet who began by saying that "The word must be put down for itself, not as a symbol of nature but a part, cognizant of the whole" (SAA, 102), who praised Gertrude Stein "for her formal insistence on words in their literal, structural quality of being words" (A, 265), has now turned, whether

[37] *The Nation,* 166 (19 June 1948); rpt. in *William Carlos Williams, a Critical Anthology,* ed. Charles Tomlinson (Baltimore: Penguin Books, 1972), pp. 165-166.

unwittingly or with the caution that may have come with age, to what is for him the alien rhetoric of Symbolism:

> The scene's the Park
> upon the rock,
> female to the City
>
> —upon whose body Paterson instructs his thoughts
> (concretely)

From this opening, Book Two steadfastly juxtaposes symbols of marriage, fulfillment, creativity—"the flower of a day" (58), "a flight of empurpled wings" (62), the "grasshopper of red basalt" (62), "pouring water" (97), the "terrifying plunge" of the falls (100), a woman's "belly . . . like a white cloud" (105)—to those of divorce and sterility: the letters of the neurotic woman poet "C" which punctuate the lyric passages, the trapped mink (65), the evangelist (71-77), the Federal Reserve Bank (90-91), the Sunday afternoon picnickers (74), the "parasitic curd" (77)—all those features of modern life that tell us that "among / the working classes SOME sort / of breakdown / has occurred" (76-77).

It has been argued, most notably by James Breslin and Paul Mariani, that such thematic clusters, although present, are not the core of *Paterson*, that the poem is, in Mariani's words, "a *process* of unfolding, of discovery," or, as Breslin puts it, that "The poem . . . *is* the act of its creation, recording . . . the consciousness of its creator, whose dual fidelity to the *world* and to the *poem* constantly forces him to turn back and start all over again."[38] "Williams," Breslin argues, "takes an established literary genre, cuts away much of the complicated formal apparatus that makes it feel aloof and empty, and pushes it back toward the ground—where it can be filled with actuality."[39] Hence the constant dissolving of perspective and shifting of ground, and the

[38] Mariani, *William Carlos Williams, The Poet and the Critics*, p. 234; Breslin, *William Carlos Williams, An American Artist*, p. 171.

[39] *William Carlos Williams, An American Artist*, p. 171.

range of styles that makes *Paterson* a "pre-epic, a rough and profuse start from which some later summative genius may extract and polish . . . a beginning."[40]

This is an attractive argument, but much as I would like to read *Paterson* as a "process of discovery," a "pre-epic," successive readings have convinced me that it is, in fact, a much more "closed" poem than either Williams or his best critics care to admit. The very cover of the first complete edition of *Paterson* (1963), with its impressionistic drawing of the Passaic Falls by Earl Horter,[41] is oddly emblematic of Williams' partial return to his literary origins. Indeed, with the publication of *Paterson* I, the analogy of Williams' poetry to avant-garde painting—whether Cubist, Dada, or Surrealist—breaks down.

"Sunday in the Park" (Book Two, Part I), for example, has been read as the exploration of the poet's consciousness, his shifting moods punctuated by the repeated word "walking." Terms like "field of action" or "process poetics" imply that the "I" who is speaking quite literally doesn't know where he or she is going, that only in the course of the utterance is the path of entry chosen. David Antin's talk-poems are a good example of such a "process of discovery"; their stance, like John Ashbery's or Frank O'Hara's or Jackson Mac Low's, is that of the *improvisatore*. But a poem like "Sunday in the Park" is essentially preplanned. The poet strolling through the park ostensibly records what he sees, observes, thinks, remembers, but in fact no detail is admitted into the space of the poem that does not relate to the central marriage-divorce tension that is the theme of the book. Lowell quite rightly talks of Hegelian thesis and antithesis here. Or, as Williams says in

[40] Breslin, *Williams*, p. 173.

[41] The first edition of the complete collected *Paterson* (Books One to Five and notes for the projected Book Six) was published in October of 1963, some seven months after Williams' death. The Horter drawing thus comes as an afterthought, but its realism is nevertheless an embodiment of Williams' Paterson. See Emily Wallace, *A Bibliography of William Carlos Williams*, p. 102.

the closing line of Part I: "NO DOGS ALLOWED AT LARGE IN THIS PARK" (77).

It is no coincidence that the upbeat of the line, "He is led forward by their announcing wings" is followed by a particularly frustrated and accusatory letter from the poetess "C," or that the image of the peon "in the lost / Eisenstein film" ("Heavenly man!") is juxtaposed to the coarse and vulgar girl in the park: "the leg raised, verisimilitude. / even to the coarse contours of the leg, the / bovine touch!" (74). The arrangement of images and incidents, in short, follows an orderly plan. Accordingly, Williams' symbolic constructs demand to be taken seriously; such patterns as the man-city identity in Book One, the deployment of the four elements in Book Three, or the introduction in Book Four of Madame Curie as "pregnant" both literally and figuratively (in that she is about to discover radium)—all these devices hark back to the Symbolism of an earlier generation.

This Symbolist landscape, I would posit, was a world in which Williams never really felt at home. He had no Heavenly City to match Yeats's Byzantium, and when he tries, not very successfully, to introduce a comparable element in lines like "Chapultepec! grasshopper hill!" he must return to the exclamation point discarded a quarter of a century earlier in *Spring and All*, as if to impress us with the importance of this exotic site in Mexico City. Unlike Stevens, he had no "major man," no McCullough, so he talks of the "Heavenly man!" in the Eisenstein film, again using the exclamation point to emphasize the peon's significance. A poet characterized by what Robert Lowell calls a "secular knowingness," Williams knew only too well that fire is only fire and water, water, and so the images of fire and flood in Book Three remain peculiarly inert, quite unlike the complex fire and water symbols in *The Waste Land* or the *Four Quartets*.

Many readers of *Paterson* have remarked that the prose sections—for example, the letter about "Billie" by the halfwit (37-38), or the description of the dwarf as seen by

General Washington (18-19), are the most exciting passages in the poem. The documentary prose evidently resisted the poet's increasing tendency to turn image into symbol, "thing" into "idea of the thing," a tendency that came to a head in *Paterson*, Book Five (1958), where the fabled unicorn in the Cloisters tapestry becomes the ruling symbol for beauty, resurrection, the fulfillment of the artist's quest.

In one of the last poetry readings he was able to give, at Wellesley in 1956, Williams read "Asphodel, that Greeny Flower."[42] Lowell movingly recalls the hush that fell over the enormous audience when the now-famous poet, "one whole side partly paralysed, his voice just audible," read this "triumph of simple confession":[43]

And so
            with fear in my heart
                        I drag it out

and keep on talking
            for I dare not stop.
                        Listen while I talk on

against time.
            It will not be
                        for long.

(PB, 154)

Like "Paterson, Five," "Asphodel" marks a return to tradition, in this case the pastoral love poem in which the penitent husband makes amends to his long-suffering wife. No more snatches of documentary prose, no Cubist or Surrealist superpositions or dislocations. The poem is stately and consistent, an autobiographical lyric in the Romantic tradition.

"Asphodel, that Greeny Flower" can be regarded as a

[42] For Williams' own account of this reading, see IWWP, 94-95.

[43] "William Carlos Williams," *Hudson Review*, 14 (1961-1962); rpt. in *William Carlos Williams*, ed. J. Hillis Miller, p. 159. Cf. Steven Gould Axelrod, *Robert Lowell: Life and Art* (Princeton: Princeton University Press, 1978), pp. 89-91.

garland for the fifties. But the Williams who speaks to the poets of our own generation is, I think, less the loving, apologetic husband of "Asphodel" or the aspiring American bard of *Paterson* than he is a Voyager to Pagany, to the Paris of the twenties; he is the poet as passionate defender of the faith that "to engage roses / becomes a geometry."

CHAPTER FIVE

"No Edges, No Convexities" Ezra Pound and the Circle of Fragments

—the fragment is like the musical idea of a song cycle. . . . each piece is self-sufficient, and yet it is never anything but the interstice of its neighbors.

—*Roland Barthes* by Roland Barthes

—Practically the whole development of the English verse-art has been achieved by steals from the French.

—Ezra Pound in *Poetry* (1913)

I

MY TITLE comes from W. B. Yeats, whose severe judgment of the *Cantos* in his *Oxford Book of Modern Verse* (1936) had, so said his old friend Ezra Pound, "done more to prevent people reading Cantos for what is *on the page* than any other smoke screen."[1] "Like other readers," said Yeats in his Preface, "I discover at present merely exquisite or grotesque fragments. He [Pound] hopes to give the impression that all is living, that there are no edges, no

The following abbreviations for Pound's works are used throughout this chapter: Where there are two dates, the first is that of original publication; the second, that of the New Directions (New York) edition used.

P	*Personae. The Collected Poems of Ezra Pound* (1926; 1949).
C	*The Cantos of Ezra Pound* (1971). The designation (VIII, 30) means "Canto VIII, p. 30."
GB	*Gaudier-Brzeska* (1916; 1970).
LE	*The Literary Essays of Ezra Pound*, ed. with an introduction by T. S. Eliot (1954; 1968).
SL	*The Selected Letters of Ezra Pound*, ed. D. D. Paige (1950).
SPr	*Selected Prose* 1909-1965 (1973).

[1] Letter to Hubert Creekmore, Rapallo 1939, SL, 321.

convexities, nothing to check the flow. . . ." There follows the "bloody paragraph" that so angered Pound:

> When I consider his work as a whole I find more style, more deliberate nobility and the means to convey it than in any contemporary poet known to me, but it is constantly interrupted, broken, twisted into nothing by its direct opposite, nervous obsession, nightmare, stammering confusion. . . . Style and its opposite can alternate, but form must be full, sphere-like, single. Even where there is no interruption, he is often content, if certain verses and lines have style, to leave unbridged transitions, unexplained ejaculations, that make his meaning unintelligible. . . . Even where the style is sustained throughout one gets an impression, especially when he is writing in *vers libre*, that he has not got all the wine into the bowl, that he is a brilliant improvisator. . . .[2]

To read this commentary today is to learn to what a surprising extent "Modernism" has already become part of literary history. For Yeats's negatives have become the positives of a later generation of poets, of those like Allen Ginsberg or Frank O'Hara or Ed Dorn who want precisely to convey the "living flow" of experience, to dispense with "edges" and "convexities" in favor of the poem as a "field of action." Interruptions and twists, "unbridged transitions" and "unexplained ejaculations," the poetic act as "brilliant improvisa[tion]"—these are accepted as a matter of course by contemporary poets and their readers. And few would maintain that "form must be full, sphere-like, single," that the poet's task is to get "all the wine into the bowl."[3]

[2] *The Oxford Book of Modern Verse* 1892-1935, ed. W. B. Yeats (Oxford: Clarendon Press, 1936), pp. xxiv-xxvi. For further discussion of the Yeats-Pound relationship, see Richard Ellmann, "Ez and Old Billyum," *Eminent Domain, Yeats Among Wilde, Joyce, Pound, Eliot, and Auden* (New York: Oxford, 1967), pp. 57-87, esp. pp. 82-85.

[3] Most critics of the thirties shared Yeats's view. See, for example, Geoffrey Grigson, "The Methodism of Ezra Pound," *New Verse*, no. 5 (October 1933); rpt. in *Ezra Pound: The Critical Heritage*, ed. Eric Homberger (Lon-

One poet who did understand the structural principle behind Pound's continually expanding long poem was his American friend, William Carlos Williams. When *A Draft of XXX Cantos* appeared in 1930, Williams remarked, "A criticism of Pound's *Cantos* could not be better concerned, I think, than in considering them in relation to the principal move in imaginative writing today—that away from the word as symbol toward the word as reality."[4] It is this "move"—Pound's gradual turn from a Symbolist mode to the art of montage, of "documentary" surface upon which dislocated fragments are juxtaposed—that is my concern in the present chapter. Here once again I would like to begin with the Rimbaud connection.

In 1957, a year after the publication of *Rock-Drill* (Cantos LXXV-XCV), Pound brought out, in a limited edition of 500 copies printed in Milan, a slender volume called *Rimbaud,* which contains five French poems with Pound's translations on the facing page: Rimbaud's "Au Cabaret-Vert," "Comedie en trois baisers," "Venus Anadyomène," and "Les Chercheuses de poux," as well as Laurent Tailhade's "Rus." In his introductory note, Pound explains:

> The *Study* [*in*] *French Poets* appeared in the *Little Review* nearly 40 years ago. The student hoped that it would stimulate thought and possibly one or two of the thousands of aspirants to literary glory would take up the

---

don: Routledge & Kegan Paul, 1972), pp. 259-264. Grigson writes: "on an unfinished poem of the length of the *Cantos* judgment must be unfinished . . . though as far as it goes the structure should be clear, like the cellular structure of a rounded organism when half dissected. This cellular analogy is important. . . . The *Cantos* must be part of an organism, growing from and round certain foci" (pp. 260-261).

This demand for "clear" structure and organic form lingers on: in *The Barb of Time: On The Unity of Ezra Pound's Cantos* (New York: Oxford, 1969), Daniel D. Pearlman tries to prove that the Cantos do in fact have "*major form*—an over-all design in which the parts are significantly related to the whole" (p. 3).

[4] "Excerpts from a Critical Sketch: *A Draft of XXX Cantos* by Ezra Pound," *Selected Essays* (New York: Random House, 1954), p. 107.

> matter. As no adequate translations have appeared, he now takes pity on those who hadn't had time to learn French but might like to know what the French authors were writing about, and herewith starts to provide a *guide* to the meaning of the poems then given in the original only.[5]

But the translation project was never carried out, perhaps because Pound realized, by 1957, that his 1918 *Little Review* anthology included much that was by then dated.[6] Only Rimbaud was translated, and even then Pound gives us no more than four early, relatively minor lyrics. Here is the first quatrain of "Au Cabaret-Vert":

> Depuis huit jours, j'avais dechiré mes bottines
> Aux cailloux des chemins. J'entrais à Charleroi.
> —Au Cabaret-Vert: je demandai des tartines
> De beurre et du jambon qui fût à moitié froid.
> (*Rimbaud*, pp. 10-11)

Pound's free translation renders in colloquial, idiomatic English the anecdotal immediacy and concreteness of the original:

> Wearing out my shoes, 8th day
> On the bad roads, I got into Charleroi.
> —Bread, butter, at the Green Cabaret
> And the ham half cold.

Pound's advocacy of what he called Rimbaud's "direct-

[5] *Rimbaud* (Milan: Scheiwiller, 1957), p. 5. Pound's translations of these five poems are reprinted in Ezra Pound, *Translations* (New York: New Directions, 1963), pp. 434-438. Note that Pound translates only the octave of the sonnet "Venus Anadyomène," and that the poem he calls, following earlier texts, "Comedie en trois baisers" is known, in all editions of Rimbaud's poetry subsequent to 1934, as "Première Soirée." See Rimbaud, *Œuvres*, ed. Suzanne Bernard (Paris: Garnier, 1960), p. 374.

[6] The thirteen poets, in order of appearance, are Jules Laforgue, Tristan Corbière, Rimbaud, Rémy de Gourmont, Henri de Régnier, Emile Verhaeren, Francis Viélé-Griffin, Stuart Merrill, Laurent Tailhade, Francis Jammes, Jean Moréas, Charles Vildrac, and Jules Romains.

ness of presentation"[7] must be seen against the background of an ongoing quarrel with Symbolism that began, in theory if not yet in practice, as early as 1913 when Pound compared Yeats unfavorably to Ford Madox Ford:

> Mr. Yeats has been subjective; believes in the glamour and associations which hang near words. . . . He has much in common with the French symbolists. [Mr. Hueffer] Ford believes in an exact rendering of things. He would strip words of all "association" for the sake of getting a precise meaning.[8]

Both Herbert Schneidau and Donald Davie have argued convincingly that Imagism, as Pound construed it, was never merely a latter-day or local version of Symbolism; that it was, on the contrary, "a radical alternative to it."[9] Following Ford, Flaubert, and Fenollosa, Pound insisted that "The touchstone of an art is its precision," that "if a man use 'symbols' he must so use them that their symbolic function does not obtrude."[10] In *Gaudier-Brzeska* (1916), he was even more emphatic: "Imagisme is not symbolism. The symbolists dealt in 'association,' that is, in a sort of allusion, almost of allegory. They degraded the symbol to the status of a word. . . . Moreover, one does not want to be called a symbolist, because symbolism has usually been associated

[7] "How to Read" (1928) in SE, 33.

[8] "Status Rerum," *Poetry*, 1 (1913), 125.

[9] See Herbert Schneidau, *Ezra Pound: The Image and the Real* (Baton Rouge: Louisiana State University Press, 1969), Chapters 1 and 2 passim; Donald Davie, *Ezra Pound* (London: Fontana/Collins, 1975), p. 43. Both Schneidau and Davie take issue with Frank Kermode's view in *Romantic Image* (1956; rpt. New York: Vintage, 1964) that "the Hulmian Image—the precise, orderly, anti-discursive, the product of intuition—is the Symbol of the French poets given a new philosophical suit" (p. 130). Schneidau (pp. 38-39) nicely refutes Kermode's assertion that "The *Cantos* . . . are the only kind of long poem the Symbolist aesthetic will admit" (p. 136).

See also Donald Davie's earlier *Ezra Pound: Poet as Sculptor* (1964; rpt. New York: Galaxy Books, 1968), Chapter III and pp. 228-229; and Hugh Kenner *The Pound Era* (Berkeley and Los Angeles: University of California Press, 1971), pp. 128-144, 173-191.

[10] "The Serious Artist" (1913), SE, 48; "A Retrospect" (1118), SE, 9.

with mushy technique" (GB, 84-85). Or again, "to use a symbol *with an ascribed or intended meaning* is, usually, to produce very bad art" (GB, 86).[11]

Such a reductionist view of Symbolism (*a* stands for *b*) has little to do with the realities of a Baudelaire or a Yeats poem. But Pound may have purposely overstated his case because he longed to replace the dense, polysemous discourse characteristic of Symbolist poetry with what he called "constatation of fact" or the "presentative method."[12] "If I had the energy," he remarks in *Gaudier-Brzeska*, "to get paints and brushes and keep at it, I might found a new school of painting, of 'non-representative' painting, a painting that would speak only by arrangements in colour" (GB, 87). This recalls a comment made by Rimbaud in 1872: "We must root out painting's old habit of copying, and we must make painting sovereign. Instead of reproducing objects, painting must compel agitation by means of lines, colors, and shapes that are drawn from the outer world but simplified and restrained: genuine magic."[13]

By 1916, then, Pound was advocating a new non-mimetic art which he called "Vorticist":

> The image is not an idea. It is a radiant node or cluster; it is what I can, and must perforce, call a VORTEX, from which and through which, and into which, ideas are constantly rushing. In decency one can only call it a VORTEX. And from this necessity came the name "vorticism." *Nomina sunt consequentia rerum*, and never was that statement of Aquinas more true than in the case of the vorticist movement.
>
> (GB, 92)

[11] By Pound's own account, this chapter of *Gaudier-Brzeska* was originally published in essay form as "Vorticism" in the *Fortnightly Review* (September 1914). See GB, 81.

[12] "The Approach to Paris, V," *The New Age*, 13 (October 2, 1913), 662.

[13] See Hugo Friedrich, *The Structure of Modern Poetry* (1956), trans. Joachim Neugroschel (Evanston: Northwestern University Press, 1974), p. 57.

The "VORTEX" is further defined as "the point of maximum energy," and we are told that "the vorticist relies on the 'primary pigment,' and on that alone" (GB, 81). It is in the spirit of this anti-Symbolist manifesto that Pound compiled his 1918 anthology of French poets.

"I do not aim at completeness," Pound announces in the Introduction. "I believe that the American-English reader has heard in a general way of Baudelaire and Verlaine and Mallarmé; that Mallarmé, perhaps unread, is apt to be slightly overestimated" (SFP, 4). This offhand statement sounds as though Pound were trying to be a bit outrageous, to *épater*, as it were, his fellow poets, Yeats and Eliot. For both Yeats and the young Eliot viewed French poetry through the lens of Arthur Symons, whose *Symbolist Movement in English Literature* (1899) made the case for Mallarmé as the high priest of poetry. Looking back at Pound's anthology in 1946, Eliot remarked somewhat acidly: "a different approach would be appropriate now. . . . Mallarmé is not discussed; and Valéry's finest work was not known. The essay reads like the report of a tourist in French poetry."[14]

But this "tourist," who was never to display any interest in Valéry, had a pantheon of his own. "After Gautier," he declares in the *Study*, "France produced, as nearly as I understand, three chief and admirable poets: Tristan Corbière, perhaps the most poignant writer since Villon; Rimbaud, a vivid and indisputable genius; and Laforgue—a slighter, but in some ways, a finer 'artist' than either of the others. I do not mean that he writes 'better' than Rimbaud. . . . Laforgue always knows what he is at; Rimbaud, the 'genius' in the narrowest and deepest sense of the term,

[14] "Ezra Pound," *Poetry*, 68 (September 1946); rpt. in *Ezra Pound: A Collection of Critical Essays* (Englewood Cliffs: Prentice-Hall, Inc., 1963), p. 21. Yeats's debt to Symons is well known, Eliot's less so. According to Lyndall Gordon in *Eliot's Early Years* (New York: Oxford, 1977), pp. 28-29, Eliot discovered Symons' *Symbolist Movement* in 1908 when the second edition arrived at Harvard. His first reaction was to order the poems of Laforgue from France.

the 'most modern,' seems, almost without knowing it, to hit on the various ways in which the best writers were to follow him, slowly" (SFP, 6-7). And he continues to stress Rimbaud's astonishing originality: "The actual writing of poetry has advanced little or not at all since Rimbaud. Cézanne was the first to paint, as Rimbaud had written—in, for example, 'Les Assis':

> Ils ont greffé dans des amours épileptiques
> Leurs fantasque ossature aux grands squelettes noirs
> De leurs chaises; leurs pieds aux barreaux rachitiques
> S'entrelacent pour les matins et pour les soirs!
>
> Ces vieillards ont toujours fait tresse avec leurs sièges."
> (SFP, 23)[15]

What Pound means here, I think, is that Rimbaud's images, like Cézanne's, are framed, not as symbols pointing beyond themselves, but as metonymic displacements that convey, in this particular case, a sense of overwhelming ugliness. "Les Assis" is a poem about the old men who haunt public libraries, but we never *see* the sitters as human beings. Rather, the poem presents parts without wholes, human frames grafted in epileptic passion onto chairs, feet intertwining over the rachitic bars of furniture, skin turning into calico, and coat buttons that have the eyes of beasts. Rimbaud thus decomposes reality; he uses palpable visual images, but they are such as the human eye has never encountered. "Les Assis" is a surrealist fantasy in which bundles of tonsils and other bits and pieces of human anatomy merge mysteriously with inanimate objects. The mode of the *Illuminations* is contained here in embryo.

Pound concludes: "The thing that stuns me in preparing

[15] A literal translation into English:

> They have grafted in their epileptic loves
> Their odd bone structure onto the large black skeletons
> Of their chairs; their feet on the rickety rails
> Are entwined for the morning and for the evening!
>
> These old men have always been braided to their seats.

this section of my essay is HOW, HOW, HOW! so much could have escaped me when I read him five years ago. How much I might have learned from the printed page that I have learned slowly from actuality. . . . I wonder in what other poet will we find such firmness of colouring and such certitude" (SFP, 26). It is interesting that Pound, never one to be modest about his accomplishments, here talks of "learn[ing] slowly." Perhaps he sensed that his own poems of this period were not without Symbolist traces. For although Pound's adaptations—notably *Cathay* (1915) and *Sextus Propertius* (1918)—do embody the new aesthetic of presentational condensation, of Rimbaldian "flat surface,"[16] his first attempt to write the "long imagiste or vorticist poem" (GB, 94) that was to become the *Cantos* was not a success. Indeed, the so-called *Ur-Cantos* published in *Poetry* in 1917 look back to the Browningesque dramatic monologues of *Personae* (1909).[17]

The original Canto I, for example, is an uneasy mixture of expostulation and image, in which the speaker alternately praises Browning, quarrels with his ghost, and wonders somewhat querulously whether he himself should "give up th'intaglio method"—the technique of his short Imagist poems—and write a long poem that might rival *Sordello*.[18] He has self-doubts because Browning has already "worked out new form, the meditative, / Semi-dramatic, semi-epic story, / And we will say: What's left for me to

[16] See Schneidau, *The Image and the Real*, pp. 31-32; Kenner, *Pound Era*, pp. 28-29, 191-222; Davie, *Pound*, pp. 58-61.

[17] For a thorough discussion of the relation of these early Cantos to Pound's final versions, see Ronald Bush, *The Genesis of Ezra Pound's Cantos* (Princeton: Princeton University Press, 1976), especially Chapter III. Although I sometimes disagree with Bush's arguments for specific influences on the evolving Cantos, I have found his study enormously helpful and am indebted to it throughout. See also Myles Slatin, "A History of Pound's Cantos I-XVI, 1915-1925," *American Literature*, 35 (May 1963), 183-195.

[18] *Three Cantos*, as Ronald Bush calls the "Ur-Cantos," appeared in the June, July, and August 1917 numbers of *Poetry* respectively, but they were composed in late 1915. Bush reproduces them on pp. 53-73; my citations are to the Bush text.

do?" (p. 56). These doubts are not without foundation: even the rather monotonous blank verse and archaic speech patterns of Canto I echo Browning's, for example:

> Were't nót *òur* lífe, your lífe, my lífe exténded?
>
> (p. 54)

And the Canto's imagery is frequently conventional. After referring to the form of Browning's poem as the "rag-bag" the modern world needs "to stuff all its thoughts in," the poet wonders:

> Say that I dump my catch, shiny and silvery
> As fresh sardines flapping and slipping on the
>   marginal cobbles?
>
> (p. 53)

This comparison of poetic invention to a creative "spilling out"—the dumping of a huge sardine catch on the "marginal cobbles" of Sirmio (Sirmione), his beloved village on Lake Garda[19]—is the sort of explicit analogy Pound takes pains to repudiate in *Gaudier-Brzeska*. And although the narrator tells "Mr. Browning" that he should have learned from "Will Wordsworth" how to "avoid speech figurative / And set our matter, as I do, in straight simple phrases" (p. 57), he is still looking for a hero upon whom he can confer his "shimmering garment," his "feathery mantle"—the "*hagomoro*" of Noh drama by means of which man attains knowledge of supernatural things.[20]

Pound evidently understood that the form he was establishing in Cantos I-III was not appropriate for his "long imagiste or vorticist poem" for almost as soon as these Cantos appeared in print, he began to tinker with them.[21] The ubiquitous first-person pronoun was eliminated, redundant passages excised, and transitions made more elliptical. But there is another long poem of this period that

[19] See Kenner, *Pound Era*, p. 357.

[20] See Bush, p. 56 and his explanatory note on p. 135.

[21] See Bush, pp. 184-190 for a detailed account of Pound's revisions for the *Lustra* (New York: Alfred A. Knopf, 1917) publication of *Three Cantos*.

seems to have satisfied not only Pound but his more skeptical readers as well. I am thinking, of course, of *Hugh Selwyn Mauberley* (1920).

II

Mauberley has a problematic place in the Pound canon. Throughout the twenties and early thirties, it was hailed as Pound's one indisputable masterpiece; thus Eliot declared in 1928: "I am quite certain of *Mauberley*, whatever else I am certain of. . . . This seems to me a great poem . . . a document of an epoch; it is . . . in the best sense of Arnold's worn phrase, a 'criticism of life'."[22] F. R. Leavis called *Mauberley* "a great poem, and a weightier achievement than any single thing . . . to be found in Yeats."[23] The New Critics generally followed this lead, the assumption being that whereas the *Cantos* suffered from what Eliot called, rather wistfully and apologetically, "an increasing defect of communication,"[24] *Mauberley*, at least, had what Ronald Bottrall defined as a "method based on a symbolism having various strata of interpretation."[25]

In recent years, as the greatness of the *Cantos* has come to be increasingly recognized, the pendulum has swung the other way. The current stand is that *Mauberley*, far from being unlike the *Cantos*, is to be seen as an early sketch for them, a slighter work containing in embryo many of Pound's later themes and techniques. Hugh Witemeyer, for example, writes: "To unify his sequence *Mauberley*, Pound employed the same device that he was to use in *The Cantos*: the assimilation of a number of historical and pseu-

[22] "Introduction to Ezra Pound: *Selected Poems* (1928)," rpt. in *Ezra Pound: A Critical Anthology*, ed. J. P. Sullivan (Baltimore: Penguin Books, 1970), pp. 108-109.

[23] *New Bearings in English Poetry* (1932; London: Chatto and Windus, 1954), p. 235.

[24] "Ezra Pound," *Poetry*, 68 (September 1946); rpt. in *Ezra Pound*, ed. Sutton, p. 23.

[25] "XXX Cantos of Ezra Pound: An Incursion into Poetics," *Scrutiny*, 2 (1933); rpt. in *Ezra Pound*, ed. Sullivan, p. 139.

dohistorical figures to the archetypal patterns of quest and heroic struggle found in Homer's *Odyssey*."[26]

This is true enough with respect to what *Mauberley says*. But if we look at the way the poem *works*, a rather different picture emerges. Take, for example, III (Part I), which contains Pound's scathing attack on the bad taste of the modern age, whether in art, religion, or politics. It begins:

The tea-rose tea-gown, etc.
Supplants the mousseline of Cos,
The pianola "replaces"
Sappho's barbitos.

Christ follows Dionysus
Phallic and ambrosial
Made way for macerations;
Caliban casts out Ariel.

(P, 189)

"To use a symbol *with an ascribed or intended* meaning," Pound had insisted in *Gaudier-Brzeska*, "is, usually, to produce very bad art" (GB, 86). Yet I count eight such "ascribing" symbols in these eight lines. Briefly, the "tea-rose tea-gown" symbolizes the vulgarity of modern dress in contrast to the delicate and beautiful "mousseline of Cos"—the Propertian tunic of Coan silk.[27] The pianola, which

[26] *The Poetry of Ezra Pound: Forms of Renewal, 1908-1920* (Berkeley and Los Angeles: University of California Press, 1969), p. 163. Cf. Sr. Bernetta Quinn, *Ezra Pound: An Introduction to the Poetry* (New York: Columbia University Press, 1972), p. 74. An exception is Donald Davie, both in *Ezra Pound: Poet as Sculptor*, p. 101 and in *Pound*, pp. 52-55. In the latter book, Davie calls *Mauberley* "a poem one must grow through, and grow out of," and observes: "Too much of *Hugh Selwyn Mauberley* is *attitudinizing*. The poem is the elaborate culmination of Pound's attempts to be urbane, but urbanity did not come naturally to him" (pp. 54-55). Interestingly, Davie's first essay on *Mauberley* was a straightforward, appreciative explication: see "Ezra Pound's *Hugh Selwyn Mauberley*," in *The Modern Age*, Vol. 7 of *The Pelican Guide to English Literature*, ed. Boris Ford (Baltimore: Penguin Books, 1963), pp. 315-329.

[27] See K. K. Ruthven, *A Guide to Ezra Pound's Personae* (1926) (Berkeley and Los Angeles: University of California Press, 1969), p. 106.

reduces music to a punched sheet of paper to be played mechanically, is contrasted to Sappho's barbitos, that is, to the original lyre of poetry, which represents, as Witemeyer puts it, "the ideal relationship between the musician and his music" as well as "the ideal relationship between music and poetry."[28] In the second stanza, Dionysus symbolizes the "Phallic and ambrosial" rites of pagan fertility, which have unfortunately been replaced by the "macerations" typical of Christianity. Ariel, the symbol of all that is delicate, airy, light, poetic, and spiritual, is cast out by Caliban, the symbol of earth, mindlessness, joylessness—the anti-poetic.

These rather facile contrasts between an idealized past and a vulgarized present continue throughout the poem as Pound produces symbol after symbol "with an ascribed or intended meaning." The "wafer," to give another example, symbolizes true communion; it is replaced by "the press," symbol of meaningless, vulgar communication—that is, of false communion. And so on. One feels that Pound begins with an idea, not with an image, and then sets about to find an objective correlative for that idea. Caliban vs. Ariel, pianola vs. Sappho's barbitos—all these items could be replaced by others without a real change in poetic effect. Moreover, despite its allusiveness and ellipses, the poem moves sequentially and logically from *a* to *b*; it is not a collage of "super-pository" images or a "VORTEX, from which, and through which, and into which, ideas are constantly rushing."

We can find similar symbolic substitutions throughout *Mauberley*, and it would be tedious to go through this over-explicated poem step by step, pointing to all the examples. Let me note just a few of the more important. Here is Stanza 4 of the opening poem, "E. P. Ode Pour L'Election de son Sepulchre":

His true Penelope was Flaubert,
He fished by obstinate isles;

[28] *Forms of Renewal*, p. 189.

Observed the elegance of Circe's hair
Rather than the mottoes on sun-dials.

(P, 187)

Here Flaubert represents the ideal of disciplined craftsmanship—*le mot juste*—that "E. P." longs to attain; the French novelist is the "Penelope" of this Odysseus, the object of his long circuitous voyage, in the course of which he is almost undone by the Sirens' song, "Caught in the unstopped ear" (stanza 4), and "fishe(s) by obstinate isles"—a reference to Pound's experiments with Provençal, Anglo-Saxon, Chinese and Japanese, Latin and Greek verse forms, but also, as Hugh Kenner points out, an allusion to the smug British Isles, whose citizens cast a cold eye on "E. P.'s" aestheticism. For this poet prefers the dangerous beauty of a Circe (cf. the refrain "Beauty is difficult" in Canto LXXIV) to the banalities inscribed on sundials, the moral platitudes of "normal" society.[29]

In XII, a dramatic monologue in the vein of Eliot's "Prufrock" and "Portrait of a Lady," Pound's symbolism is especially one-dimensional. The "stuffed-satin drawing room" of the Lady Valentine all too obviously represents the emptiness of upper-class British society, and the final quatrain about Fleet Street bristles with indignation:

Beside this thoroughfare
The sale of half-hose has

[29] In *The Poetry of Ezra Pound* (New York: New Directions, 1951), Hugh Kenner finds multiple ironies in the stanza. For example: "The first line . . . renders with astonishing concision an intricate set of cultural perspectives. Pound's voyages to China, to Tuscany, to Provence, his battles with Polyphemic editors and his dallyings with pre-Raphaelite Sirens, are transformed, as in the *Cantos*, into an Odyssey of discovery and frustration." See *Ezra Pound, A Collection of Critical Essays*, ed. Walter Sutton (Englewood Cliffs: Prentice-Hall, Inc., 1963), p. 46. No doubt, these allusions do stand behind Pound's text, but the *mode* of symbolism as distinct from the referents still strikes me as reductive: good guys (Flaubert) versus bad things like "mottoes on sundials." Most commentators, however, follow Kenner's lead: see John Espey, *Ezra Pound's Mauberley, A Study in Composition* (Berkeley and Los Angeles: University of California Press, 1955; rpt. 1974), p. 85.

Long since superseded the cultivation
Of Pierian roses.

(P, 196)

Pieria was the place near Mount Olympus where the Muses were worshipped; the allusion is, once again, to a Sappho lyric.[30] Pound's contempt for a London in which "the cultivation / Of Pierian roses" has been "superseded" by the sale of "half-hose" is a simplified version of such Eliot passages as the following:

Where are the eagles and the trumpets?

Buried beneath some snow-deep Alps.
Over buttered scones and crumpets
Weeping, weeping multitudes
Droop in a hundred A.B.C.'s[31]

"A Cooking Egg," from which these lines come, skirts sentimentality by suggesting that the debased London of seedy A.B.C.'s is at least partly a projection of the speaker's state of mind, a figment of his troubled imagination. In Pound's lyric, on the other hand, the attack on modernity is head-on.

The continuing controversy over the status of Mauberley (is he Pound? a persona who represents the failed aesthete? or sometimes Pound and sometimes this persona? or neither?) has obscured what seems to me much more important: that Pound was never quite at ease with the poetic materials of *Mauberley*, that he was trying too hard to compose in the Eliot mode. As he later put it:

> . . . at a particular date in a particular room, two authors, neither engaged in picking the other's pocket, decided that the dilutation of *vers libre*, Amygism, Lee Masterism, general floppiness had gone too far and that some

[30] See Ruthven, p. 140. The allusion is to Sappho, LXXI: "for you have no part in the roses that come from Pieria."

[31] T. S. Eliot, *Collected Poems 1909-1962* (New York: Harcourt, Brace & World, 1963), p. 37. All subsequent references to Eliot's poetry are to this edition.

counter-current must be set going. Parallel situations centuries ago in China. Remedy prescribed: 'Emaux et Camées' (or the Bay State Hymn Book). Rhyme and regular strophes.

Results: Poems in Mr. Eliot's *second* volume, not contained in his first ('Prufrock', *Egoist*, 1917), also 'H. S. Mauberley'.

Divergence later.[32]

Interestingly, the "remedy prescribed" proved to be difficult for both poets. Under Pound's tutelage, Eliot studied Gautier and produced, between 1917 and 1919, seven quatrain poems in an impersonal, "hard," allusive, satiric, highly condensed mode. Pound found these quatrains quite "diverting" (SL, 136). In 1938, he recalled nostalgically that "Eliot's real criticism of England" antedated his British citizenship and conversion to the Anglican church; it was found, so Pound believed, in poems like "Whispers of Immortality," which ends with the lines: "But our lot crawls between dry ribs / To keep our metaphysics warm." Of this passage, Pound says approvingly: "Out of Gautier and the Bay State Hymn Book, but no soft Victorian slither converging."[33] The typescripts of the quatrain poems in the Berg Collection of the New York Public Library testify to Pound's excision of such "Victorian slither" as passive constructions, prepositional phrases, and weak verbs.[34]

[32] *Criterion* (July 1932), cited by John Espey in *Ezra Pound's Mauberley*, p. 25. Espey (pp. 49-61) and Ronald Bush (pp. 256, 259, 263) also argue for a strong Henry James influence on *Mauberley*. I find this doubtful because Pound had none of James' consuming interest in psychological complexities. As he wrote in a letter to Williams in 1908: "To me the short so-called dramatic lyric . . . is the poetic part of a drama the rest of which . . . is left to the reader's imagination or implied or set in a short note. I catch the character I happen to be interested in at the moment he interests me, usually a moment of song, self-analysis, or sudden understanding or revelation. And the rest of the play would bore me and presumably the reader" (SL, 3-4).

[33] "National Culture, A Manifesto 1938," *Impact* (Regnery, 1960); rpt. in SPr, 164.

[34] See Bush, p. 208.

But in the summer of 1919, Eliot wrote a very different sort of poem—"Gerontion." Although the typescript is again annotated by Pound, here Eliot chose not to follow Pound's advice, although he later agreed not to include "Gerontion" as a prelude to *The Waste Land*.[35] Indeed, this dense Symbolist poem with its "contrived corridors" and "Vacant shuttles / Weav(ing) the wind," did not square with Pound's Imagist-Vorticist aesthetic. For where in "Gerontion" is "direct treatment of the thing"?

In the juvescence of the year
Came Christ the tiger
In depraved May, dogwood and chestnut, flowering
judas,
To be eaten, to be divided, to be drunk
Among whispers; by Mr. Silvero
With caressing hands, at Limoges
Who walked all night in the next room;

By Hakagawa, bowing among the Titians;
By Madame de Tornquist, in the dark room
Shifting the candles; Fraülein von Kulp
Who turned in the hall, one hand on the door.
(pp. 29-30)

Here, on the contrary, indirection is the order of the day. Every word resonates. Christ the Tiger who visits His wrath upon the slothful and cowardly, upon those who, like Gerontion himself, have made the grand refusal, recalls both Blake's Tiger and Jonathan Edwards' image of God as an angry wild beast. This is a Christ who has come not to send peace but a sword, for the "juvescence of the year" in which He came, has turned out to be the "depraved May" of "flowering judas," the season of man's denial of the Incarnation. In the Black Mass that follows, this Christ is "eaten," "divided," and "drunk / Among whispers" by a disreputable and shadowy group of international types. Eliot's use of proper names here and elsewhere immedi-

[35] See SL, p. 171; Bush, pp. 209-211.

ately sets him apart from Pound. Whereas Pound increasingly uses the real names of real people—Mr. Jefferson, Wyndham Lewis, Sir Edward Coke, Isotta degli Atti, Confucius—in what are essentially metonymic structures, Eliot invents symbolic figures: Mr. Silvero (silver) of the "caressing hands," perhaps a collector of fine china, perhaps engaged in sexual games; the Japanese art patron Hakagawa, incongruously "bowing among the Titians," Madame de Tornquist, whose "dark room" activities recall not only Madame Blavatsky but Eliot's own Madame Sosostris, and whose hybrid name evokes the decay of national identity and culture; and finally the mysterious Fraülein von Kulp (*culpa*), who performs unspecified and hence seemingly unspeakable acts.

Eliot's dramatic presentation of these sinister persons functions, of course, as the objective correlative of his conviction that a civilization that has rejected the Christian dispensation is doomed to decay, and that, accordingly, "De Bailhache, Fresca, Mrs. Cammel" and their like are ultimately "whirled / Beyond the circuit of the shuddering Bear / In fractured atoms." For Pound, such a powerful symbolic embodiment of human weakness and deprivation may well have seemed excessive. In his 1930 "Credo," he remarked:

> Mr. Eliot who is at times an excellent poet and who has arrived at the supreme Eminence among English critics largely through disguising himself as a corpse once asked in the course of an amiable article what 'I believed'.
>
> Having a strong disbelief in abstract and general statement as a means of conveying one's thought to others I have for a number of years answered such questions by telling the enquirer to read Confucius and Ovid. . . .
>
> Given the material means I would replace the statue of Venus on the cliffs of Terracina. I would erect a temple to Artemis in Park Lane. . . .
>
> I believe that postwar 'returns to christianity' . . . have

been merely the gran' rifiuto and, in general, signs of fatigue.

(SPr, 53)

Not Christ the Tiger or the shuddering Bear but a *real* Venus or a *real* temple to Artemis—this is what Pound wanted poetry to deal with. "The natural object is always the adequate symbol." What one wants is *constatation of fact.*

It is against this background that we must reconsider the Eliot-Pound collaboration on *The Waste Land.* For despite all the stylistic changes that Pound brought about in Eliot's long poem, changes that have recently been submitted to careful study[36]—the thematic strains of the original *Waste Land* are not significantly altered in the final version. Indeed, one might argue that Pound's excisions and revisions made Eliot's central themes and symbols more prominent than they would otherwise have been, buried as they were under the weight of such satirical intrusions as "He Do the Police in Different Voices" (Part I) or the Popean couplets about Fresca at her toilet at the beginning of Part III.[37]

Consider what happens to "Death by Water," which Pound reduced from ninety-two lines to ten. The first section, written in quatrains rhyming *abab,* introduces a parodic version of Ulysses in the person of a foolish sailor on shore leave, regaling his cronies in the public bars, who are "Staggering, or limping with a comic gonorrhea," with stories of the "much seen and much endured" (p. 55). In the margin of the manuscript, Pound wrote, "Bad—but cant attack until I get typescript." The second section, written in rather slack Tennysonian blank verse, is the dramatic

[36] See especially the essays by A. Walton Litz, Hugh Kenner, Richard Ellmann, and Helen Gardner in *Eliot in His Time, Essays on the Occasion of the Fiftieth Anniversary of The Waste Land,* ed. A. Walton Litz (Princeton: Princeton University Press, 1973). The early stages of Eliot's composition are discussed fully by Lyndall Gordon in *Eliot's Early Years,* pp. 86-120.

[37] See T. S. Eliot, *The Waste Land, A Facsimile and Transcript of the Original Drafts Including the Annotations of Ezra Pound,* ed. Valerie Eliot (London: Faber and Faber, 1971), pp. 4-5, 39-41. Subsequent page numbers refer to this text.

monologue of the sailor, telling of a fishing expedition from the Dry Salvages north to the Outer Banks of Nova Scotia. Even as the sailor meditates on the significance of a mysterious Sirens' song heard one night on watch (lines 65-72), a song that makes him question the relationship of reality to dream, the ship hits an iceberg and is destroyed. After this ending ("And if *Another* knows, I know I know not, / Who only knows that there is no more noise now"—p. 61) comes the "Phlebas the Phoenician" lyric, which is the only part of the original that remains in the finished poem.

Pound seems to have decided that the long account of the sailor's voyage was an unnecessary digression. But when Eliot wrote from London, "Perhaps better omit Phlebas also???" Pound replied, "I DO advise keeping Phlebas. In fact I more'n advise. Phlebas is an integral part of the poem; the card pack introduces him, the drowned phoen. sailor. And he is needed ABSOLOOTLY where he is. Must stay in" (SL, 171). Pound understood, in other words, that "Death by Water" is the essential link between the Madame Sosostris passage and the following lines near the end of Part V:

> *Damyata*: The boat responded
> Gaily, to the hand expert with sail and oar
> The sea was calm, your heart would have responded
> Gaily, when invited, beating obedient
> To controlling hands
>
> I sat upon the shore
> Fishing, with the arid plain behind me
> Shall I at least set my lands in order?
>
> (*Collected Poems*, p. 69)

Phlebas' "death by water" is the necessary prelude to the hints of rebirth contained in these lines, whereas the actual sea voyage, as described in the cancelled narrative portion, is irrelevant to the poem's life-in-death theme. Curiously, then, Pound seems to have understood Eliot's purpose better than did Eliot himself.

Figure 1. Pablo Picasso. *Ma Jolie (Woman with Guitar).*

Figure 2. Marcel Duchamp.

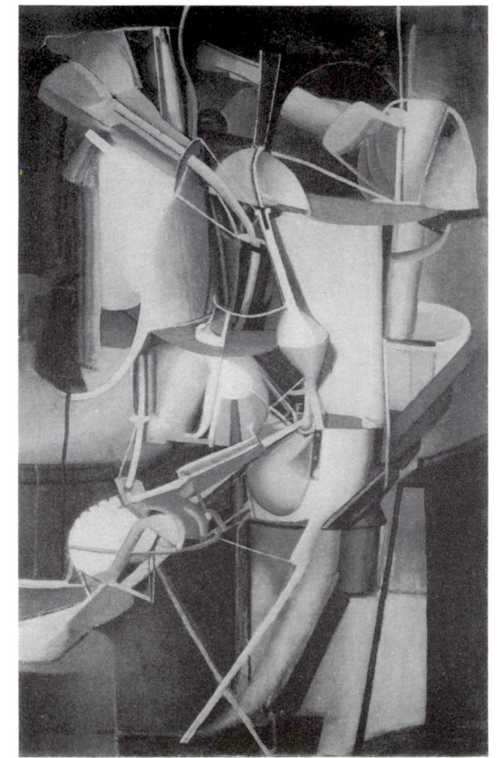

Figure 3. Marcel Duchamp. *The Bride*.

Figure 4. Juan Gris. *Still Life before an Open Window.*

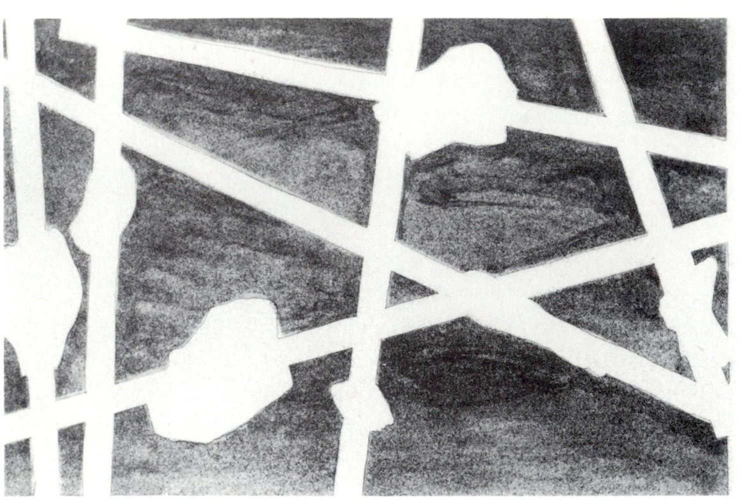

Figure 7. Jasper Johns. Plate from *Fizzles/Foirades*.

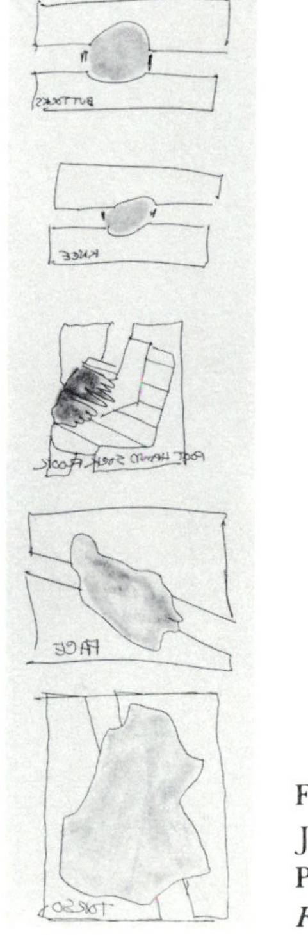
Figure 8. Jasper Johns. Plate from *Fizzles/Foirades*.

Figure 9. Jasper Johns. Plate from *Fizzles/Foirades*.

Figure 10. Jasper Johns. Plate from *Fizzles/Foirades*.

Figure 11. Jasper Johns. Plate from *Fizzles/Foirades*.

d'ôter mes lunettes, pour qu'elles se brouillent. C'est un avantage. Mais ce n'est pas une véritable protection, comme nous allons voir. C'est pourquoi je me tiens de préférence, quand je me lève, devant une surface unie, semblable à celle que je commande depuis mon lit, je parle du plafond. Car je commence de nouveau à me lever. Je croyais avoir fait mon dernier voyage, celui où maintenant je dois encore une fois essayer de voir clair, afin qu'il me serve de leçon, et dont j'aurais mieux fait de ne pas revenir. Mais l'impression me gagne que je vais être obligé d'en entreprendre un autre. Je commence donc de nouveau à me lever et à faire quelques pas dans ma chambre, en me tenant aux barreaux du lit. C'est l'athlétisme au fond qui m'a perdu. D'avoir tant sauté et couru, boxé et lutté, dans ma jeunesse, et bien au-delà pour certaines spécialités, j'ai usé la machine avant l'heure. J'avais dépassé la quarantaine que je lançais encore le javelin.

Figure 12. Jasper Johns. Plate from *Fizzles/Foirades*.

Figure 13. René Magritte. *The Field-Glass.*

In discussing Pound's "operation upon *The Waste Land*," Eliot notes:

> I have sometimes tried to perform the same sort of maieutic task; and I know that one of the temptations against which I have to be on guard, is trying to re-write somebody's poem in the way I should have written it myself if I had wanted to write that poem. Pound never did that: he tried first to understand what one was attempting to do, and then tried to help one do it in one's own way.[38]

This is an important distinction. Pound did *not* try to transform *The Waste Land* into the sort of city poem he himself might have written. Rather, he helped Eliot to write it in his own way. "What the Thunder Said," for example, is left virtually untouched by Pound, for here Eliot discovered his quest theme and brought it to a swift and dramatic conclusion.

In assessing Pound's response to *The Waste Land*, critics invariably cite the famous letter to Eliot (24 December 1921) in which Pound says: "Complimenti, you bitch. I am wracked by the seven jealousies, and cogitating an excuse for always exuding my deformative secretions in my own stuff, and never getting an outline. I go into nacre and objets d'art" (SL, 169). But the fact is that, despite these self-depreciating words, Pound knew well enough that *The Waste Land*, like "Gerontion," was not his sort of poem. As Eliot himself observes, after thanking Pound for "helping one to do it in one's own way," "There did come a point, of course, at which difference of outlook and belief became too wide" (Sutton, p. 23).

In the late spring of 1922, Pound resumed work on the *Cantos* after an almost three-year interval that followed the completion of Canto VII. In May, Canto VIII, not previously referred to in Pound's correspondence, appeared in *The Dial*; it was to become, with some changes, the present

[38] "Ezra Pound," *Poetry*, 68 (September 1946); rpt. in *Ezra Pound*, ed. Sutton, pp. 22-23.

Canto II. "The appearance of this Canto," writes Myles Slatin, "signalled the beginning of another period of intensive work on the long poem. This period, stretching from the spring of 1922 to the early part of 1925, was the climactic period of the poem's composition, for during it the poem—at least the first part of it—took what is now its final shape."[39]

Canto IX—the future Canto VIII—was a Malatesta Canto. Pound refers to it in a letter to his mother on 20 August 1922, and the four Malatesta Cantos were finished by the summer of 1923 and published in the July *Criterion*. Significantly, Pound's revisions of these Cantos for the 1925 book publication were minor, generally restricted to changes in lineation and occasional phrasing.[40] "What is more important," says Slatin, "the design of the poem suddenly crystallized, perhaps partly as a result of the long and intensive labor which went into the Malatesta group. Within a month or perhaps two months of the publication of these Cantos, Pound had entirely revised the beginning of the poem and had come to the end of the composition of the first sixteen Cantos" (p. 191).

Interestingly, the design that now "crystallized" was no longer the symbolic design of *Mauberley*, with its elaborate oppositions between the tawdry present and the splendors of a lost Achaia. It is as if Pound's revisions of the *Waste Land* manuscript had taught him that collaboration between himself and Eliot was no longer possible. By 1925, he was remarking that Eliot's "literary production has been reduced to a minimum, and that not of his best potentiality, from fatigue" (SL, 196). And after this, his references to Eliot become increasingly caustic.[41]

[39] "A History of Pound's Cantos I-XVI," *American Literature*, 189; cf. Bush, p. 251.

[40] *Criterion*, 1, no. 4 (July 1923), 363-384. In revising Canto IX—the future Canto VIII—Pound added four lines to the beginning: "These fragments you have shelved (shored)," and so on. See C, 28. In the original version of this Canto, the word "and" that ends the poem was set off in a separate line. Such minor changes in lineation are typical of Pound's revision of the Malatesta Cantos.

[41] One of the most interesting comments is made in "A Visiting Card"

By the early twenties, then, Pound had put the Symbolist masters of his youth squarely behind him. In Paris, where *A Draft of XVI Cantos* took shape, Pound turned to new models. The example of *Ulysses* is often cited, for example by Ronald Bush, who argues that the radical condensation, "juxtaposed *contrast*," and documentary realism of the *Cantos* derive from Joyce's novel.[42] Yet, despite the many parallels, both verbal and thematic, between *Ulysses* and the *Cantos*, there seems to be a basic opposition between Joyce's scholastically organized novel, that "Aquinas-map" in which each episode has its own Homeric analogue, symbol, technique, organ, color, and so on, and the *Cantos*, with their "constatation of fact," their cuts, their paratactic structure and autobiographical intrusions.

Dada, which Pound regarded with some suspicion but which nevertheless attracted him during the Paris years, is perhaps a more important analogue. In his "Island of Paris" letters for *The Dial*, Pound expressed admiration for the Dada poets' irreverence and daring, the willingness of these "young and very ferocious" artists to satirize the sanctimonious attitude of the art-buying public.[43] On the other

---

(1942); rpt. SPr, 306-335. In a section called "Style," Pound reiterates his distinction between the three forms of poetry—*phanopoeia*, *melopoeia*, and *logopoeia*—and remarks: "In this last category Eliot surpasses me; in the second I surpass him. Part of his logopoeia is incompatible with my main purpose" (SPr, 321). See also the "Prefatio Aut Cimicium Tumulus," *Active Anthology* (1933); rpt. in SPr, 389-400. Here Pound attacks Eliot's criticism with such comments as "Mr. Eliot's misfortune was to find himself surrounded by a horrible and microcephalous bureaucracy which disliked poetry" (SPr, 392).

[42] Bush, pp. 194-197. Cf. Forrest Read, "Pound, Joyce, and Flaubert: The Odysseans," in *New Approaches to Ezra Pound*, ed. Eva Hesse (Berkeley and Los Angeles: University of California Press, 1969), pp. 124-144. Read has important things to say about the relationship of Pound to Joyce as transmitters of the Odyssean tradition.

[43] *The Dial*, 69 (September 1920), 407-408. See Andrew Clearfield, "Pound, Paris, and Dada," *Paideuma*, 7 (Spring & Fall 1978), 113-140. In this important background essay, Clearfield establishes Pound's connection to such periodicals as Tristan Tzara's *Dadaphone* and André Breton's *Littérature*; he also traces Pound's published comments on the Dada movement.

hand, Pound always regarded art itself as sacred, and the humorous anti-art stance of the Dadaists must have irritated him. Thus he tended to dismiss Apollinaire, even though the *Cantos* have much in common with Apollinaire's poetry: for example, the spatial arrangement of words on the page, the incorporation of extra-poetic materials, the use of slang and advertising jargon, the abolition of all transition between blocks of material.[44]

The Dada poets usually claimed Rimbaud as their poetic father, the first anti-artist. In this allegiance, Pound and Picabia could meet. In 1928, Pound wrote a long letter to René Taupin, in response to the specific questions that Taupin (who was preparing his book, *L'Influence du symbolisme français sur la poésie americaine*) had posed. This letter helps to place the technique of the evolving Cantos in the context of what Pound himself called his "steals from the French" and contains Pound's strongest statement in praise of Rimbaud. Despite the slapdash French, cryptic shorthand references, and misspellings that characterize Pound's long, rambling letter, its central points are perfectly clear:

(1) Pound strenuously objects to Taupin's hypothesis that Imagism derived from French Symbolism. "Symbole???" he asks, "je n'ai jamais lu 'les idées des symbolistes' sur ce sujet. . . . Mais 'voui': l'idée de l'image doit 'quelque chose' aux symbolistes français via T. E. Hulme, via Yeats < Symons < Mallarmé. Come le pain doit quelque chose au vanneur de blé, etc" (SL, 218). He concedes that Imagist concepts of condensation and concentration may owe something to Symbolism by way of the Hulme cénacle of 1908 but points out that his own version of Imagism was never quite that of Amy Lowell, F. S. Flint, etc. "Fort difference entre Flint: (*tolerance* pour *tous* les fautes et imbécillités des poètes français). Mois—examen très sévère—et intolérance" (p. 216).

(2) Pound came to nineteenth-century French poetry, in his own words, "relativement tard" (p. 216). "Ma connais-

[44] See Clearfield, p. 132.

ance des poètes fr. mod. et ma propagande pour ces poètes en Amerique (1912-17-23) venait en sens genérale *aprés* l'inception de l'Imagisme à Londres (1908-13-14)" (p. 218). This explanation squares with Pound's admission in *A Study in French Poets* that much had escaped him when he first read Rimbaud in 1913.

(3) Despite the inherent disparity between the French and American imaginations, the *technique* of French poetry from the time of Gautier to 1912 could serve as an example to any American poet of Pound's generation. "Que les poétes *essentials* à cette étude se reduissent à Gautier, Corbière, Laforgue, Rimbaud. Que depuis Rimbaud, aucun poète en France n'a inventé rien de fondamentale" (p. 217).

(4) Pound cites as one of his central aims the attempt to forge a systematic aesthetic based on Rimbaud's intuitive stylistic habits: "Ce que Rimbaud atteint par intuition (génie) dans certaines poèmes, érigé en esthetique conscient (?? peut-être)—je ne veux pas prendre une gloire injuste—mais pour tant que je sais. J'en ai fais une esthétique plus ou moins systématique—et j'ai pu citer certaines poèmes de R. comme example" (p. 217).

Pound thus regards his own poetic as a systematized version of Rimbaud's. But he admits that it is all but impossible to write Rimbaldian verse in English. "Est-ce-que il existe une langue anglais pour exprimer les lignes de Rimbaud? Je ne *dis pas* un traducteur capable de le faire, mais est-ce-que cette langue existe? (comme moyen)—et depuis quand?" (p. 218). The question is rhetorical: Pound hopes, of course, that his own poetic language might be the counterpart of Rimbaud's. In "How to Read," published the following year, he therefore relates this language to "PHANOPOEIA, which is a casting of images upon the visual imagination." Indeed, "Rimbaud brought back to *phanopoeia* its clarity and directness" (LE, 25, 33).

Rimbaldian—or Poundian—*phanopoeia* is not, of course, a mere aggregate of concrete visual images. Eisenstein, who shared Pound's predilection for the ideogrammic technique of Chinese poetry, defined *montage* as follows:

> . . . the juxtaposition of two separate shots by splicing them together resembles not so much a simple sum of one shot plus another shot—as it does a *creation.* It resembles a creation—rather than a sum of its parts—from the circumstance that in every such juxtaposition *the result is qualitatively* distinguishable from each component element viewed separately.[45]

To put it another way, when image A is juxtaposed to image B, it loses its status as A and becomes a link in what Eisenstein calls "a chain of representations."[46] It is the making of such chains, such metonymic sequences in which "the whole is something else than the sum of its parts,"[47] that I wish to examine in the *Cantos.* I begin with the Malatesta Cantos, in which, as Myles Slatin notes, the design of Pound's long poem begins to crystallize, and then turn to the sequence generally considered to be the highpoint of Pound's long poem: the *Pisan Cantos* (LXXIV-LXXXIV) of 1948.

III

Much has been written on the background and themes of the Malatesta Cantos, and I don't wish here to go over familiar ground. Thomas Jackson has shown, quite conclusively, I think, that Malatesta is not simply, as many commentators have assumed, Pound's hero—the Renaissance ruler as beneficent patron of art—but that the emphasis in these Cantos is on Sigismundo's very mixed motives and consequently dubious successes.[48] From the

[45] Sergei M. Eisenstein, *The Film Sense*, trans. and ed. Jay Leyda (1947; rpt. New York: Harcourt Brace Jovanovich, Inc., 1975), pp. 7-8. See also Eisenstein, "The Cinematographic Principle and the Ideogram" (1929), *Film Form* (New York: Harcourt, Brace & World, Inc., 1949), pp. 28-44.

[46] *Film Sense*, p. 19.

[47] Kurt Koffka, *Principles of Gestalt Psychology* (New York: Harcourt, Brace, 1935), p. 176, as cited by Eisenstein, *Film Sense*, p. 8.

[48] "The Adventures of Messire Wrong-Head," ELH, 32 (June 1965), 242. For the view that Malatesta is one of Pound's heroes, see Sr. Bernetta Quinn, *Ezra Pound: An Introduction to the Poetry*, pp. 105-106.

beginning of Canto VIII, Sigismundo is depicted as a man torn between his love for the arts and his concern for war-politics and "service money"; the public man, in Jackson's words, "is forever undoing the private man." If Sigismundo was responsible for the architectural splendors of the Tempio at Rimini, he was also the first man to use metal cannonballs. If he wrote beautiful love poems to Isotta degli Atti, he also engaged in the most petty materialistic power struggles with the Sforza and Medici dynasties.

The portrait of Malatesta that emerges from these Cantos is thus hardly novel: it takes us back to Burckhardt's understanding of the Italian Renaissance as a time of incredible tension between sexual brutality and courtly love, between physical violence and artistic delicacy. To paraphrase Samuel Johnson, "if you were to read the Malatesta Cantos for their thematic interest, your patience would be so much fretted that you would hang yourself." And this is precisely how some readers have responded. "Reading," says Donald Davie, "is an unsatisfactory word for what the eye does as it resentfully labors over and among these blocks of dusty historical debris."[49]

Yet, on closer inspection, Pound's manipulation of these "blocks of dusty historical debris" exerts a peculiar fascination. It is not just a matter of "cultural overlayering" or of alternating a love letter with a list of building materials, a list of building materials with a papal edict. I would posit that Pound's basic strategy in the *Cantos* is to create a flat surface, as in a Cubist or early Dada collage, upon which verbal elements, fragmented images, and truncated bits of narrative, drawn from the most disparate contexts, are brought into collision. Such "collage poetry," as David Antin points out, "no longer yield(s) an iconic representation, even of a fractured sort, though bristling with significations."[50] It thus occupies a middle space between the mi-

[49] *Ezra Pound: Poet as Sculptor*, p. 126.

[50] "Some Questions About Modernism," *Occident*, 8, new series (Spring 1974), 19.

metic on the one hand and the non-objective or "abstract" on the other; the referential process is not cut off but it is subordinated to a concern for sequential or spatial arrangement. Indeed, in the case of the Malatesta Cantos, the text becomes a surface of linguistic distortions and contradictions that force the reader to participate in the poem's action. Just as Rimbaud invents cityscapes in which Swiss chalets on magic pulleys dissolve into Vesuvian craters and then into gorges spanned by little footbridges, so Pound dislocates language so as to create new verbal landscapes.

The 1923 version of Canto VIII opens as follows:

Frater tamquam et compater carissime
(*tergo*
. . hanni de
. . dicis
. . entia
Equivalent to: Giohanni of the Medici, Florence)
Letter received, and in the matter of our Messire
Gianozio
One from him also, sent on in form and with all due
dispatch,
Having added your wishes and memoranda.[51]

Unlike, say, the opening of "Gerontion" or the first page of *Ulysses,* this passage is not polysemous. As D. S. Carne-Ross, in a general discussion of the *Cantos,* puts it: "Pound's first level doesn't point beyond itself. . . . the whole reverberating dimension of inwardness is missing. There is no murmuring echo chamber where deeps supposedly answer to deeps."[52] But neither is the passage a ragbag of dusty historical debris. Its strategy is best understood if we compare it to its source: a 1449 letter from Sigismundo to Giovanni di Medici. The original begins with the address:

[51] *Criterion,* 1 (July 1923), 364; cf. C, VIII, 28.

[52] " 'The Music of a Lost Dynasty': Pound in the Classroom," *Boston University Journal,* 21 (Winter 1973), 38. Carne-Ross's is one of the best discussions we have of the problems of interpreting the *Cantos,* and I owe a great deal to it.

Magnifice vir tamquam frater, et compater carissime.[53]

Pound lops off the standard form of address ("Magnifice vir") and reverses the next two words, emphasizing Sigismundo's rather oily appeal to his Medici patron as a *true brother.* Next, the sonorous formality of the address is undercut by a series of incomplete words, meant to reproduce what is on the back of the envelope ("*tergo*"). Here the reader has to fill in the first few letters of each word in order to make sense of the address: "*Jo*hanni de / *Me*dicis / *Flo*rentia." The poet thus insists on our participation; it is up to us to fill in the blanks, to play the game. But just when we become accustomed to this strategy, Pound does a further turnabout and tells us matter-of-factly: "Equivalent to: Giohanni of the Medici, Florence."

The lines, in short, do not convey information; rather, they take certain facts and present them from different linguistic perspectives (formal, florid Italian; broken Italian words; English translation) as if to undercut their historicity. Fact, in other words, is repeatedly transformed into fiction. Thus in the body of the letter, Pound takes Sigismundo's perfectly straightforward "Ho ricevuto vostra lettera" ("I have received your letter") and turns it into business English—"Letter received"—whereas the phrase "li preghi et recordi vestri" ("your best wishes and remembrances") becomes, by an absurd sleight-of-hand, "your wishes and memoranda," as if Rimini were dissolving into Wall Street.

Such linguistic indeterminacy is one of the central devices of these Cantos. Pound uses a variety of techniques to command our attention. Perhaps the simplest is condensation and modernization. In Canto VIII, for example, Sigismundo's letter to Giovanni di Medici regarding his renewed alliance with Venice is a seven-line condensation of the original eighteen lines of prose, in which Sigismundo gives a formal explanation of the precise terms the Vene-

[53] Pound's main source is Charles Yriarte, *Un Condottiere au Xv Siècle* (Paris, 1882), especially the appendix, "Notes-Documents-Commentaries." This particular letter is cited in full on p. 381.

tians have offered him, his military troubles caused by renewed flooding, and so on. Here is Pound's rendition:

Venice has taken me on again
            At 7,000 a month, *fiorini di Camera.*
For 2,000 horse and four hundred footmen,
And it rains here by the gallon,
We have had to dig a new ditch.
In three or four days
I shall try to set up the bombards.

(VIII, 30)

Such updating of history would not in itself make the Malatesta Cantos unique; it is a device many poets have used. But Pound's forte is to take a passage like the one just cited and then suddenly to switch back to the voice of the Renaissance chronicler, in this case describing the wedding of Bianca Visconti to Francesco Sforza:

Under the plumes, with the flakes and small wads of colour
Showering from the balconies
With the sheets spread from windows,
            with leaves and small branches pinned on them,
Arras hung from the railings; out of the dust,
With pheasant tails upright on their forelocks,
            The small white horses, the
Twelve girls riding in order, green satin in pannier'd habits.

(VIII, 30-31)

Another frequent form of montage is to set the original Italian side by side with a correct English translation so as to intensify and reinforce a central image; thus "*non gli manchera la provixione mai*" is followed by "never lacking provision," and the line "With his horsemen and his footmen" precedes "*gente di cavallo e da pie.*" Or again, Pound may translate a given letter or document written in highly formal Italian so literally that it sounds like a parody in

English. The best example of such satiric super-literalism is the letter of Sigismundo's five-year-old son, which Pound translates in Canto IX with tongue-in-cheek pedantic fidelity:

> "Magnificent and Exalted Lord and Father in especial my
> "lord with due recommendation: your letter has been pre-
> "sented to me by Gentilino da Gradara and with it the bay
> "pony (ronzino baiectino) the which you have sent me, and
> "which appears in my eyes a fine caparison'd charger, upon
> "which I intend to learn all there is to know about riding, in
> "consideration of yr. paternal affection for which I thank
> "your excellency thus briefly and pray you continue to hold
> "me in this esteem. . . .
>
> (IX, 39)[54]

In English, the endless "the which," "upon which," and "for which" clauses, the consistent circumlocution, and the involuted address sound wholly absurd, especially since the subject of the letter is no more than the gift of a bay pony. Translated thus literally, the letter has neither the status of fifteenth-century document nor twentieth-century adaptation; it remains a curiosity, removed from a specific time-space context. The introduction of the Italian phrase "ronzino baiectino" is particularly skillful: "ronzino baiectino" does mean "bay pony," but in the context it sounds more like a zoological specimen or a rare disease.

The Malatesta Cantos "cut" back and forth between such literal translation on the one hand and intentional mistranslation on the other. We have one example of the latter in the above passage. Pound translates "uno grosso et apreciato corsiero" as "a fine caparison'd charger." "Apreciato" means "worthy" or "admirable"; "caparison'd" is a pure invention, used to enhance the bombastic formality of the child's letter. Frequently in the Malatesta Cantos, the straightforward expository prose of the original gives way to business English ("This to advise," "the said load");

[54] See Yriarte, p. 445.

illiterate spelling ("I think it advisabl that I shud go to rome to talk to mister Albert so as I can no what he thinks about it rite"—IX, 38); abbreviations ("yr. Lordship," "The Illus. Sgr. Mr. Fedricho d'Orbino," "Sidg"); modern slang ("that nicknosed s.o.b. Feddy," "And old Sforza bitched us at Pesaro," "worked the wangle," "And he found 'em, the anti-Aragons, / busted and weeping in their beards"); regional American dialects ("provided you don't get too ornry," "But dey got de mos' bloody rottenes' peace on us"); and comic name-calling ("old Wattle-Wattle," "Siggy darlint," the transformation of Giorgio Ranbutino into "Giorgio Rambottom").

Closely related to such artful mistranslation is the purposely incorrect rendering of the Italian itself. In the letter to Giovanni di Medici which opens Canto VIII, for example, Pound has Sigismundo say: "And tell the *Maestro di pentore* / That there can be no question of / His painting the walls for the moment, / As the mortar is not yet dry / And it wd. be merely work chucked away / (*buttato via*) . . ." (VIII, 28). In the original,[55] the Italian phrase is *gettata via*, which means "thrown away." Pound substitutes the harsh "*buttato via*," partly to suit his own meaning—"chucked away"—and partly, no doubt, for comic sound effect.

One of Pound's most effective ways of distorting perspective is to juxtapose a snatch of Italian with the "official" Latin document relating to the same thing, and then to tack on an English conclusion, thus incorporating linguistic conventions of various centuries. Canto IX, for instance, begins on a note of quasi-Biblical repetition—"One year floods rose, / One year they fought in the snows, / One year hail fell"—then moves through a series of paratactic "And . . ." clauses ("And the Emperor came down and knighted us, / And they had a wooden castle set up for fiesta"), gives way to the series of "real" letters discussed above, and then comes to the following climax:

[55] See Yriarte, p. 381.

"et amava perdutamente Ixotta degli Atti"
e *"ne fu degna"*
"constans in proposito
"Placuit oculis principis
"pulchra aspectu"
"populo grata (Italiaeque decus)

"and built a temple so full of pagan works"
i. e. Sigismund
and in the style "Past ruin'd Latium"
The filigree hiding the gothic,
with a touch of rhetoric in the whole
And the old sarcophagi,
such as lie, smothered in grass, by San Vitale.
(IX, 41)

The Italian lines (1-2) were written by Pope Pius II. The four Latin lines that follow come from a fifteenth-century chronicle attributed to Alessandro da Rimini, although Pound condenses and rephrases the original. The conjunction of the Italian and Latin encomia emphasizes Isotta's special charms and justifies Sigismundo's boundless passion for her. But now both are further set off by the English conclusion, which begins with a translation from the Latin chronicle ("and built a temple so full of pagan works"), modulates into American shorthand ("i.e. Sigismund"), and then provides a variation of Walter Savage Landor's Victorian poem, "Past ruined Ilion Helen lived." The love affair of Sigismundo and Isotta degli Atti is thus viewed in the perspective of three centuries as well as three languages. In the final lines of the Canto, Pound reverses the movement, and we come back to the old sarcophagi, "such as lie, smothered in grass, by San Vitale"—that is, to the early Christian world. We also come back to the poet who contemplates all these things, whose vision of the sarcophagi at San Vitale has prompted his meditation on the Malatesta in the first place.

The Malatesta Cantos do not, then, recreate history; they decompose and fragment historical time and action so as to draw the "events" recorded into the world of the text. This is not to say that Pound updates the annals of the Malatesta family; he is, on the contrary, quite faithful to the record. But the linguistic deformations I have been describing project the world of the Renaissance *condottiere* onto a flat picture plane or shallow film screen, upon which categories like "past" and "present" become irrelevant.

Here a comparison of Pound and Yeats is instructive. For Yeats, the "broken wall, the burning roof and tower" of Troy embody certain basic human conflicts that recur at other moments in history. Troy, like Byzantium, or like the "Romantic Ireland" of Robert Emmet and Wolfe Tone, is a symbolic landscape. Pound's history collage, on the other hand, retains fidelity to the literal events but brings those events into the reader's circle by transforming the history lesson into a kind of "VORTEX, from which and through which, and into which, ideas are constantly rushing." History becomes the impetus for the play of language. Thus the lengthy Latin statement describing the *auto-da-fé* of Sigismundo, complete with bibliographical references to its sources (X, 43-44) is exploded by the slangy passage that follows it:

> So that in the end that pot-scraping little runt Andreas
>   Benzi, da Siena
> Got up to spout out the bunkum
> That that monstrous swollen, swelling s. o. b.
>   Papa Pio Secundo
>   Aeneas Silvius Piccolomini
>   da Siena
> Had told him to spout, in their best bear's-greased
>   latinity . . .

And this narrative, rendered in Pound's best Western twang, is again displaced by a Latin passage, listing the sins for which Sigismundo was excommunicated: "*Stupro, caede, adulter, / homicida, parricida ac periurus*," and so on. Neither "Renaissance" nor "modern" characters, Andreas Benzi, Aeneas Silvius Piccolomini (Pius II), and Sigismundo

Malatesta exist only in the collage-text of the poem. And the reader, making his way through Pound's paste-ups and film-splices, finds himself inside the circle of fragments.

IV

In the middle of Canto LXXIV, the first Pisan Canto, we find these lines:

Le Paradis n'est pas artificiel

but spezzato apparently
it exists only in fragments unexpected excellent sausage
(LXXIV, 438)

In the later Cantos, the verbal units that Yeats called "exquisite or grotesque fragments" become smaller and smaller, the cuts more radical and "unexpected," the "unbridged transitions" more frequent, the lines more jagged, and the movement of the whole accordingly swifter. Of the *Pisan Cantos*, one can say, as Leo Steinberg says of Robert Rauschenberg's "flatbed" paintings: "the images—each in itself illusionistic—keep interfering with one another; intimations of spatial meaning forever cancelling out to subside in a kind of optical noise."[56] It is this *interference* that is important; the text becomes what Steinberg calls "a kind of flat documentary surface to which anything reachable-thinkable can adhere" (p. 88).

One hears much about the "autobiographical element" in the *Pisan Cantos*; the sequence is often described as the meditation or reverie of the aging poet, confined in his "cage" at the Pisa detention camp. But on reflection, one realizes that although autobiography *is* ubiquitous in the Pisan sequence, it enters the text in a very odd way. Most of the references are, strictly speaking, personal—Pound calls up the names of old friends, former teachers, artists, headwaiters, and fellow inmates of the DTC. Yet there is

[56] *Other Criteria: Confrontations with Twentieth-Century Art* (New York: Oxford, 1972), pp. 87-88.

nothing "confessional" about these personal references, nothing that points to the poet's inner life or reveals his psychological complexity. Rather, images, "each in itself illusionistic," are brought into collision on a kind of shallow film screen, a flat documentary surface or movable aerial map. If we take a given passage from these Cantos, we can see how this movement works. Here are eighty-five lines from the center of the long Canto LXXIV:

"beauty is difficult" sd/ Mr. Beardsley
          and sd/ Mr. Kettlewell looking up from a
pseudo-Beardsley of his freshman composition
  and speaking to W. Lawrence:
                              Pity, you didn't finish the job
while you were at it"
          W. L. having run into the future non-sovereign Edvardus
on a bicycle equally freshman
                    a. d. 1910 or about that
beauty is difficult
in the days of the Berlin to Bagdad project
        and of Tom L's photos of rock temples in Arabia Petra
but he wd/ not talk of
          L.L.G. and the frogbassador, he wanted to
  talk modern art (T. L. did)
  but of second rate, not the first rate
  beauty is difficult.
He said I protested too much   he wanted to start a press
and print the greek classics. . . . periplum
          and the very *very* aged Snow created considerable
hilarity quoting the φαίνε-τ-τ-τ-τττ-αί μοι
in reply to *l'aer tremare*
                    beauty is difficult
But on the other hand the President of Magdalen
(rhyming dawdlin') said there were
too many words in "The Hound of Heaven"
               a moddddun opohem he had read
and there was no doubt that the dons lived well
                                        in the kawledg
it was if I remember rightly the burn and freeze that the freshmen
had failed to follow
or else a mere desire to titter etc.

and it is (in parenthesis) doubtless
easier to teach them to roar like gorillas
than to scan φαινεται μοι
inferior gorillas
of course, lacking the wind sack
and although Siki was quite observable
we have not yet calculated the sum gorilla + bayonet
and there was a good man named Burr
descendant of Aaron during the other war
who was amused by the British
but he didn't last long AND /
Corporal Casey tells me that Stalin
le bonhomme Staline
has no sense of humour (dear Koba!)
and old Rhys, Ernest, was a lover of beauty
and when he was still engineer in a coal mine
a man passed him at high speed radiant in the mine gallery
his face shining with ecstasy
"A'hv joost . . . . Tommy Luff."
and as Luff was twice the fellow's size, Rhys was puzzled
The Muses are daughters of memory
Clio, Terpsichore
and Granville was a lover of beauty
and the three ladies all waited

"and with a name to come"

εσσομένοισι

aram vult nemus

Came Madame Lucrezia
and on the back of the door in Cesena
are, or were, still the initials
joli quart d'heure, (nella Malatestiana)
Torquato where art thou?
to the click of hooves on the cobbles by Tevere
and "my fondest knight lie dead" . . or la Stuarda
"ghosts move about me" "patched with histories"
but as Mead said: if they were,
what have they done in the interval,
eh, to arrive by metempsychosis at. . . . ?

and there are also the conjectures of the Fortean Society
Beauty is difficult. . . . the plain ground
                                        precedes the colours
and this grass or whatever here under the tentflaps
        is, indubitably, bambooiform
representative brush strokes wd/ be similar
. . . . cheek bone, by verbal manifestation,
        her eyes as in "La Nascita"
        whereas the child's face
is at Capoquadri in the fresco square over the doorway
        centre background
the form beached under Helios
                funge la purezza,
and that certain images be formed in the mind
                to remain there
                        formato locho

(LXXIV, 444-446)

In scanning Pound's "aerial map," I shall begin by tracing what Hugh Kenner calls "the rhythms of recurrence."[57] For once we have seen what the continuities are, we are in a better position to see how the cuts operate. Consider the following metonymic chains:

I. Time: The Present The Prison Camp and the War
"a good man named Burr / descendant of Aaron during the other war"—"Corporal Casey," telling Pound that "Stalin / le bonhomme Staline / has no sense of humour (dear Koba!)"—the "grass or whatever here under the tentflaps" which "is, indubitably, bambooiform"

II. Time: The Near-Present
A. The University
"Mr. Kettlewell looking up from a / pseudo-Beardsley of his freshman composition / and speaking to W. Lawrence"—"the very *very* aged Snow" [a teacher of Greek at Eton][58],

[57] *The Poetry of Ezra Pound*, p. 300.

[58] This and subsequent identifications, unless otherwise designated, are taken from John Hamilton Edwards and William W. Vasse, *Annotated*

who "created considerable / hilarity quoting" Sappho at the wrong moment—"the President of Magdalen (rhymes with dawdlin')" who "said there were / too many words in 'The Hound of Heaven' / a moddddun opohem he had read"—"the dons who lived well / in the kawledg"—the tittering freshmen whom "it is easier to teach to roar like gorillas / than to scan φαίνεταί μοι"

B. The Art World

"Mr. Beardsley"—"Tom L's [T. E. Lawrence's] photos of rock temples in Arabia Petra" and his desire "to talk modern art . . . but of second rate, not the first rate"—Francis Thompson's "The Hound of Heaven"—"Old Rhys, Ernest . . . a lover of beauty"—"Granville [Barker] . . . a lover of beauty"—"Torquato [the librarian of the Malatestiana]"[59]—G. S. Mead's investigations into metempsychosis—"the conjectures of the Fortean Society"

C. The Political World

"the future non-sovereign Edvardus" [Edward VII] almost run down by W. Lawrence "on a bicycle equally freshman / a. d. 1910 or about that"—"the days of the Berlin to Bagdad project"—"L.L.G. [Lloyd George] and the frogbassador" in relation to T. E. Lawrence

III. Time: The Historical Past The Italian Renaissance

"l'aer tremare" [Cavalcanti]—the assignation of "Madame Lucrezia" [Borgia] at Cesena—the "Malatestiana" [Tempio at Rimini]—"la Stuarda" [Mary Stuart, Queen of Scots] and her "advisor" David Rizzio—Botticelli's "La Nascita" and his fresco at Capoquadri

---

Index to the Cantos of Ezra Pound (Berkeley and Los Angeles: University of California Press, 1971).

[59] I owe this identification to Daniel Pearlman, *The Barb of Time*, p. 258. The librarian of the Malatestiana was Manlio Torquato Dazzi, to whom Pound dedicated his *Cavalcanti*.

IV. Time: Ancient Past   Greek Myth and Literature
T. E. Lawrence's desire "to start a press / and print the greek classics—periplum"—Sappho (the "φαίνεται μοι")—"The Muses . . . daughters of memory / Clio, Terpsichore"—Homer's *Odyssey*: Elpenor, " 'And with a name to come' / εσσομένοισι" — "aram vult nemus" (the grove needs an altar) from Ovid—"the form beached under Helios"

V. Time: Continuous   Refrain: "Beauty if difficult"
The refrain is repeated five times. Each time its meaning shifts slightly. "Beauty is difficult" for Aubrey Beardsley in a very different sense from the way it is "difficult" for the old Eton teacher Snow, whose recitation of Sappho brings on "hilarity." Again, "beauty is difficult" in a comic sense for those in the various Occult societies of the day who make "conjectures." The refrain further modulates into a secondary refrain: "lover of beauty," applied both to Ernest Rhys and to Harley Granville-Barker; both refrains lead up to the final phrase, "certain images to be formed in the mind / to remain there / *formato locho*." All that has preceded these lines becomes part of the graven image, fixed in its prepared place.

One of Pound's detractors, George P. Elliott, complained that "rhythms of recurrence" cannot constitute a structure: "Anybody can concoct ten dozen disparate themes, subjects, image-types, rhythms, attitudes, cultural quiddities, and keep popping them up one and another in patterns of varying complication and banality. This is merely technique."[60]

True enough if the items in question are simply repeated. But one of the special pleasures of reading the *Cantos* is to observe with what agility and grace Pound cuts across the metonymic chains he has created. The opening

[60] "Poet of Many Voices," *The Carleton Miscellany*, 2 (Summer 1961); rpt. *Ezra Pound*, ed. Sutton, p. 161.

passage about the student Kettlewell and his freshman composition, for example, quickly cuts into the Edward VII "plane," the two being related by the word "freshman." Or again, the "conversation" between Pound and Corporal Casey about Stalin is the structural analogue of Ernest Rhys's one-time conversation with the comical coal miner who tells the proper Rhys that "A'hv joost . . . . Tommy Luff." The "bambooiform grass" dissolves into "representative brush strokes"; these, in turn, recall Botticelli's painting. The words of Elpenor, "And with a name to come," cut into the line "Came Madame Lucrezia." They also lead, of course, back to the very first Canto where Elpenor tells Odysseus to "heap up mine arms, by tomb by sea-bord, and inscribed: / '*A man of no fortune, and with a name to come*' " (I, 4). Indeed, most of the references in the passage cut across to earlier or later Cantos. The circle of fragments becomes wider and wider.

So far, I have considered only the referential planes in Canto LXXIV, but of course perspectivism is further generated by the complex verbal and rhythmic play, rather like that of the Malatesta Cantos. On the prosodic level, the "rhythm of recurrence" is the anapestic-trochaic line, as in "on a bicycle equally freshman," or " 'beauty is difficult' sd/ Mr Beardsley." But despite this preponderant rhythmic curve, the lines themselves range from five to eighteen syllables and are distinguished by their enormous variability: no two consecutive lines follow precisely the same pattern either metrically or spatially.

Pound's language ranges from the "poetic diction" of "Torquato, where art thou?" and "to the click of hooves on the cobbles by Tevere" to the casual conversation of "Pity you didn't finish the job / while you were at it" and to such comical asides as "and as Luff was twice the fellow's size, Rhys was puzzled." "Normal" prose idiom is broken up by modern typographical abbreviations ("sd.," "wd.," "etc."); parenthetical bits ("talk modern art [T. L. did]");

sound imitations ("Magdalen [rhyming dawdlin']"), "a moddddun opohem," "kawledge," " 'A'hv joost . . . . Tommy Luff' "; comic coinages ("the frogbassador"); and foreign tags that range from French ("le bonhomme Staline"; "joli quart d'heure") to Italian ("funge la purezza"; "*formato locho*") to Latin ("aram vult nemus") to Greek. In most of these Cantos there would, of course, also be Chinese phrases.

Pound's individual word units and images are, as we have seen, insistently illusionistic. Unlike, say, Gertrude Stein or, for that matter, Rimbaud, he does not call into question the relationship of signifier to signified. We can readily identify the fresco "at Capoquadri . . . over the doorway," Francis Thompson's then modern poem, "The Hound of Heaven," or T. E. Lawrence's photographs of "rock temples in Arabia Petra." We can look up the biography of the writer Ernest Rhys and find that he did indeed put in a stint as engineer in a coal mine. Again, there is grass under the tentflaps in Pound's Canto for no better reason than that Pound, sitting inside his tent in the detention camp, saw it growing there.

But these illusionistic, literal images are consistently "interfering" with one another, so as to remind us that the world of the poem is not, after all, the real world. As soon as we pause over a particular reference—say "the Berlin to Bagdad project"—and try to treat it as a topical allusion, we run into another line or phrase that explodes the veracity of the first: in this case, the reference to "L.L.G. and the frogbassador" makes the "Berlin to Bagdad project" sound like an event in a comic opera. Certainly, no one would read these lines in order to get some sort of "meaningful" portrait of T. E. Lawrence. Thus what is sometimes taken for the poetry of statement becomes something quite different. Pound would deny his landscape any Symbolist depth, for only on a flat screen can Corporal Casey stand beside Clio or Lucrezia Borgia coexist with Lloyd George. Neither historical nor archetypal, these characters dwell in what can only be called Pound country.

The poetry of the *Cantos* looks ahead to our own documentary collages, whether in poetry or film or painting. Leo Steinberg's assessment of Rauschenberg's procedure is applicable here:

> Any flat documentary surface that tabulates information is a relevant analogue to his picture plane—radically different from the transparent projection plane with its optical correspondence to man's visual field. And it seemed at times that Rauschenberg's work surface stood for the mind itself—dump, reservoir, switching center, abundant with concrete reference freely associated as in an internal monologue—the outward symbol of the mind as running transformer of the external world, constantly ingesting incoming unprocessed data to be mapped in an overcharged field.
>
> (p. 88)

The notion of the mind as "running transformer . . . constantly ingesting incoming unprocessed data" would surely have appealed to Pound; his own Vorticist manifesto of 1914, for that matter, anticipates Steinberg's image of the "work surface" as "switching center" or "overcharged field." In the later Cantos, these ideas are put into action. Toward the end of Canto LXXIV, we read:

> the frescoes in S. Pietro and the madonna in Ortolo
> e "fa di clarità l'aer tremare"
> as in the manuscript of the Capitolare
> Trattoria degli Apostoli (dodici)
> "Ecco il tè" said the head waiter
> in 1912 explaining its mysteries to the piccolo
> with a teapot from another hotel
> but coffee came to Assisi much later
> that is, so one cd/ drink it
> when it was lost in Orleans and France semi-ruin'd
> thus the coffee-house facts of Vienna
>
> (LXXIV, 448)

Of this elaborate verbal montage, we could say, as

Barthes says of film, that "the *having-been-there* of the photograph gives way before a *being-there* of the thing."[61] No mediating terms are necessary: one fresco dissolves into another; a painted portrait of a beautiful lady (by Stefano di Giovanni) is juxtaposed to a verbal one (the Cavalcanti sonnet again); a shot of St. Peter's is spliced with one of the Capitoline Museum and its manuscript room. The Church of the Apostles gives way to the "Trattoria degli Apostoli"; there are twelve (dodici) apostles and it is 1912; Assisi has replaced Rome and Pound is once more a "piccolo." The headwaiter in this filmic sequence has a teapot but the boy seems to want coffee, which is, unfortunately, undrinkable. In any case, the Assisi image is replaced by those of Orleans and France, and some doubt is cast on the preceding narrative by the cryptic aside: "thus the coffee-house facts of Vienna."

To follow Pound's cinematic dissolves—to see how *church* becomes *museum* becomes *trattoria*, or again, how the art of fresco painting points to the art of poetry which points in turn to the art of making coffee—is not easy. The *Cantos* force us to readjust our habits of reading. For, as D.S. Carne-Ross says:

> Not merely does the thing, in Pound's best verse, not point beyond itself: *it doesn't point to us*. The green tip that pushes through the earth in spring does not stand for or symbolize man's power of spiritual renewal. . . . The green thrust is itself the divine event. . . . Meant as literally as Pound means it, this is very hard to take. Not only does it offend against the ways we have been taught to read literature, it is an offense against the great principle of inwardness or internalization that has put us at the center of things and laid waste the visible world.[62]

[61] "Rhetoric of the Image," *Image—Music—Text*, Essays selected and translated by Stephen Heath (New York: Hill and Wang), p. 45.

[62] " 'The Music of a Lost Dynasty,' " 38. See also Herbert Schneidau's important discussion of metaphor vs. metonymy in Pound's poetry in "Pound, Olson, and Objective Verse," *Paideuma*, 5 (Spring 1976), 15-30.

This is not to say that Pound is not present in a text like Canto LXXIV. But the poet's "I," as Keith Cohen says in his study of film esthetic, is now projected onto an other: "the creating subject participates in the object, perhaps even becomes immersed in it, and in so doing charges the object with an 'attitude,' a visual configuration that reaches out to meet the consciousness of the spectator."[63] The *Cantos* is one of the first modern poems to question the centrality of personal emotion. Its "flat documentary surface" stands in brash opposition to the "organic" poem of the Symbolists; its "composition by field," to use Charles Olson's phrase, is a challenge we are still trying to meet.

[63] *Film and Fiction: The Dynamics of Exchange* (New Haven: Yale University Press, 1979), p. 72.

CHAPTER SIX

"The Space of a Door": Beckett and the Poetry of Absence

—This fragility of the outer meaning had a bad effect on Watt.
—Beckett, *Watt* (1944)

—It is easier to raise a shrine than to bring the deity down to haunt it.
—Beckett, The Unnamable (1958)

I

THE "interfering" images that jostle one another on the "documentary surface" or "shallow screen" of Pound's *Cantos* are, we have seen, insistently illusionistic. We can, after all, go to San Vitale or to Magdalen ("rhyming dawdlin' ") College, Oxford, and we know that "Kung" (Confucius) and "Uncle William" (Yeats) are people who once were alive. Pound's "shrines," that is to say, have real deities in them. It is their collision that creates "the opening of the field."

The indeterminacy of Beckett's verbal compositions is of a very different order. The frame of reference is at once wider and narrower. Beckett does not people his fictions with Greek goddesses, Renaissance war lords, or old friends. His characters, when they have names at all, are called Pim and Bom, Winnie and Willie, Hamm and Clov. They dwell neither on Mt. Taishan nor in Kensington but in an unspecified room or in an open space, which may or may not be in a town. For in Beckett's world, it is not the *juxtaposition* of items drawn from disparate contexts that creates semantic gaps. Rather, the enigma is created by the "fragility" of the words themselves, words whose meanings are constantly eroded and reformulated.

As a point of entry into Beckett's poetic frame, I should like to consider one of his most recent texts; the prose poems called *Fizzles,* which Beckett translated from his French version *Foirades* in 1973-1974, expressly for the collaboration he undertook with Jasper Johns.[1] *Foirades / Fizzles* (1976) contains five prose fragments by Beckett and thirty-three etchings by Johns, which act not as illustrations of individual poems but as important visual analogues. "Fizzle 5" is characteristic of Beckett's late style:

> Closed place. All needed to be known for say is known. There is nothing but what is said. Beyond what is said there is nothing. What goes on in the arena is not said. Did it need to be known it would be. No interest. Not for imagining. Place consisting of an arena and a ditch. Between the two skirting the latter a track. Closed place. Beyond the ditch there is nothing. This is known because it needs to be said. Arena black vast. Room for millions.

[1] *Fizzles* (farts, hissing sounds, failures) is a mild translation of *Foirades* which means "shit" or "diarrhea." The Jasper Johns-Samuel Beckett collaboration *Foirades/Fizzles* was published in a limited signed edition of 250 copies by Petersburg Press, South America, 1976. The etchings were proofed and printed at the Atelier Crommelynck in Paris in 1975-1976. The publication was edited by Vera Lindsay, who conceived of the project and brought Beckett and Johns together.

Fizzles 1-6 were written in French, c. 1960 and translated by Beckett in 1973-1974 for the collaboration. Johns used all except #3 but changed their order. For the Grove Press edition (New York: 1976), Beckett restored #3 and added two more Fizzles: "Still," written in English in 1972 and "For to end yet again," originally written in French and translated by Beckett in 1975. All subsequent references are to the Grove Press edition, subsequently noted as F. The French text *Foirades* was published in Paris by Éditions de Minuit in 1976.

I refer to the Fizzles by their Grove Press edition number; the Johns-Beckett numbering is as follows:

Grove Press (F)	Johns-Beckett
1	2
2	5
4	1
5	6
6	3

> Wandering and still. Never seeing never hearing one another. Never touching. No more is known. Depth of ditch. See from the edge all the bodies on its bed. The millions still there. They appear six times smaller than life. Bed divided into lots. Dark and bright. They take up all its width. The lots still bright are square. Appear square. Just room for the average-sized body. Stretched out diagonally. Bigger it has to curl up. Thus the width of the ditch is known. It would have been in any case. Sum the bright lots. The dark. Outnumber the former by far. The place is already old. The ditch is old. In the beginning it was all bright. All bright lots. Almost touching. Faintly edged with shadow. The ditch seems straight. Then reappears a body seen before. A closed curve therefore. Brilliance of the bright lots. It does not encroach on the dark. Adamantine blackness of these. As dense at the edge as at the centre. But vertically it diffuses unimpeded. High above the level of the arena. As high above as the ditch is deep. In the black air towers of pale light. So many bright lots so many towers. So many bodies visible on the bed. The track follows the ditch all the way along. All the way round. It is on a higher level than the arena. A step higher. It is made of dead leaves. A reminder of bedlam nature. They are dry. The heat and the dry air. Dead but not rotting. Crumbling into dust rather. Just wide enough for one. On it no two ever meet.
>
> (F, 37-39)

The sound structure of this highly elliptical text is our first anomaly. Its phrasing is that of a telegram, but instead of limiting his words, Beckett repeats them again and again:

Closed place.

All needed to be known for say is known.
There is nothing but what is said.
Beyond what is said there is nothing.

What goes on in the arena is not said.
Did it need to be known it would be. . . .
Closed place.

There is much anaphora:

Never seeing
never hearing one another
Never touching

So many bright lots
so many towers
So many bodies visible on the bed

Complex patterns of alliteration and assonance are pervasive:

*A*s d*e*nse *a*t the *e*dge *a*s *a*t the c*e*ntre

*A*d*a*m*a*ntine bl*a*ckness

the w*idth* of the d*itch*

*Brill*iance of the *br*igh*t lot*s

On it no two ever *meet*

And since more than a third of the sixty-six sentences are short nominal or participial phrases, a two-stress rhythm is a recurrent feature:

Clósed pláce

nó ínterest

Róom for míllions

Wándering and stíll

Néver toúching

Dépth of dítch

Dárk and bríght

A stép hígher

Phonemically, then, Beckett's text *is* a kind of "closed place," the rhythm of recurrence being carefully foregrounded. But there is a curious disjunction between sound and meaning. For if we try to draw a diagram of Beckett's minimal landscape, we soon discover that it is impossible to visualize or conceptualize. If the "Place consisting of an arena and a ditch" is a "closed place," the scene is evidently indoors—walled and roofed in. But the impersonal voice that speaks tells us that "Beyond the ditch there is nothing," and that "the towers of pale light" diffused from the bright lots shoot up into the black air. So the arena would have to be an open place, some sort of amphitheater, but situated in an empty landscape.

This arena evidently has room for millions. Does this mean that the millions are actually *in* the arena or only that they could be? How can they be wandering and still at the same time? And why can these figures never see, hear, or touch one another? More striking: when the millions are next sighted as "still there," they are seen to be "six times smaller than life." "There" is presumably the bed of the ditch, a bed "divided into lots. Dark and bright," the bright ones appearing to be square. These squares have "Just room for the average-sized body. Stretched out diagonally." But if the bodies as seen from the "edge" (of the track above?) "appear six times smaller than life," how does the narrator know that they are average-sized? Again, if the width of the ditch is calculated as being the sum of the bright lots, and these lots are, in turn, squares whose diagonal is the length of the average-sized body, how wide would that be? We cannot possibly say for we have no idea how many of the lots are "still bright," although we do know that "In the beginning it was all bright," and that "So many bright lots so many towers." Furthermore, if the bed is divided up into square lots, the ditch would have to mark a straight line. Indeed, "The ditch seems to be straight." But "Then reappears a body seen before. A closed curve therefore." Since closed curves cannot be divided into squares, the vision of the "Closed place" becomes increasingly fictive.

The vantage point of the narrator is never fixed: hence the directional signals, numbers, and measurements are constantly shifting in import. At first, the observer would seem to be outside the visual field, able to take in the whole scene. But to know that the "millions" are "Never seeing never hearing one another" and that a tall person would have to curl up so as to fit into a lot, is to be one of the crowd. A moment later, the spectator looks down from the "edge" and sees figures the size of rodents. Yet he seems to have been here for a long time, to know, like the voice of Genesis, that "In the beginning it was all bright." Is he the lone person on the track alluded to in the penultimate sentence? Or some kind of tourist, inspecting the scene and recreating its probable past?

What is Beckett depicting? Perhaps the "Closed place" is a giant crematorium strewn with the bodies of the newly dead. Certainly the references to "the heat and the dry air," the leaves that are "Dead but not rotting" supports such a reading. In this case, the track is "Just wide enough for one" because one victim is released into it at a time and then gassed and dropped into the ditch. Accordingly, "no two ever meet" within its confines.

But if the arena encircled by the ditch brings to mind images of World War II horrors, it also evokes, as so often in Beckett, the dimensions of Dante's hell, in this case the image of Malebolge at the opening of *Inferno XVIII*:

Loco è in inferno detto Malebolge
 tutto di pietra e di color ferrigno,
 come la cerchia che d'intorno il volge.

Nel dritto mezzo del camp maligno
 vaneggia un pozzo assai largo e profondo,
 di cui suo loco dicerò l'ordigno.

Quel cinghio che rimane adunque è tondo,
 tra il pozzo e il piè dell' alta ripa dura,
 ed ha distinto in dieci valli il fondo.[2]

[2] *The Divine Comedy*, with translation and comment by John D. Sinclair (New York: Oxford University Press, 1939), pp. 226-227.

(There is a place in Hell called Malebolge, all stone of iron color, like the wall that goes round it. Right in the middle of the baleful space yawns a pit of great breadth and depth, of whose structure I shall tell in its own place, so that the belt left between the pit and the high rocky bank is round, and its bottom is divided into ten valleys.)

But unlike Dante's Malebolge or the hell of the concentration camp, Beckett's "Closed place" is empty of all life; we are aware of no struggle, no suffering, no killing. Indeed, it might be that "no two ever meet" for the simple reason that no one is there. Moreover, the "towers of light" may have positive rather than negative connotations. As Beckett said in an interview with Tom Driver (1961): "If there were only darkness, there would be no inscrutability—but there is also light."[3] Perhaps the "Closed place" is best seen as an analogue to the white vault of "Imagination Dead Imagine" or to the rubber cylinder of *The Lost Ones*, or again, as the Unnamable puts it: "the place where . . . I have always been is purely perhaps the inside of my distant skull where once I wandered, now am fixed, lost for tininess, or straining against the walls. . . ."[4] In this context, the body recognized as "seen before" can be construed as something remembered: the ditch seems to be circling round the narrator rather than vice versa. Think of placing an object on the window-ledge of one of those revolving rooftop restaurants in our new skyscraper hotels: it will indeed return, an hour or so later, a "body seen before" that reminds us of our persistent rotation.

Of Jasper Johns' painting *According to What*, John Ashbery has written: "It is a sort of equation with insufficient conditions for determining the unknown."[5] "Closed place" poses the same problem. Consider the permutations of the

[3] *Columbia University Forum*, Summer 1961; rpt. in *Samuel Beckett: The Critical Heritage*, ed. Lawrence Graver and Raymond Federman (London and Boston: Routledge & Kegan Paul, 1979), p. 220.

[4] *The Unnamable*, in *Three Novels* by Samuel Beckett (New York: Grove Press, 1958), pp. 302-303.

[5] "Brooms and Prisms," *Art News*, 65 (March 1966), 59.

verbs *say* and *know*. At the beginning, the voice informs us that "All needed to be known for say is known. There is nothing but what is said. Beyond what is said there is nothing." It is the lesson of Wittgenstein: "Wovon man nicht sprechen kann darüber muss man schweigen" (Whereof one cannot speak, thereof one must be silent).[6] Logically, then, there is nothing further to say for all that needs to be known is that this is a "Closed place." "What goes on in the arena is not said" and therefore it cannot be known. But no sooner has the narrator remarked "No interest. Not for imagining," then he starts to imagine what does or might go on in the arena. Such speculation seems to be forbidden for the voice now utters "No more is known." But immediately we are given information (something said, hence known) about the depth of the ditch, the bodies on the bed, the lots "Dark and bright," the position of the bodies on the squares. Then we are told that "The width of the ditch is known." How can this be true when it has not been "said"? And furthermore, the equation W (width) = XY (where X is the side of the square and Y the number of squares) has two unknowns and is accordingly insoluble.

Perhaps, then, what is "said" cannot be "known" under any circumstances. Beckett has been implying as much at least since the composition of *Watt* (1944):

> For Watt now found himself in the midst of things which, if they consented to be named, did so as it were with reluctance. And the state in which Watt found himself

[6] This is Proposition 6.54 of the *Tractatus Logic-Philosophicus*. For an excellent discussion of the relation of Beckett's *Watt* to Wittgenstein, see Jacqueline Hoefer, "Watt," *Perspective*, 11 (1950), 166-182; rpt. in *Samuel Beckett: A Collection of Critical Essays*, ed. Martin Esslin (Englewood Cliffs: Prentice-Hall, 1965), pp. 62-76. Although John Fletcher in *The Novels of Samuel Beckett* (London: Chatto & Windus, 1964), p. 88, reports that Beckett told him that he did not read Wittgenstein until 1959 or so and hence could not have alluded to his philosophy in *Watt* (1944), it remains true that, as Gerald Bruns observes, "the problem of language posed in *Watt* is precisely that with which Wittgenstein was most deeply concerned," *Modern Poetry and the Idea of Language* (New Haven: Yale University Press, 1974), p. 278. Certainly in *Fizzles*, the allusion is clear.

> resisted formulation in a way no state had ever done, in which Watt had ever found himself. . . . Looking at a pot, for example, or thinking of a pot, at one of Mr. Knott's pots . . . it was in vain that Watt said, Pot, pot. Well, perhaps not quite in vain, but very nearly. For it was not a pot, the more he looked, the more he reflected, the more he felt sure of that, that it was not a pot at all.[7]

And in a late text like *Fizzles*, we read typically:

> Old earth, no more lies, I've seen you, it was me, with my other's ravening eyes, too late. You'll be on me, it will be you, it will be me, it will be us, it was never us. It won't be long now, perhaps not tomorrow, nor the day after, but too late.
>
> ("Fizzle 6," p. 43)

To read enigma texts like these is rather like being sent out on a snipe-hunt, that popular children's game in which the players disperse in the dark, equipped with pillowcases, flashlights, sticks, and a set of rules, in search of birds they know are not to be caught. Not *product* as in the treasure hunt but *process* is the key. Analogously, the reader of "Closed place" makes his way through the repeated negatives—"nothing," "no," "not," "never"—and the ambiguous references to "it" ("Did it need to be known it would be" or "This is known because it needs to be said"), responding to such seemingly careful placements as "between the two," "beyond the ditch," "High above," "A step higher," "skirting the latter," "Faintly edged with shadow," "Just wide enough for one," "Just room for the average-sized body," "As high above as the ditch is deep," and so on. The process of specification is seen as urgent, and yet we don't know what it is that is specified.

"Closed place" thus becomes a paradigm for the mystery of being.[8] Like Gertrude Stein, Beckett creates an intricate

[7] *Watt* (1944; New York: Grove Press, 1959), p. 81.

[8] For a related discussion of "Fizzle 7" ("Still"), see Enoch Brater's "Still / Beckett: the Essential and the Incidental," *Journal of Modern Literature*:

system of repetitions and permutations, but whereas Stein explodes all syntactic rules, relying on relational metonymic structures to create a particular impression, Beckett does not violate the syntax; on the contrary, he uses the simple declarative sentence or noun phrase. In Stein's "A Substance in a Cushion," the activity presented—probably the making of a new suit on the sewing machine—is only gradually revealed by the contiguities of "circle," "cover," "wear," "feather," "cotton," "change," "difference," "ribbon," "pink," "purple." Her individual sentences, however, make no "sense." Beckett's procedure is the opposite. "The ditch is old," "They are dry," "It is on a higher level than the arena"—these sentences are perfectly grammatical. But the words placed in these neat syntactic slots—subject-verb-object—elude our grasp. "The ditch is old" looks like a sentence in a first-grade reader except that we don't know what the ditch is. Nor can we determine what it means to be on a higher level than the arena. In reading Stein, we cut across sentence boundaries and locate the items to be related. In reading Beckett, we move from sentence A to sentence B with some measure of self-satisfaction until we realize that the syntactic order is only an illusion. "The official business of the Beckett sentence," writes Hugh Kenner, "is to affirm a tidy control it cannot quite achieve."[9] Thus the seeming progress of the narrative is really a persistent decreation.

Here the interplay between Beckett's texts and Jasper Johns' visual images is revealing. For although Johns has made no effort to match his plates to the individual prose poems, *Foirades/Fizzles* emerges as a coherent verbal-visual system. We begin, in each case, with a number; and the numbers, as always in Johns, run in a proper sequence:

Samuel Beckett Special Number," ed. Enoch Brater, 6 (Summer 1977), 3-16. This special issue contains some of the best essays available on Beckett's late style and structure: see, aside from Brater's article, the contributions by J. E. Dearlove, Elizabeth Bregman Segré, and Susan D. Brienza.

[9] "Shades of Syntax," in *Samuel Beckett: A Collection of Criticism*, ed. Ruby Cohn (New York: McGraw Hill, 1975), p. 28.

after 4 comes 5 (Figure 5). To introduce numbers into the visual field is to reduce the power of images to achieve concretion. Not five apples in a bowl, as Cézanne might have painted them, but the number 5 itself—a man-made, abstract sign whose conventional form cannot be altered. For, as Leo Steinberg says, "No likeness nor image of a 5 is paintable, only the thing itself."[10] This "thing itself" points to certainty and fixity, like Beckett's careful placement of the track *between* the arena and the ditch or the "five or six minutes" of Horn's visit to the narrator in "Fizzle 2."

Yet, in painting over and behind his numbers, using brushstroke so as to create a broken, textured surface, Johns dissolves the distinction between figure and ground and creates a peculiar tension; he makes the viewer aware of the flatness of the picture plane as well as the non-functioning of the number. We don't, in other words, scan this picture for the sake of information—to find out the price of an item in a shop window, for example. The number merely *is*. And, just as Beckett's references to the "width of the ditch" or the "millions" in the arena are contradicted by the context in which such numbers and measurements are presented, so Johns' numbers challenge the viewer to accept a world devoid of real specifications.

It is also a world emptied of human presence. As in "Closed place," only objects are left; the persons who have made the objects are missing. Just as Beckett assembles a limited set of properties—a track, a ditch, towers of pale light, dry leaves, bodies stretched out diagonally—so, in a series of etchings based on his 1972 four-panel painting *Untitled*,[11] Johns presents images of plaster casts of body

[10] *Other Criteria: Confrontations with Twentieth-Century Art* (New York: Oxford, 1972), p. 28.

[11] See Michael Crighton, *Jasper Johns* (exhibition catalogue) (New York: Harry N. Abrams, Inc. in association with the Whitney Museum of Modern Art, 1977), pp. 59-60; Judith Goldman, "Introduction," *Foirades/Fizzles* (New York: Whitney Museum of American Art, 1977), p. 1 of 4 unpaginated pages in the exhibition catalogue.

parts—buttocks, a knee, a foot, a leg, a torso—attached to some crossed wooden strips fastened by wing nuts (Figure 6). But the "subject" of these pictures is only ostensibly the human body. For the anatomical parts are mere fragments and they belong, not to a body, but to a collage made of wood and plaster; they become, like the numerals, part of a man-made system. Moreover, the shapes themselves don't really look like hands and feet, knees or buttocks; we see them, rather, as peculiar excrescences that grow mysteriously on wooden poles just as the "body seen before" of Beckett's text reappears in the closed curve of the ditch. Or again (Figure 7), Johns labels each form with the name of the designated body part. Perhaps the word KNEE is more "real" than the painted image of a knee could be. Hands, feet, eyes, buttocks—these can only be simulated on canvas whereas the word KNEE, even when seen in a mirror (Figure 8) names the real thing. Or does it? Figure 7 contains a shape, roughly as big as the one labelled "BUTTOCKS," that contains the words "FOOT HAND SOCK FLOOR"—which is to say that the label really tells us nothing at all about the human body. In this case, as in Beckett's text, "There is nothing but what is said."

Johns raises still other possibilities. In Figure 9, which faces the French text of "Fizzle 2" ("Horn venait toujours la nuit"), we see what look like plaster casts of two legs from the calf down, the feet encased perhaps in black slippers. But to whom do these mysterious legs, speckled with paint and lumps of plaster, belong? The triangular white shape on the right, covered by black-line squiggles, affords no clue; neither does the dark background in which we can discern the barest outlines of the top of a number 5. Is there a body lying in some sort of ditch here? What is the jagged shape behind the leg, whose imprint is oddly crossed out by a black line? Do these body parts relate, in some mysterious way, to the torsos depicted earlier in the book (Figures 10, 11)? There is no way of knowing. "Johns' pictures," says Steinberg, "are situations wherein the subjects are constantly found and lost, submerged and recovered."[12] Just so, of Beckett's "Closed place" we are told that "Beyond the ditch there is nothing." And yet "towers of pale light" shoot up into the black air.

Fragmented body parts attached to wooden sticks, mirror images of words referring to the body, abstract forms that dimly suggest body shapes—these are the visual analogues to Beckett's enigmatic verbal landscape. *Foirades/Fizzles* is an unusually happy conjunction of word and image. For just as a leg may be designated by a plaster cast or by the painted image of a leg shape, or by the letters that spell the word L-E-G in English, and yet elude all attempts to reproduce the "real" leg of a particular person, so Beckett's text creates a structural model that questions the very nature of the "real." Consider the following passage from "Fizzle 2":

> Then suddenly it was dark again and Horn went away, the five or six minutes having presumably expired. But here one of two things, either the final extinction had coincided, by some prank of chance, with the close of the session, or else Horn, knowing his time to be up, had cut off the last dribs of current. I still see, sometimes, that waning face disclosing, more and more clearly the more it entered shadow, the one I remembered. In the end I said to myself, as unaccountably it lingered on, No doubt about it, it is he.
>
> (F, 21)

"No doubt about it, it is he." But who is he? What is the "waning face disclosing" as it enters shadow? And what is the "it" that is in "outer space not to be confused with the other"? We know that Horn went away "after five or six minutes" just as we know that in the plate accompanying the text of this Fizzle (Figure 12) there are four black lollipop shapes and two inverted balloon shapes, facing in opposite directions, attached to what look like poles. These balloon shapes recall the body parts labelled "BUTTOCKS" and "KNEE" (see Figure 7), but there is no way of determining

[12] *Other Criteria*, p. 25.

how and why they are related to what I have called the lollipops (or traffic signals?). Johns thus invents what John Ashbery has called a "way of happening" without telling us what it is that is happening. As Beckett himself puts it in a justly famous statement about *Finnegans Wake*:

> Here form IS content, content IS form. You complain that this stuff is not written in English. It is not written at all. It is not to read—or rather it is not only to be read. It is to be looked at and listened to. [Joyce's] writing is not about something; it is that something itself. . . . Here is a savage economy of hieroglyphs. Here words are not the polite contortions of 20th century printer's ink. They are alive. They elbow their way on to the page, and glow and blaze and fade and disappear.[13]

II

These fighting words were pronounced by Beckett in 1929, almost fifty years before the publication of *Fizzles*. His distrust of Symbolism was born early; it is present, for example, in the study of Proust (1931):

> Proust is too much an affectivist to be satisfied by the intellectual symbolism of a Baudelaire, abstract and discursive. The Baudelarian unity is a unity 'post rem,' a unity abstracted from plurality. His 'correspondence' is determined by a concept, therefore strictly limited and exhausted by its own definition.[14]

This is, of course, a wholly reductive view of Baudelarian symbolism but, for our purposes here, what matters is not the relative accuracy of Beckett's view of Baudelaire, but the distinction he makes between Baudelaire and Proust:

[13] "Dante . . . Bruno. Vico . . Joyce," in Beckett and others, *Our Exagmination Round his Factification for Incamination of Work in Progress* (Paris: Shakespeare and Co., 1929); rpt. in Samuel Beckett, *I Can't Go On, I'll Go On, A Selection from Samuel Beckett's Work*, ed. and introduced by Richard W. Seaver (New York: Grove Press, 1976), p. 117.

[14] *Proust* (1931; rpt. New York: Grove Press, 1957), p. 60.

> Proust does not deal in concepts, he pursues the Idea, the concrete. He admires the frescoes of the Paduan Arena because their symbolism is handled as a reality, special, literary and concrete and is not merely the pictorial transmission of a notion. . . . For Proust the object may be a living symbol, but a symbol of itself. The symbolism of Baudelaire has become the *autosymbolism* of Proust. Proust's point of departure might be situated in Symbolism, or on its outskirts.
>
> (P, 60)

What does Beckett mean by the term *autosymbolism*? In discussing the role of Albertine in the *Recherche*, Beckett notes, again and again, the indeterminacy of Proustian characterization: "All that is active, all that is enveloped in time and space, is endowed with what might be described as an abstract, ideal and absolute impermeability" (P, 41). In Proust's rendering of Albertine, "the multiple aspects [do] not bind into any positive synthesis. The object evolves, and by the time the conclusion—if any—is reached, it is already out of date" (P, 65).

In this context, the semantic structure of a Baudelaire poem would evidently strike Beckett as exhibiting too much closure. He is similarly skeptical about Rilke, whose poetry he oddly accuses of "breathless petulance" and "overstatement."[15] Jack B. Yeats's novel *The Amaranthers*, on the other hand, is praised for its "respect for the mobility and autonomy of the imagined":

> There is no allegory, that glorious double-entry, with every credit in the said account a debit in the meant, and inversely; but the single series of imaginative transactions.
>
> There is no symbol. The cream horse that carries Gil-

[15] Review of Rainer Marie Rilke, *Poems*, trans. J. B. Leishman (London: Hogarth Press, 1934), in *The Criterion*, 13 (1933-34), 705-706. This and the related reviews of the early thirties are discussed by Lawrence E. Harvey, *Samuel Beckett, Poet & Critic* (Princeton: Princeton University Press, 1970), pp. 414-415.

> foyle and the cream coach that carries Gilfoyle are related, not by rule of three, as two values to a third, but directly as stages of an image.[16]

"No symbols where none intended."[17] Not the "Baudelarian unity" but the "autosymbolism" of a Proust or the "incoherent continuum" of a Rimbaud—this was the choice Beckett made in the early thirties. In the unpublished *Dream of Fair to Middling Women* (1932), he praises Rimbaud's "audibilities [that] are no more than punctuation in a statement of silences. How do they get from point to point. That is what I meant by incoherent reality. . . ." And he concludes with youthful bravado: "I shall state silences more completely than even a better man spangled the butterflies of vertigo."[18] Or, as he put it some thirty years later in the interview with Tom Driver:

> The confusion is not my invention. We cannot listen to a conversation for five minutes without being acutely aware of the confusion. It is all around us and our only chance now is to let it in. The only chance of renovation is to open our eyes and see the mess. It is not a mess you can make sense of. . . . To find a form that accommodates the mess, that is the task of the artist now.[19]

Beckett's early affinity for Rimbaud's poetic of indeterminacy can be seen in his remarkable translation of "Bateau ivre" (1932), a text long lost which has only recently, and by the purest chance, been recovered, and which appeared for the first time in the newly edited *Collected Poems in English & French* of 1977.[20] As a poetic experiment, "Drunk-

[16] *Dublin Magazine*, 12, no. 3 (July-September 1936), 81.

[17] This is the concluding sentence of the Addenda to *Watt*, p. 254.

[18] *Dream of Fair to Middling Women*, Unpub. Ms., Reading University Library, Reading, England, quoted by John Pilling, *Samuel Beckett* (London: Routledge and Kegan Paul, 1976), p. 182.

[19] See Graver and Federman, *Samuel Beckett: The Critical Heritage*, pp. 218-219.

[20] (London: John Calder, 1977 and New York: Grove Press, 1977). The Grove Press text is subsequently cited as CP.

en Boat" looks ahead to Beckett's own great French/English works written from the mid-forties on. It also affords insight into what many critics consider the "stale pretentiousness" of *Echo's Bones*, Beckett's first collection of poems (1935).[21] Read in conjunction with those few of his verse translations the author cared to preserve,[22] his early lyric, both English and French, appears as less of an anomaly in the Beckett canon.

The highly concrete but ultimately mobile and enigmatic images of "Bateau ivre," which have teased translators from Edgell Rickword (1924) and Louise Varèse (1945) down to Robert Lowell (1961), Wallace Fowlie (1966), and Paul Schmidt (1975),[23] are distinguished, in the Beckett version, by the lucid indeterminacy that characterizes the original, even though Beckett predictably darkens the landscape, introducing shadows that are only latent in Rimbaud's poem.

[21] The phrase is Donald Davie's: see his review of *Poems in English, New Statesman*, 5 (January 1962), 21; rpt. in Graver and Federman, p. 272; Davie talks of the "mish-mash of Joyce and Eliot out of English, and from French, moody abstractions and nonce words to baffle translators." Cf. Richard Coe, review of the CP in the *Times Literary Supplement*, 15 July 1977; rpt. in Graver and Federman, p. 354. Coe speaks of the "paradox that the greatest writer of our time was a poet whose formal 'poems' oscillate between the obscure, the imitative, and the awkward."

[22] Aside from "Bateau ivre," the CP includes seven poems by Paul Eluard, Apollinaire's "Zone," and some recent versions of Sebastien Chamfort's Maxims. For translations not included—for example those from Montale (*Delta*, 1930), Breton (*Transition*, 1932), and René Crevel (*This Quarter*, 1932)—see Raymond Federman and John Fletcher, *Samuel Beckett: His Works and His Critics: An Essay in Bibliography 1929-1966* (Berkeley and Los Angeles: Univ. of California Press, 1970).

[23] See Edgell Rickword, *Rimbaud—The Boy and the Poet* (1924; rpt. Essex, England: Daimon Press, 1963), Appendix; Louise Varèse, *A Season in Hell and the Drunken Boat* (1945; rpt. New York: New Directions, 1961), pp. 92-103; Robert Lowell, *Imitations* (New York: Farrar, Straus & Giroux, 1961), pp. 81-83; Wallace Fowlie, *Rimbaud, Complete Works, Selected Letters* (Chicago: Univ. of Chicago Press, 1967), pp. 114-121; Paul Schmidt, *Arthur Rimbaud, Complete Works* (New York: Harper & Row, 1975), pp. 120-123. The translations of Rickword, Lowell, and Schmidt are abridged. All page references in the text are to these editions.

Take, for example, Rimbaud's difficult sixth stanza, in which the boat plunges into the ocean depths, undergoing a sea-change at once exhilarating and ominous:

Et dès lors, je me suis baigné dans le Poème
De la Mer, infusé d'astres, et lactescent,
Dévorant les azurs verts; où, flottaison blème
Et ravie, un noyé pensif parfois descend. . . .[24]

Wallace Fowlie follows the original word for word:

And from then on I bathed in the Poem
Of the Sea, infused with stars and lactescent,
Devouring the green azure where, like a pale elated
Piece of flotsam, a pensive drowned figure sometimes
sinks. . . .

(p. 117)

A faithful translation, but somewhat awkward. "Infused with stars and lactescent" sounds as if the sea had just received an injection against measles or chicken pox. In the fourth line, "a pensive drowned figure sometimes sinks" turns Rimbaud's softly alliterating sounds into a noisy tongue-twister. "Sinks" is, moreover, a misleading translation of "descend" (all that goes down does not necessarily sink), especially in a poem that begins with the words "Comme je descendais . . ." and that regards the descent downward and inward as the path toward some sort of vision.

Louise Varèse tries to render the stanza in more "natural" English:

And since then I've been bathing in the Poem
Of star-infused and milky Sea,
Devouring the azure greens, where, flotsam pale,
A brooding corpse at times drifts by. . . .

(p. 95)

[24] Rimbaud, *Œuvres*, ed. Suzanne Bernard (Paris: Garnier, 1960). All subsequent references to Rimbaud's works are to this edition, cited as "Rimbaud."

Varèse's "star-infused and milky Sea" is preferable to Fowlie's "lactescent," and she rightly sees that the "noyé pensif" drifts rather than sinks, but "Since then I've been bathing" sounds excessively flippant, calling to mind a seaside holiday rather than Rimbaud's mysterious metamorphosis.

A much freer version is Robert Lowell's:

> Rudderless, I was driven like a plank
> on night seas stuck with stars and dribbling milk;
> I shot through greens and blues, where luminous,
> swollen, drowned sailors rose for light and sank. . . .
>
> (p. 82)

Lowell preserves Rimbaud's *b* rhyme ("milk"/"sank"); otherwise he takes great liberties with the text, eliminating "le Poème de la Mer" and making the star and milk imagery quite realistic, almost ugly. The "noyé pensif" now becomes "drowned sailors" (an interesting echo of Lowell's own "Quaker Graveyard in Nantucket" where the "drowned sailor clutched the drag-net"), again a reference so specific that Rimbaud's calculated vagueness is quite lost.[25]

Finally, here is Beckett:

> Thenceforward, fused in the poem, milk of stars,
> Of the sea, I coiled through deeps of cloudless green,
> Where, dimly, they come swaying down,
> Rapt and sad, singly, the drowned. . . .
>
> (CP, 95)

What Beckett understands is that the "I" does not merely bathe or drift in the "Poem of the Sea." Rather, the self, no longer knowing where its identity ends and the ocean's begins, fuses with its surroundings. Everything merges: the poem, the "milk of stars," the "deeps of cloudless green"

[25] Paul Schmidt's translation retains the meaning of line 1 but, like Lowell, transforms the "flottaison blême / Et ravie" into the specific "Drowned men, pale and thoughtful." Like Lowell, Schmidt also retains the *b* rhyme and he turns "astres, et lactescent" into the realistic "gruel of stars" (p. 120).

through which "I coiled." Beckett alters Rimbaud's word order, but the tone of the original is kept intact. In what is surely a masterstroke, the "pensive drowned figure" of Fowlie, the "brooding corpse" of Varèse, or the "drowned sailors" of Lowell give way to an ambiguous "they" who "come swaying down," "Rapt" (*ravie*), "sad" (*blême*), and, most important, "singly." Only when we come to the last two words of the stanza, do we learn that these intermittent apparitions are "the drowned." What the "je" really *sees* thus remains a mystery.

Rimbaud's vocabulary is so esoteric, his meanings so elusive, that translators have generally paid little attention to his use of sound beyond such obvious strategies as taking over his rhyme scheme or rendering his alexandrines in blank verse. It is all the more remarkable that Beckett is able to invent this:

> Where dimly, they come swaying down,
> Rapt and sad, singly, the drowned. . . .

"Dimly" almost rhymes with "singly" and "down" with "drowned"; the alliteration of *d*'s, assonance of *a*'s ("rapt and sad"), and ominous pauses before and after "singly" create a sense of awe and wonder. It is not quite Rimbaud's more formal sound structure and yet it serves as a nice analogue, just as Beckett's *How It Is* (1964), which I shall discuss later, is a recreation rather than an exact translation of his *Comment c'est* (1961).

The treatment of Rimbaud's imagery is especially telling. Beckett's oceans are less dazzling, his ecstasies less intense, his flowers less sparkling, his desire to have the keel burst less dramatic. Rimbaud's *fauve* landscape of azure-green, violet, and glowing phosphorus is peculiarly stripped of its exoticism. Yet, unlike Lowell's translation, which shifts without warning from word-for-word rendition to discordant images, Beckett's is entirely coherent. He regards the voyage of the "Bateau ivre" not so much as an *escape to* an ideal visionary realm as an *escape from* the nullity—"the trivial racket of trivial crews"—of everyday life. As such, the landscape of dream is less magical and the return to "reality" correspondingly less bitter than in Rimbaud.

Such "chastening" of language can be seen in the third stanza:

Dans les clapotements furieux des marées,
Moi, l'autre hiver, plus sourd que les cerveaux
  d'enfants,
Je courus! Et les Péninsules démarées
N'ont pas subi tohu-bohus plus triomphants.
(p. 128)

Wallace Fowlie renders this:

Into the furious lashings of the tides,
More heedless than children's brains, the other winter
I ran! And loosened peninsulas
Have not undergone a more triumphant hubbub.
(p. 115)

And Paul Schmidt gives the literal meaning of "sourd":

Through the wild splash and surging of the tides
Last winter, deaf as a child's dark night,
I ran and ran! And the drifting Peninsulas
Have never known such conquering delight.
(p. 120)

Beckett, however, characteristically introduces an element of withdrawal, the sense of what he once described as "existence by proxy" or "being absent":

Blanker than the brain of a child I fled
Through winter, I scoured the furious jolts of the
  tides,
In an uproar and a chaos of Peninsulas,
Exultant, from their moorings in triumph torn.
(CP, 95)

By means of delicate adjustments—"Blanker than the

brain" rather than "deaf" or "heedless"; "through winter" rather than "that winter" or "the other winter"; "fled" and "scoured" rather than the neutral "ran"; a "chaos of Peninsulas" rather than peninsulas that are "drifting" or "loosened"—Beckett transforms Rimbaud's violent ecstasy into a moment of fear. There are instances of this sort throughout the poem. "La têmpete a béni mes éveils maritimes" becomes "I started awake to tempestuous hallowings." The sense of blessing has evaporated. Again, "Plus douce qu'aux enfants la chair de pommes sures" becomes, in an interesting variation, "More firmly bland than to children apples' firm pulp." Sweet flesh has no place in the Beckett landscape. So too, "les rutilements du jour" are regarded as "the sky's haemorrhage," and "Les flots roulant au loin leur frisson de volets" become "peals of ague [that] rattle down its slats."

Beckett's journey into otherness is thus a more sombre one than Rimbaud's. Yet interestingly, his interpretation of "Bateau ivre" succeeds in drawing out certain implications of the climactic fourteenth stanza that are often ignored:

> Glaciers, soleils d'argent, flots nacreux, cieux de
> braises!
> Échouages hideux au fond des golfes bruns
> Où les serpents géants dévorés des punaises
> Choient, des arbres tordus, avec de noirs parfums!
> (p. 130)

Here the ecstasy of vision modulates into terror and most translators stress the violent contrast:

> Glaciers, suns of silver, nacreous waves, skies of
> embers!
> Hideous strands at the end of brown gulfs
> Where giant serpents devoured by bedbugs
> Fall down from gnarled trees with black scent!
> (Fowlie, p. 117)

Or

> Glaciers and silver suns, fiery skies and pearly seas,
> Hideous wrecks at the bottom of brown gulfs
> Where giant serpents vermin ridden
> Drop with black perfumes from the twisted trees!
>
> (Varèse, p. 99)

Beckett's imagery is more equivocal:

> Iridescent waters, glaciers, suns of silver, flagrant
> skies,
> And dark creeks' secret ledges, horror-strewn,
> Where giant reptiles, pullulant with lice,
> Lapse with dark perfumes from the writhing trees.
>
> (CP, 99)

The opulence of the poet's vision, Beckett implies, has been deceptive all along. The "fond des golfes bruns" and "noirs parfums" would, sooner or later, have to reveal themselves. And so the nostalgic second half of "Bateau ivre," which begins with the conditional "J'aurais voulu" of stanza 15, emphasizes, in Beckett's version, loss of self rather than rapture. A line like "Or moi, bateau perdu sous les cheveux des anses," which can be viewed as a withdrawal into a kind of pleasure dome, a "cave" of sexual delights, is rendered more literally—and therefore cruelly—by Beckett: "Now I who was wrecked in the inlets' tangled hair." Accordingly, the loss of vision and the return to the linear, one-dimensional world of reality in the last three stanzas of the poem is regarded less as a failure than as something inevitable. One must resign oneself. "But no more tears," Beckett's "I" says abruptly, giving Rimbaud's "Mais vrai, j'ai trop pleuré!" a new twist. And the childhood memory of the penultimate stanza is not wholly negative:

> I want none of Europe's waters unless it be
> The cold black puddle where a child, full of sadness,

Squatting, looses a boat as frail
As a moth into the fragrant evening.

(CP, 105)

Compare Lowell:

Shrunken and black against the twilight sky
our Europe has no water. Only a pond
the cows have left, and a boy wades to launch
his paper boat frail as a butterfly.

(p. 83)

This facile contrast between a waterless black Europe and a brightly colored oceanic dream world is quite inimical to Rimbaud's sensibility: his twilight, after all, is "embaumé"—sweet-smelling, perfumed. Beckett, taking Rimbaud's ambiguity even further, no longer makes the Romantic distinction between reality and dream. In a Beckett "vision," there is only, as we saw in the case of *Fizzles*, the abortive attempt to reach conclusion, a process in need of constant renewal because the anticipated epiphany never quite comes. His "Drunken Boat" thus makes the visionary pole less intense, less attractive than it was for Rimbaud. Thus the passionate intensity of Rimbaud's climactic line, "O que ma quille éclate! O que j'aille à la mer!" gives way to the muted anguish of "May I split from stem to stern and founder, ah founder!"

The escape motif, so prominent in the "Drunken Boat" of 1932, is central to Beckett's own poems in *Echo's Bones*.[26] Lawrence E. Harvey, the leading authority on Beckett's lyric poetry, has gone to great lengths to track down the allusions, both philosophical and literary, as well as the topical references in these early poems.[27] But *Echo's Bones*

[26] *Echo's Bones and Other Precipitates* was originally published in Paris by the Europa Press in 1935. See CP, pp. 9-36.

[27] *Samuel Beckett, Poet & Critic.* Almost a hundred pages are devoted to *Echo's Bones* (pp. 67-169). But Harvey also has long sections on the early prose and criticism; in 1961-1962, he had a series of important conversations with Beckett; these discussions of poetics are cited and paraphrased

has an immediate "French connection" that Harvey, in his concern with the Latin and Provençal models, largely ignores. Whether Beckett calls a given poem an "enueg" or a "sanie" or a "serena" turns out to be much less important than the frequency of the journey structure on the model of "Bateau ivre" or of Apollinaire's "Zone," which Beckett translated in 1950. "Enueg I," for example, begins:

> Exeo in a spasm
> tired of my darling's red sputum
> from the Portobello Private Nursing Home
> its secret things
> and toil to the crest of the surge of the steep perilous
>   bridge
> and lapse down blankly under the scream of the
>   hoarding
> round the bright stiff banner of the hoarding
> into a black west
> throttled with clouds.
>
> (CP, 10)

An *enueg*, Harvey tells us, is a Provençal lyric that catalogues the annoyances of life from mere trifles to serious insults: the word literally means *vexation*. The enueg is characterized by discontinuity of thought, the only unifying device usually being the poet's dislike, applied indiscriminately. The genre tends toward the witty and epigrammatic but, as Harvey further notes, Beckett's enuegs are really closer to another Provençal form, the *planh*, which is a poem expressing the great displeasure and sor-

---

in the book. Harvey's is thus an indispensable guide. Unfortunately, some of his readings are labored; source study gets in the way of his perception of the poems as poems.

John Fletcher has two good general essays about the poetry: "The Private Pain and the Whey of Words: A Survey of Beckett's Verse," in *Samuel Beckett*, ed. Esslin, pp. 23-32; and "Beckett as Poet," in *Samuel Beckett*, ed. Cohn, pp. 51-62. The best short treatment of the poetry is, I think, Hugh Kenner's in *A Reader's Guide to Samuel Beckett* (New York: Farrar, Straus & Giroux, 1973), pp. 42-48.

row one feels at loss or misfortune, whether of a loved person or of an object (pp. 79-81).

"Enueg I" does follow these models. Beckett begins by lamenting the fatal illness of a girl he loved and goes on to rail against the squalor of Dublin with its "grey verminous hens, / perishing out in the sunk field" and its "sweaty heroes, / in their Sunday best." There are echoes of Eliot ("the stillborn evening turning a filthy green") and Joyce ("on the hill down from the Fox and Geese into Chapelizod" and the "Isolde Stores"—both from *Finnegans Wake*).[28] But structurally, "Enueg I" has a much more direct analogue in Apollinaire's "Zone," which Beckett has chosen to include in the new *Collected Poems* together with his translation. The poem opens:

> À la fin tu es las de ce monde ancien
>
> Bergère ô tour Eiffel le troupeau des ponts bêle ce
> matin

which Beckett renders:

> In the end you are weary of this ancient world
>
> This morning the bridges are bleating Eiffel Tower oh
> herd
>
> (CP, 106-107)

"Zone" (1913) explores the geography of self, the location of individual identity in space/time. As the poet—sometimes "je," sometimes "tu"—wanders through present-day Paris, he relives incidents from his past life, incidents that take him from one geographic "zone" to another until all merge. Thus the images of "bleating bridges," "bellowing buses," "the handbills the catalogues the singing posters" are juxtaposed to memories of the poet's pious

[28] On the Joyce allusions, see Melvin J. Friedman, "Introductory Notes to Beckett's Poetry," in *Samuel Beckett: The Art of Rhetoric,* ed. Edouard Morot-Sir, Howard Harper, and Douglas McMillan, North Carolina Studies in the Romance Languages and Literatures (Chapel Hill: Univ. of North Carolina Press, 1976), pp. 146-149.

Christian childhood, painful puppy love, and voyages to exotic places:

> Here you are in Marseilles among the water-melons
>
> Here you are in Coblentz at the Giant's Hostelry
>
> Here you are in Rome under a Japanese medlar tree
>
> (CP, 115)

The tempo accelerates, becoming increasingly frenetic until suddenly, just as the poet comes within sight of his own house at Auteuil and, totally exhausted from his all-night wanderings, longs for sleep "Among your fetishes from Guinea and the South Seas," he turns around and sees the sunrise:

> Soleil cou coupé

which Beckett renders in an especially tense image

> Sun corseless head
>
> (CP, 120-121)

The deathnote of this image (the sun as maimed body) sounds throughout "Enueg I," which, like "Zone," presents the poet wandering through the city and its suburbs, crossing and recrossing the river (here the Liffey), pointing to everything he sees as if it might provide him with an identity:

> I trundle along rapidly now on my ruined feet
> flush with the livid canal;
> at Parnell Bridge a dying barge
> carrying a cargo of nails and timber
> rocks itself softly in the foaming cloister of the lock. . . .
>
> Blotches of doomed yellow in the pit of the Liffey
> the fingers of the ladders hooked over the parapet,
> soliciting. . . .
>
> (CP, 11-12)

And in "Serena I" (a *serena* is an evening song in which the lover longs for the night which will bring him his beloved), we read:

I find me taking the Crystal Palace
for the Blessed Isles from Primrose Hill
alas I must be that kind of person
hence in Ken Wood who shall find me
my breath held in the midst of thickets
none but the most quarried lovers. . . .

but in Ken Wood
who shall find me. . . .

(CP, 21-22)

Here the fear of engulfment recalls Apollinaire's

Tu es à Paris chez le juge d'instruction
Comme un criminel on te met en état d'arrestation. . . .
Tu n'oses plus regarder tes mains et à tous moments
je voudrais sangloter

which Beckett translates:

You are in Paris with the examining magistrate
They clap you in gaol like a common reprobate. . . .
You dare not look at your hands tears haunt my eyes
(CP, 116-117)

Here the peculiar absence of punctuation between "hands" and "tears," which places the nouns in a kind of false apposition, and the shift from "your" to "my" as forms of self-address, all within the space of one line, are stylistic features of Apollinaire's poetry that Beckett was to make peculiarly his own.

Echo's Bones also contains specific allusions to Rimbaud. "Enueg I," which dates from the same year as Beckett's translation of "Bateau ivre," ends with a passage taken from "Barbare":

Ah the banner
the banner of meat bleeding

on the silk of the seas and the arctic flowers
that do not exist.

(CP, 12)

In the original, this reads:

> Oh! Le pavillon en viande saignante sur la soie des mers et des fleurs arctiques; (elles n'existent pas.)
>
> (Rimbaud, 292)

This sentence has already appeared once in the prose poem; when it reappears in the final line, it is abruptly broken off: "Le pavillon. . . ." The elocution is typically Rimbaldian: the erotic longing for what are, in fact, fictive entities that do not normally coexist—a banner of bleeding meat on silken seas, arctic flowers—coupled with the realization that "elles n'existent pas."

But in Beckett's version, the syntax is skewed ever so slightly so that it is now the exotic "arctic flowers / that do not exist," whereas the rather grotesque banner of meat is visualized as "bleeding on [wounding, soiling] the silk, of the seas." Beckett thus rejects what we might call Rimbaud's magic-lantern show, just as he is ultimately quite different from the Apollinaire who could say in "Zone":

J'aime la grâce de cette rue industrielle
Située à Paris entre la rue Aumont-Thiéville et
l'avenue des Ternes

I love the grace of this industrial street
In Paris between the Avenue des Ternes and the Rue
Aumont-Thiéville.

(CP, 108-109)

Beckett, who is not likely to find "grace" in any street, industrial or otherwise, talks in "Serena I" of the city as a place where the "grey hold of the ambulance / is throbbing on the brink ebb of sights" (CP, 22). And the lines cited from "Barbare" are juxtaposed to "Blotches of doomed yellow in the pit of the Liffey; / the fingers of the ladders hooked over the parapet, / soliciting." Indeed, Beckett's response to Rimbaud and Apollinaire is stylistic and structural rather than thematic; his "Drunken Boat" is like a black-and-white print of a color film called "Bateau ivre."

But of course it is in these black-and-white prints that we can locate the origins of such later poetic fictions as *How It Is* (1964), "Imagination Dead Imagine" (1966), *The Lost Ones* (1971), and *Fizzles*. None of these works are, strictly speaking, "poems," and accordingly they are never mentioned in discussions of contemporary poetry. This is a puzzling situation, for the fictions Beckett has been writing since the early sixties are not, of course, "novels" or "stories" either. All retain some element of narrative, but a narrative dislocated and truncated, that tends to lead nowhere. Again, all foreground what Northrop Frye calls "an associative phrase-rhythm" based on various devices of repetition, a rhythm that acts "to break down or through the whole structure of verbal articulation."[29] These "Residua," as Beckett calls them, point the way to the "free prose" of such texts as Ashbery's *Three Poems*.

III

—les vrais paradis sont les paradis qu'on a perdus.
—Proust, *Le Temps Retrouvé*

How It Is, especially Part I with its delicate permutations on that "long vast stretch of time" that existed "before Pim," is, I think, Beckett's most Proustian composition—a truncated, tickertape version of Proust, in which the nameless narrator, crawling on his belly through the mud, bearing his sack, his cord, his cans of fish and can-opener, experiences, in a series of privileged moments that partly follow, partly parody the Proustian model, visitations from the "life the other above in the light said to have been mine,"[30] dream images of "my beginnings," or of, as Beckett

[29] *The Well-Tempered Critic* (Bloomington: Indiana University Press, 1963), pp. 73, 92.

[30] (New York: Grove Press, 1964). Subsequently cited as H.

puts it in *Proust*, "the only Paradise that is not the dream of a madman, the Paradise that has been lost" (P, 14).

Most of the commentary on *How It Is* has concerned itself with the book's tripartite structure—"before Pim with Pim after Pim"—and the meaning of these three stages of development. "Literally and metaphorically," writes Ruby Cohn, "the central event of the book is the couple, the meeting of two beings, which has haunted Beckett at least since A and C of *Molloy*."[31] The meeting itself establishes the pairing of tormentor (the narrator) and victim (Pim), a pairing that is reversed when the narrator himself subsequently becomes the victim of a new character named Bom. The sequence, Beckett implies, could go on indefinitely:

> each one of us is at the same time Bom and Pim tormentor and tormented pedant and dunce wooer and wooed speechless and reafflicted with speech in the dark the mud nothing to emend there
>
> (H, 140)

But we also know that in the dramatic reversal at the end of *How It Is*, the narrator denies that these meetings have ever occurred:

> that wasn't how it was no not at all no how then no answer how it was then no answer HOW WAS IT screams good. . . .
>
> no nor any journey no never any Pim no nor any Bom no never anyone no only me no answer only me yes so that was true yes it was true about me yes and what's my name no answer WHAT'S MY NAME screams good
>
> (H, 144-146)

Indeed, the hypothetical journey toward Pim is, like the journey of Rimbaud's "Bateau ivre," a paradigm of the descent into the self. As Marcel says at the end of the

[31] *Back to Beckett* (Princeton: Princeton University Press, 1973), p. 230. Cf. Michael Robinson, *The Long Sonata of the Dead, A Study of Samuel Beckett* (New York: Grove Press, 1969), pp. 213-214.

Recherche, when he relives the childhood moment of the tinkling garden bell, announcing Swann's visit: "Pour tâcher de l'entendre de plus près, c'est en moi même que j'étais obligé de redescendre" ("To hear it better, it was into my own depths that I had to re-descend").[32] In *Proust*, Beckett provides a chart of the novel's eleven privileged moments when "some immediate and fortuitous act of perception" points the way toward "salvation in the midst of life" (P, 22-23). In the minimalist landscape of *How It Is*, we find the same longing "to go back":

> only one thing to do go back or at least only other thrash round where I lie and I go on zigzag give me my due conformably to my complexion present formulation seeking that which I have lost there where I have never been
>
> dear figures when all fails a few figures to wind up with part one before Pim the golden age the good moments the losses of the species I was young. . . .
>
> . . . we're talking of the base in the old line of march which I thus revisit an instant between two vertices one yard and a half a little less dear figures golden age so it ends part one before Pim my travelling days vast stretch of time I was young all that all those words chevrons golden vertices. . . .
>
> (H, 46-47)

"Only one thing to do go back"; the "golden age the good moments"; "all those words chevrons golden vertices"—Beckett's origin here is Proustian but of course, as the above quotations reveal, the modernist text has undergone radical deformation. "These gobbets of utterance," writes Hugh Kenner, "are paced and cadenced like elegiac

[32] *A La Recherche du Temps Perdu*, III (Paris: Gallimard, Bibliothèque de la Pléiade, 1954), p. 1046; *The Past Recaptured*, trans. Andreas Mayor (New York: Random House, 1970), p. 971. Subsequent page references are to these editions; the translator of the Random House edition, prior to *The Past Recaptured*, is C. K. Scott Moncrieff.

vers libre, though the reader, sharing the protagonist's vigil, must detect for himself the boundaries of the phrases and reconstitute the muted *bel canto*."[33]

In the blocks of type that constitute *How It Is*, main verbs and definite articles are omitted, punctuation and capitalization (except for proper names) eliminated. But even when we succeed in determining the boundaries of Beckett's fragmented phrases, the condensed text remains an enigma. Consider the lines cited above:

> only one thing to do go back or at least only other thrash round where I lie

This looks like Basic English, every word a monosyllable and readily understood. It is, moreover, quite easy to fill in the words and punctuation that would turn Beckett's fragment into a complete sentence: "[There is] only one thing to do [:] [to] go back or at least [the] only other [thing to do] is [to] thrash [a]round where I lie." Supplying the missing links is thus not the reader's main problem; the real puzzle is semantic. Why is the "only thing to do" to "go back"? Why is the inertia of "thrash[ing] round where I lie" "at least" the "only other" thing to do? There is no way of deciding. Again, when the narrator says: "we're talking of the base in the old line of march which I thus revisit an instant between two vertices one yard and a half a little less," we cannot make out what "the base in the old line of march" is, nor can we identify the "two vertices" so carefully pinpointed as "one yard and a half a little less." It is the same indeterminacy we encountered in *Fizzles*.

[33] *Reader's Guide to Samuel Beckett*, p. 139. On the Dantean source, Kenner writes: "one point of departure for the book may have been Inferno VII, where the souls of the Sullen . . . lie immersed in mud, and gurgle a statement of the case in their thoughts since the mud prevents their speaking or singing plainly. . . . And earlier in the same Canto Dante displays a tribe who move perpetually back and forth along a semi-circle, banging each other, cursing, about-facing. This may have contributed to the vision of the endless procession of tormentors and tormented in the third part of *How It Is*, though the special logistics of Beckett's formulations are his own (p. 138)."

The neat tripartite structure of *How It Is* is thus an empty container, within which "bits and scraps" coalesce for a moment and then separate to form new configurations. In this "narrative without narration," as Gerald Bruns calls it,[34] there is neither logic nor sequence; indeed, it makes better sense to read the book, at least Part 1, as a dream vision, in which time and space are dislocated, the present in the mud giving way at any moment to unpredictable fantasy and memory.

Consider the four opening paragraphs:

> how it was I quote before Pim with Pim after Pim how it is three parts I say it as I hear it
>
> voice once without quaqua on all sides then in me when the panting stops tell me again finish telling me invocation
>
> past moments old dreams back again or fresh like those that pass or things things always and memories I say them as I hear them murmur them in the mud
>
> in me that were without when the panting stops scraps of an ancient voice in me not mine
>
> (H, 7)

First a statement or, more accurately, a non-statement of the theme, since all that happens is finally disavowed. Secondly, an invocation to the Muse, the "voice once without," "an ancient voice in me not mine." In a conversation with Lawrence Harvey, held shortly after the publication of *Comment c'est*, Beckett speaks of "a presence, embryonic, undeveloped, a self that might have been but never got born, an *être manqué*." One finds this "lost self" in "images of getting down, getting below the surface, concentrating, listening."[35] Such splitting of the self recalls, of course, Rimbaud's "*Je* est un Autre." It is this "Other" who will be evoked in the dream sequences of the text. Indeed, the

[34] *Modern Poetry and the Idea of Language*, p. 183.
[35] See *Samuel Beckett, Poet & Critic*, p. 247.

dream motif is introduced immediately after the "invocation" in the third paragraph:

> past moments old dreams back again or fresh like those that pass or things things always and memories I say them as I hear them murmur them in the mud

The sound patterning here is densely woven: note the anaphora of "past" / "pass", the alliteration of *m*'s in "*m*o*m*ents," "drea*m*s," "*m*e*m*ories," "*m*ur*m*ur the*m* in the *m*ud," the assonance in "m*o*ments *o*ld," "m*u*rm*u*r . . . m*u*d," and the "z" endings of "dream*s*," "thing*s*," "memorie*s*," "alway*s*." Rhythmically, the utterance is characterized by heavy stressing and strong caesurae: "past moments // old dreams // back again" or "things // things // always."

Having foregrounded the *dream-memory-moment* axis, Beckett juxtaposes it to the present "reality":

> my life last state last version ill-said ill-heard ill-recaptured ill-murmured in the mud brief movements of the lower face losses everywhere

Such alternation between the narrator's present ("murmur in the mud") and the "golden vertices" of the recreated past ("a dream I am given a dream. . . . a llama emergency dream") continues throughout Part 1. Interestingly, the narrator's "moments . . . all lost" are not, as in Proust, dependent upon a particular sensation that releases the involuntary memory. Beckett's moments simply come and go, quite independently of the protagonist's actual movements in the mud, his handling of the can-opener, and so on. The past cannot be recaptured; it can only be glimpsed at random and unpredictable intervals:

> life life the other above in the light said to have been mine on and off no going back up there no question no one asking that of me never there a few images on and off in the mud
>
> (H, 8)

In the narrator's circle of hell[36]—"the sacks the tins the mud in the dark the silence the solitude"—images of "life the other above in the light" thus flash fitfully on and off. The most obviously Proustian of these—although Beckett slyly turns Proust inside out—begins with the image of "my mother's face I see it from below it's like nothing I ever saw"—a self-cancelling image that recalls Rimbaud's "les fleurs arctiques (elles n'existent pas)":

> we are on a veranda smothered in verbena the scented sun dapples the red tiles yes I assure you
>
> the huge head hatted with birds and flowers is bowed down over my curls the eyes burn with severe love I offer her mine pale upcast to the sky whence cometh our help and which I know perhaps even then with time shall pass away
>
> in a word bolt upright on a cushion on my knees whelmed in a nightshirt I pray according to her instructions
>
> that's not all she closes her eyes and drones a snatch of the so-called Apostles' Creed I steal a look at her lips
>
> she stops her eyes burn down on me again I cast up mine in haste and repeat awry
>
> the air thrills with the hum of insects
>
> that's all it goes out like a lamp blown out
>
> (H, 15-16)

In her biography of Beckett, Deirdre Bair reproduces a photograph (c. 1908) that closely corresponds to the autobiographical image in the above passage: Mrs. Beckett

[36] See Kenner, *Reader's Guide*, p. 138. I don't think it is correct to say, as does Robinson in *Long Sonata of the Dead*: "The mud of *How It Is* is the spiritually empty counterpart to Ezekiel's valley of dry bones where nothing is because God is not" (p. 215). Beckett may allude to Dante but his is not a Christian hell.

is depicted in a large hat, bending over her small boy who is dressed in white and kneels on a little pillow.[37] Curiously, the photograph is just as equivocal as the text: is it the standard portrait of a "loving" mother and child or is the primary tone one of hostility?

Here it is interesting to compare Beckett's scene with what is probably its source: the Combray sequence in *Du Côté de chez Swann*, in which Marcel awaits his mother's goodnight kiss, while his family, seated in the little front garden in the early evening, looks forward to the timid ring of the visitors' bell that announces Swann's visit. In the Proustian narrative, the goodnight kiss has the force of religious rite, singularly providing the little boy with a short-lived moment of tranquillity:

> . . . [Maman] avait penché vers mon lit sa figure aimante, et me l'avait tendue comme une hostie pour une communion de paix où mes lèvres puiseraient sa présence réelle et le pouvoir de m'endormir.
>
> (I, 13)
>
> . . . [Maman] bent her loving face down over my bed and held it out to me like a Host, for an act of Communion in which my lips might drink deeply the sense of her real presence, and with it the power to sleep.
>
> (p. 17)

In *How It Is*, the mother's figure is similarly "bowed down over my curls," but interestingly, Proust's "figure aimante" is replaced by the anonymity of "the huge head hatted with birds and flowers," an image that gives us pause, for we expect hats, but not heads, to be huge. Maternal love as an act of communion is replaced by a "severe love" that is "smothered" in the "verbena" of religious rote: the voice of an impersonal "she" who "drones a snatch of the so-called Apostles' Creed." The Proustian kiss gives way to

[37] *Beckett* (New York: Harcourt Brace Jovanovitch, 1978), p. 17. The photograph by Dorothy Kay is supplied by the Reading University Library; it is opposite p. 114.

separation—the child sits "bolt upright on a cushion" and prays "according to her instructions"—and the moment is characterized by fear: "she stops her eyes burn down on me again I cast up mine in haste and repeat awry."

Nevertheless, something of the Proustian tone remains. The parenthetical "yes I assure you" strikes a note of emotional engagement, a desire to remember, as does the "offering" of the child's "pale upcast" eyes to his mother's "severe love." As in the Combray garden, "the scented sun dapples the red tiles" and "the air thrills with the hum of insects." Accordingly, when the privileged moment is over ("that's all it goes out like a lamp blown out"), something seems to have been lost. Indeed, the voice utters:

> the space of a moment the passing moment that's all my past little rat at my heels the rest false

But why this "passing moment" is valuable remains a mystery. The dream image defies explanation.

A similar play on the Proustian theme (this time on the adoration of "les jeunes filles en fleur") occurs in the "old dream of flowers and seasons" in which the narrator recreates a scene of adolescent love:

> I look to me about sixteen and to crown all glorious weather egg-blue sky and scamper of little clouds I have my back turned to me and the girl too whom I hold who holds me by the hand the arse I have
>
> (H, 29)

The introduction of the "arse" into this pastoral scene looks ahead to the bitter reversal that comes six paragraphs later:

> seen full face the girl is less hideous it's not with her I am concerned me pale staring hair red pudding face with pimples protruding belly gaping fly spindle legs sagging knocking at the knees. . . .
>
> (H, 29-30)

There follows a passage in which "puppy love" is taken

quite literally: the girl's "ash-grey dog" creating so much commotion that the two "lovers" are interrupted in their "mingling of hands":

> suddenly yip left right off we go chins up arms swinging the dog follows head sunk tail on balls no reference to us

The ensuing comic chase scene modulates into the farce of the sandwich-eating ritual ("I bite she swallows my sweet boy she bites I swallow"), and before long the narrator loses interest in his verbal invention: the playful pastoral idyl fades out:

> blue and white of sky a moment still April morning in the mud it's over it's done I've had the image the scene is empty a few animals still then goes out no more blue I stay there
>
> way off on the right in the mud the hand opens and closes that helps me it's going let it go I realize I'm still smiling there's no sense in that now been none for a long time now
>
> (H, 31)

Here the effect is oddly equivocal. The romance itself has been related in mock-scientific parody style—"we let go our hands and turn about I dextrogyre she sinistro"—and Beckett seems to be having a good laugh. But when "the hand opens and closes that helps me it's going," the speaker, having "had the image," finds himself peculiarly alone. "Still smiling," he notes that "the scene is empty" and yet "I must stay there." Like the empty desert of Rimbaud's *Saison en enfer*, Beckett's hell seems to be characterized by the absence of others:

> Du même désert, à la même nuit, toujours mes yeux las se réveillent à l'étoile d'argent, toujours, sans que s'émeuvent les Rois de la vie, les trois mages, le coeur, l'âme, l'esprit.
>
> (Rimbaud, 238)

> (From the same desert, in the same night, always my tired eyes awaken to the silver star, always, without any reaction from the Kings of life, the three magi, the heart, the soul, the spirit.)

To see the silver star rise in an empty sky—this is analogous to the condition of Beckett's "I" as he watches the last animal disappear and sees that there is "no more blue."

The absence of others signifies, of course, an absence of self. This emptying out of the self, reflected in the narrator's halting utterances that never quite succeed in becoming whole sentences, much less coherent paragraphs, is presented in a series of dislocated verbal fragments, dream images more mysterious than the two memory pictures discussed so far. Here is what Beckett calls the "first image":

> life in the light first image some creature or other I watched him after my fashion from afar through my spy-glass sidelong in mirrors through windows at night first image
>
> saying to myself he's better than he was better than yesterday less ugly less stupid less cruel less dirty less old less wretched and you saying to myself and you bad to worse bad to worse steadily
>
> (H, 9)

The ambiguity of this dream image invites all sorts of speculation. On the one hand, the references to a "he" who is hoped to be "less cruel less dirty less old" than he was "yesterday," call to mind an oppressive father figure, a man so feared that the child has to keep telling himself: "he's better than he was." On the other, the images of mirrors and "windows at night" suggest that the child's vision is not of another person but simply of himself, distanced and turned into an object by being addressed first as "he" and then as "you."[38] But in this case, what can "less dirty less

[38] In the original French of *Comment c'est* (Paris: Editions de Minuit, 1961) the wording of the second block of type is different:

old" mean? Can these words refer to the child himself? It seems unlikely, for we learn a few lines later that "I pissed and shat another image in my crib never so clean since." The identity of the "creature" who is "watched" thus remains a mystery. We know that the voyeuristic child, watching "him" from afar through his "spy-glass," experiences some kind of fear; he seems, further, to feel profoundly guilty about something ("saying to myself and you bad to worse bad to worse steadily"). But we never know what crime, if any, he has committed.

Another way to absent the self is to fantasize the scene of one's death as it might be viewed by someone living:

> another image so soon again a woman looks up looks at me the images come at the beginning part one they will cease I say it as I hear it murmur it in the mud the images part one how it was before Pim I see them in the mud a light goes on they will cease a woman I see her in the mud
>
> she sits aloof ten yards fifteen yards she looks up looks at me says at last to herself all is well he is working
>
> my head where is my head it rests on the table my hand trembles on the table she sees I am not sleeping the wind blows tempestuous the little clouds drive before it the table glides from light to darkness darkness to light
>
> that's not all she stoops to her work again the needle stops in midstitch she straightens up and looks at me

---

je me disais il est mieux mieux qu'hier moins laid
moins bête moins mechant moins sale moins
vieux moins malheureux et moi je me disais et moi
suite ininterrompue d'altérations définitives (p. 12)

Here the narrator does not address himself as "you" and the change described in the last line is unspecified. The English version seems to put more blame on the self, which is reproved: "you bad to worse steadily." But the identity of the "creature" referred to is just as ambiguous in the French as in the English text.

> again she has only to call me by my name get up come and feel me but no
>
> I don't move her anxiety grows she suddenly leaves the house and runs to friends
>
> (H, 10-11)

This strange scene is rather like a film scenario in which some of the directions are very explicit while others are missing. The narrator is now seen from the outside, from the point of view of the "woman" who may be mother or wife and who watches, while she sews, his every movement. The image of the self is decomposed into a series of body parts: "my head rests on the table," "my hand trembles on the table." The woman evidently tries to read these signs, and when she finally realizes that "I don't move," "her anxiety grows she suddenly leaves the house and runs to friends." Has she, then, witnessed his death? Or is he merely playing dead so as to avoid her scrutiny? "She has," after all, "only to call me by my name get up come and feel me but no."

The sharply defined images of this passage remain curiously enigmatic. "The little clouds drive before it the table glides from light to darkness to light"—how do such things happen? Or again, why does the "needle stop[s] in midstitch"? Does "she" see or hear something that arrests her attention? We can only say that this dream narrative, full as it is of missing links, echoes the fear-guilt motif of the "first image." Perhaps the "I" wills to die so as to destroy the woman's habitual routine; perhaps he wants somehow to make the needle stop "in midstitch." Then again, perhaps it is all an accident. In any case, we are no nearer to the meaning of the story when the narrator disavows it by saying: "it wasn't a dream I didn't dream that nor a memory . . . it was an image" (H, 11).

One of the related anomalies of *How It Is* is that the man who speaks obsessively of his longing to meet Pim is also a man who rejects all human contact, all the "callers in my life." Take the following frightening dream sequence:

nor callers in my life this time no wish for callers hastening from all sides all sorts to talk to me about themselves life too and death as though nothing had happened me perhaps too in the end to help me last then goodbye till we meet again each back the way he came

all sorts old men how they had dandled me on their knees little bundle of swaddle and lace then followed in my career

others knowing nothing of my beginnings save what they could glean by hearsay or in public records nothing of my beginnings in life

others who had always known me here in my last place they talk to me of themselves of me perhaps too in the end of fleeting joys and of sorrows of empires that are born and die as though nothing had happened

others finally who do not know me yet they pass with heavy tread murmuring to themselves they have sought refuge in a desert place to be alone at last and vent their sorrows unheard

if they see me I am a monster of the solitudes he sees man for the first time and does not flee before him explorers bring home his skin among their trophies

(H, 12-13)

Again the parent text here seems to be Rimbaud's *Saison*, specifically "Mauvais Sang," in which the narrator describes his nightly rambles: "Au matin, j'avais le regard si perdu et la contenance si morte, que ceux que j'ai rencontrés *ne m'ont peut-être pas vu*" ("In the morning, I had a look so vacant and an expression so dead, that those I met perhaps did not see me" [Rimbaud, 216]). The longing to be invisible, the dread of being seen, is a characteristically schizoid gesture, for to be seen is to suffer engulfment, the implosion of the self.[39] The nameless and faceless callers

[39] See R. D. Laing, *The Divided Self* (Baltimore: Penguin Books, 1965), pp. 43-46.

of *How It Is* are frightening because they exhaust all possible categories: "old men [who] had dandled me on their knees," those "who had always known me here in my last place," those "knowing nothing of my beginnings save what they could glean by hearsay," and finally those "who do not know yet they pass with heavy tread." As the "callers in my life"—even those who are total strangers—close in on him, the narrator's "I" gives way to "he," and that distanced "he" becomes a passive victim: "he sees man for the first time and does not flee before him explorers bring home his skin among their trophies."

To be skinned alive by unknown and nameless "explorers" is to experience a total loss of identity, a kind of death. The present "life without callers" is thus a life in the void—"the silence I must break when I can bear it no more" (H, 13). And a few pages later, the voice insists: "a witness I'd need a witness" (H, 18).

In the midst of this "journey" that "can't last it lasts," whose protagonist is "calm calmer you think you're calm," and who perceives himself as "in the lowest depths" as well as "on the edge" (H, 20), a surrealistic image flashes on the poet's mindscreen:

> . . . I see a crocus in a pot in an area in a basement a saffron the sun creeps up the wall a hand keeps it in the sun this yellow flower with a string I see the hand long image hours long the sun goes the pot goes down lights on the ground the hand goes the wall goes
>
> (H, 21)

Here is a haunting image of futility. The "crocus in a pot" is neither inherently beautiful nor in any way special; Beckett sees it as "this yellow flower with a string." Nevertheless, it becomes a fetish for the speaker; he is absorbed in the meaningless ritual in which an unidentified hand keeps the pot in the sun. This hand, like Jasper Johns' detached body parts, seems to be attached to the pot ("long image hours long"); it doesn't disappear until "the sun goes the pot goes down lights on the ground." And when it does "go" it is only because the observer can't see it in the dark ("the hand goes the wall goes"). When "the light goes on" again, two paragraphs later, the crocus has become an item in a list: "the prayer the head on the table the crocus the old man in tears the tears behind the hands skies all sorts different sorts on land and sea blue of a sudden gold and green of the earth of a sudden in the mud" (H, 21). Whose is the "head on the table"? Is it the same head that "rests on the table" in the vision of the woman sewing? Again, is the "prayer" the Apostle's Creed, which the poet's mother used to drone? Is "the old man in tears" an image of the "I" or is this the ugly old "creature" seen through the spy-glass in what Beckett calls the "first image"? And what does the crocus have to do with it all? A crocus is, of course, a harbinger of spring, but here it exists pointlessly between "the head on the table" and "the old man in tears."

Beckett's images of the "paradise before" (H, 23) as it must have been in the "first asparagus burst" of his "happiness" (H, 25) are thus brought to life by the poet as Proustian "dream greenhorn" (H, 23). But these images, fragile and unstable, have an irreducible ambiguity. No symbols where none intended. As for the journey toward Pim, we must remember that the narrator himself observes: "go right leg right arm push pull towards Pim he does not exist" (H, 27).

Never, then, do we come to know "how it is." "The speaker," observes Gerald Bruns, "speaks only to disavow his speech, thus to place all within the empty space of indeterminacy."[40] Thus the "Pim" who exists does not exist, and when the speaker momentarily forgets himself and pronounces the word "mamma" twice (p. 26), he quickly reminds himself that the word composed of these particular sounds may just as well "signify some other thing" (H, 26).

But the "empty space of indeterminacy" provides Beckett with a remarkable "subject." In a lyric poem written in

[40] *Modern Poetry and the Idea of Language*, p. 181.

French in 1948, the dream sequences of *How It Is* exist in embryo:

je suis ce cours de sable qui glisse
entre le galet et la dune
la pluie d'été pleut sur ma vie
sur moi ma vie qui me fuit me poursuit
et finira le jour de son commencement

cher instant je te vois
dans ce rideau de brume qui recule
où je n'aurai plus à fouler ces long seuils mouvants
et vivrai le temps d'une porte
qui s'ouvre et se referme

(CP, 56)

Beckett's rather loose English translation is on the facing page:

my way is in the sand flowing
between the shingle and the dune
the summer rain rains on my life
on me my life harrying fleeing
to its beginning to its end

my peace is there in the receding mist
where I may cease from treading these long shifting thresholds
and live the space of a door
that opens and shuts

(CP, 57)[41]

What does it mean to exist in the shifting sands "between the shingle and the dune," to "live the space of a door /

[41] This is a case where Beckett doesn't do justice to his own poem. The English version has none of the subtle sound patterning found in the French (e.g., "je *s*ui*s* *c*e cours de *s*able qui gli*ss*e"); the meaning of lines 4-5 is largely lost: a literal translation would give us "on me my life which escapes me pursues me / and will end on the day of its beginning"; the important sixth line is omitted altogether as is the image of "the curtain of receding mist." Finally "time" (of a door) oddly becomes "space."

that opens and shuts"? Suggestive as they are, Beckett's dream images refuse to divulge what he called a "notion." "Je suis ce cours de sable" brings to mind a painting by Magritte, say *The Field-Glass* of 1963 (Figure 13). Here too, "le temps d'une porte" (or "the space of a door" as it is altered to read in the English version) becomes an unsolvable mystery. For on this canvas, in the left-hand pane of the door-window, we see cloud shapes that may be (1) the real sky seen through the glass; (2) the reflection of the sky from another source; or (3) a painted window-shade. But the right half of the window defies the logic of any of these possibilities. For the skyscape is now, oddly, behind the window frame, eliminating the second and third possibilities just mentioned. And the window is slightly ajar on the darkness beyond, thus negating the first one.[42] As Magritte explains such phenomena:

> A door could very well open on a landscape seen upside down, or the landscape could be painted on the door. Let us try something less arbitrary: next to the door let us make a hole in the wall which is another door also. This encounter will be perfected if we reduce these two objects to a single one. The hole takes its position, therefore, quite naturally in the door, and through this hole one can see the darkness. This image could be enriched still more if one were to illuminate the invisible thing hidden by the darkness.[43]

"The invisible thing hidden by the darkness"—it is the same possibility that haunts Beckett when he says: "Chèr instant je te vois / dans ce rideau de brume qui recule." This "chèr instant" is, in Jasper Johns' words, the moment when a thing "becomes other than it is," "the moment in

[42] On this point, see Suzy Gablik, *Magritte* (Boston: New York Graphic Society, 1976), p. 97. The analogy to Magritte is also made by Hugh Kenner (*Reader's Guide*, pp. 56-57), although Kenner does not refer to a specific painting.

[43] Cited by Suzy Gablik, *Magritte*, p. 97.

which one identifies a thing precisely."[44] But the door, enigmatically planted on the empty beach, opens and shuts over and over again, leaving the poet to wrestle with the curtain of receding mist, with "the fragility of the outer meaning."

[44] See John Ashbery, "Brooms and Prisms," *Art News*, 65 (March 1966), 82.

CHAPTER SEVEN

"Mysteries of Construction": The Dream Songs of John Ashbery

—I wrote about what I didn't see. The experience that eluded me somehow intrigued me more than the one I was having, and this has happened to me down through the years.

—John Ashbery[1]

I

In 1955 both Frank O'Hara and John Ashbery entered the annual competition for the Yale Younger Poets Award. The outcome of this contest is one of the nice ironies of literary history. The judge that year was W. H. Auden, and he originally declared that none of the manuscripts submitted deserved to win the prize. But then, by Ashbery's account, the following happened:

> . . . someone, a mutual friend, possibly Chester Kallman, told Auden—by that time he'd gone to Ischia for the summer—that Frank and I both submitted. And he asked us through his friend to send our manuscripts, which we did, and then he chose mine, although I never had felt that he particularly liked my poetry, and his introduction to the book is rather curious, since it doesn't really talk about the poetry. He mentions me as being a kind of successor to Rimbaud, which is very flattering, but at the same time I've always had the feeling that Auden probably never read Rimbaud. He was very outspokenly anti-French.[2]

[1] Sue Gangel, "An Interview with John Ashbery," *San Francisco Review of Books*, 3 (November 1977), 12.

[2] See David Kermani, excerpts from unpublished interview with John

Auden's Foreword to *Some Trees*, published by Yale in 1956, *is* a curious document. The comparison between Ashbery and Rimbaud leads Auden to the following rather back-handed compliment:

> Where Wordsworth had asked the question, "What is the language really used by men?" Rimbaud substituted the question, "What is the language really used by the imagining mind?"
>
> In "Les Illuminations" he attempted to discover this new rhetoric, and every poet who, like Mr. Ashbery, has similar interests has the same problem. . . . the danger for a poet working with the subjective life is . . . realizing that, if he is to be true to nature in this world, he must accept strange juxtapositions of imagery, singular associations of ideas, he is tempted to manufacture calculated oddities as if the subjectively sacred were necessarily and on all accounts odd.[3]

This emphasis on Ashbery's "calculated oddities," his "strange juxtapositions of imagery" is put even more bluntly in Auden's letter of rejection to O'Hara:

> I'm sorry to have to tell you that, after much heart searching I chose John's poems. It's really very awkward when the only two possible candidates are both friends.
>
> This doesn't mean that I don't like your work; lots of the poems I like very much, in particular *Jane Awake*.
>
> I think you (and John too, for that matter) must watch what is always the great danger with any "surrealistic" style, namely of confusing authentic non-logical relations

---

Ashbery, New York City, 2 June 1974, in *John Ashbery: A Comprehensive Bibliography* (New York and London: Garland Publishing, Inc., 1976), p. 6.

[3] Foreword to *Some Trees*, Yale Series of Younger Poets, 52 (New Haven: Yale University Press, 1956), p. 16. This foreword was not reprinted in the second edition (New York: Corinth Books, 1970), nor is it included in the reprint of that edition by the Ecco Press, New York, 1978.

which arouse wonder with accidental ones which arouse mere surprise and in the end fatigue.[4]

It is hardly surprising that Auden would have misgivings about a poetic style so seemingly unlike his own, and so startling a departure from the carefully controlled neo-Symbolist poetry that dominated the early fifties.[5] What I find especially interesting, however, is that, despite Auden's evident reservations about Ashbery's poetry, he did make precisely the right connections:

> From Rimbaud down to Mr. Ashbery, an important school of modern poets has been concerned with the discovery that, in childhood largely, in dreams and daydreams entirely, the imaginative life of the human individual stubbornly continues to live by the old magical notions. Its world is one of sacred images and ritual acts . . . a numinous landscape inhabited by demons and strange beasts.
>
> (p. 13)

Or, as Ashbery was to put it in *Three Poems* (1972), "the magic world really does exist" (TP, 16).[6] When, for ex-

[4] Unpublished letter to Frank O'Hara, 3 June 1955. Quoted by permission of Edward Mendelson, Literary Executor of the Estate of W. H. Auden. Copyright © 1977 by the Estate of W. H. Auden.

[5] See my *Frank O'Hara: Poet among Painters* (New York: George Braziller, 1977; rpt. Austin: University of Texas Press, 1979), Chapter One, passim; and my essay " 'Transparent Selves': The Poetry of John Ashbery and Frank O'Hara," *The Yearbook of English Studies*: American Literature Special Number, 8 (Modern Humanities Research Association, 1978), pp. 171-196.

[6] The following abbreviations of Ashbery's books are used throughout this chapter:

ST	*Some Trees* (1956; rpt. New York: Ecco Press, 1978).
TCO	*The Tennis Court Oath* (Middletown: Wesleyan University Press, 1962).
RM	*Rivers and Mountains* (1966; rpt. New York: Ecco Press, 1977).
DDS	*The Double Dream of Spring* (1970; rpt. New York: Ecco Press, 1976).
TP	*Three Poems* (New York: Viking Press, 1972).
SP	*Self-Portrait in a Convex Mirror* (New York: Viking Press, 1975).

ample, Robert Frost's "I" came upon "two roads" that "diverged in a yellow wood," he felt he had to choose one or the other. In the dream landscape of "The System," it works out differently:

> That's the way it goes. For many weeks you have been exploring what seemed to be a profitable way of doing. You discovered that there was a fork in the road, so first you followed what seemed to be the less promising, or at any rate the more obvious, of the two branches until you felt you had a good idea of where it led. Then you returned to investigate the more tangled way, and for a time its intricacies seemed to promise a more complex and therefore a more practical goal for you, one that could be picked up in any number of ways so that all its faces or applications could be thoroughly scrutinized. And in so doing you began to realize that the two branches were joined together again, farther ahead; that this *place of joining* was indeed the end, and that it was the very place you set out from, whose *intolerable mixture of reality and fantasy* had started you on the road which has now come full circle. It has been an *absorbing puzzle.* . . .
>
> (TP, 90, my italics)

Ashbery's narrator does not look forward to a time when he will be telling one and all that he "took the [road] less traveled by, / And that has made all the difference." For in the place where reality meets dream, choice becomes an irrelevancy; what matters is that two paths that are separate can mysteriously join together. Or maybe there never were two.

This "absorbing puzzle," the ongoing process of "waking up / In the middle of a dream with one's mouth full / Of unknown words" (SP, 55), is not to be confused with the Romantic yearning for transcendence, the longing to enter

---

HD *Houseboat Days* (New York: Viking Press, 1977).
AWK *As We Know* (New York: Viking Press, 1979).

some other-worldly realm. Ashbery has little in common with Yeats's "Man Who Dreamed of Faeryland." On the contrary, the poet casts a cold eye on the seemingly endless round of epiphanies his contemporaries say they are experiencing. Thus, in reviewing Philip Booth's *Weathers and Edges* in 1966, Ashbery remarks: "Rare is the grain of sand in which [Booth] can't spot the world; seagulls, dories, and schools of herring are likewise windows on eternity, until we begin to suspect that he is in direct, hot-line communication with it."[7]

Not *what* one dreams but *how*—this is Ashbery's subject. His stories "tell only of themselves," presenting the reader with the challenge of what he calls "an open field of narrative possibilities" (TP, 41). For, like Rimbaud's, his are not dreams "about" such and such characters or events; the dream structure is itself the event that haunts the poet's imagination. As he put it in an essay on Gertrude Stein, written shortly after the publication of *Some Trees*:

> *Stanzas in Meditation* gives one the feeling of time passing, of things happening, of a "plot," though it would be difficult to say precisely what is going on. Sometimes the story has the logic of a dream . . . while at other times it becomes startlingly clear for a moment, as though a change in the wind had suddenly enabled us to hear a conversation that was taking place some distance away. . . . But it is usually not events which interest Miss Stein, rather it is their "way of happening," and the story of *Stanzas in Meditation* is a general, all-purpose model which each reader can adapt to fit his own set of particulars. The poem is a hymn to possibility. . . .[8]

What Ashbery means by a "hymn to possibility" can be understood by comparing his "Rivers and Mountains" (1966) to a poem that may well have been its source, Auden's "Mountains" (1952), which begins:

[7] *New York Herald Tribune: Book World,* 3, no. 42 (4 September 1966), 2.
[8] "The Impossible," *Poetry,* 90, no. 4 (July 1957), 251.

I know a retired dentist who only paints mountains,
But the Masters rarely care
That much, who sketch them in beyond a holy face
Or a highly dangerous chair;
While a normal eye perceives them as a wall
Between worse and better, like a child, scolded in France,
Who wishes he were crying on the Italian side of the Alps:
Caesar does not rejoice when high ground
Makes a darker map,
Nor does Madam. Why should they? A serious being
Cries out for a gap.

And it is curious how often in steep places
You meet someone short who frowns,
A type you catch beheading daisies with a stick. . . .[9]

Here Auden is exploring the ideas human beings have invented about physical nature, specifically the stale Romantic notion that mountains connote strength and grandeur. For what are mountains really but objects that retired dentists like to paint? (The Old Masters knew better!) And whom do we see scaling their heights but vulgar little types who behead daisies with their walking sticks? The Julius Caesars, for whom those "dark" places on the map were a special nuisance, have been replaced by "unsmiling parties, / Clumping off at dawn in the gear of their mystery / For points up." And so it goes from stanza to stanza. Auden's tone is sophisticated, wry, bemused, gently satiric—as if to say that he himself is also a bit foolish for getting annoyed about such trivia. For isn't the idea of nature (as distinct from its particular manifestations) benign and lovable?

"Mountains" is a witty dissection of human pretensions and rationalizations. But what are we to make of Ashbery's "Rivers and Mountains"?

On the secret map the assassins
Cloistered, the Moon River was marked

[9] *Collected Poems* (New York: Random House, 1976), pp. 428-429.

Near the eighteen peaks and the city
Of humiliation and defeat—wan ending
Of the trail among dry, papery leaves
Gray-brown quills like thoughts
In the melodious but vast mass of today's
Writing through fields and swamps
Marked, on the map, with little bunches of weeds.

. . . .

Your plan was to separate the enemy into two groups
With the razor-edged mountains between.
It worked well on paper
But their camp had grown
To be the mountains and the map
Carefully peeled away and not torn
Was the light. . . .

(RM, 10-11)

We know from Auden's context how to regard "retired dentists who only paint mountains," and it is amusing to think of the child, scolded in France, wishing himself on the other side of the Alps. But what are we to make of this "secret map" where unidentifiable assassins are cloistered? Are the mountains real or do they only exist as marks on a map? Further, is the map real or are the Moon River and eighteen peaks to be found on some sort of board game in which toy soldiers battle? Is the poet alluding to a comic strip? An adventure film? A travelogue? Or is the strange landscape that emerges a fantasy on a postage-stamp scene ("a stamp could reproduce all this / In detail")? The reader can invent any number of plots and locations that fit this "all-purpose model," but there is finally no way of knowing what these war games signify. Auden playfully reminds us that "perfect monsters—remember Dracula—/Are bred on crags in castles," but Ashbery's "secret map" allows for no such connections to be made, for we can identify neither the monsters nor the crags. The land, after all, "Was made of paper."

It would be easy to conclude that Ashbery's poetry is

merely incoherent, that anything goes. Robert Boyers' strictures in the *Times Literary Supplement* (1978) are typical: "If we take meaning to refer to the possibility of shared discourse in which speaker and auditor may participate more or less equally," then "Ashbery is an instance of a poet who, through much of his career, eliminates meaning without achieving any special intensity. . . . Meaning is often left out of an Ashbery poem . . . to ensure the continuity of a quest for which ends are necessarily threatening."[10]

This is to regard *meaning* as some sort of fixed quantity (like two pounds of sugar or a dozen eggs) that the poet as speaker can either "leave out" or proffer to the expectant auditor with whom he is engaged in "shared discourse." But, as Ashbery suggests in his remarks on Gertrude Stein, there are other ways of generating meaning, of creating the "transparency" he admires in the poetry of Reverdy, for whom "a canal and a factory" are not symbolic counters but "living phenomena"[11] Consider the following poem from *Houseboat Days* (1977):

The Other Tradition

They all came, some wore sentiments
Emblazoned on T-shirts, proclaiming the lateness
Of the hour, and indeed the sun slanted its rays
Through branches of Norfolk Island pine as though
Politely clearing its throat, and all ideas settled
In a fuzz of dust under trees when it's drizzling:
The endless games of Scrabble, the boosters,
The celebrated omelette au Cantal, and through it

[10] "A Quest without an Object" (review of *Houseboat Days*), *Times Literary Supplement*, 1 September 1978, p. 962; cf. Roger Shattuck, review of *Houseboat Days*, *New York Review of Books*, 25, no. 4 (23 March 1978), 38. "Fantasia of a Nut-Brown Maid," writes Shattuck, conveys "the sense of a container without contents."

[11] See "Reverdy en Amérique," *Mercure de France* (Special Issue: Pierre Reverdy), 344 (January/April 1962), 110-111. I am translating from Ashbery's French.

The roar of time plunging unchecked through the
  sluices
Of the days, dragging every sexual moment of it
Past the lenses: the end of something.
Only then did you glance up from your book,
Unable to comprehend what had been taking place, or
Say what you had been reading. More chairs
Were brought, and lamps were lit, but it tells
Nothing of how all this proceeded to materialize
Before you and the people waiting outside and in the
  next
Street, repeating its name over and over, until silence
Moved halfway up the darkened trunks,
And the meeting was called to order.
                                        I still remember
How they found you, after a dream, in your thimble hat,
Studious as a butterfly in a parking lot.
The road home was nicer then. Dispersing, each of the
Troubadours had something to say about how charity
Had run its race and won, leaving you the ex-president
Of the event, and how, though many of those present
Had wished something to come of it, if only a distant
Wisp of smoke, yet none was so deceived as to hanker
After that cool non-being of just a few minutes before,
Now that the idea of a forest had clamped itself
Over the minutiae of the scene. You found this
Charming, but turned your face fully toward night,
Speaking into it like a megaphone, not hearing
Or caring, although these still live and are generous
And all ways contained, allowed to come and go
Indefinitely in and out of the stockade
They have so much trouble remembering, when your
  forgetting
Rescues them at last as a star absorbs the night.
(HD, 2-3)

This elusive narrative is what Ashbery calls in an earlier poem "a puzzle scene." The very verse form is equivocal, for Ashbery's loose blank verse (the lines range from four to six stresses and from nine to fifteen syllables) is overwhelmed by the prose rhythm of his purposely clumsy long sentences—sentences that spill over successive lines with their complicated subordinate clauses and qualifiers:

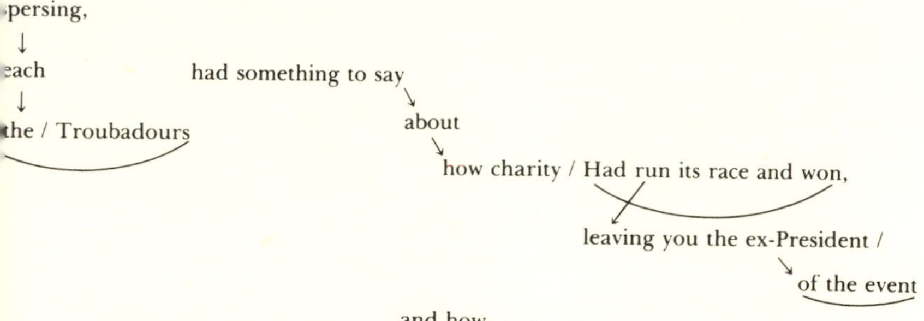
persing,
each
the / Troubadours
had something to say
about
how charity / Had run its race and won,
leaving you the ex-President /
of the event
and how. . . .

Such verse, Northrop Frye has suggested, represents a kind of inverse euphuism: "the prose element in the diction and syntax is so strong that the features of verse still remaining give it the effect of continuous parody. This is the area of intentional doggerel. . . . Here again, as with euphuism, we are moving in an atmosphere of paradox, and also discontinuity."[12]

Parody and discontinuity are, of course, also operative on the semantic level of Ashbery's poem. "The Other Tradition" presents a series of arresting visual images, akin to Reverdy's "living phenomena," that don't seem to add up. Who, to begin with, are these people who "came" late in the day to this setting of "Norfolk Island pine" and what are they doing? The "endless games of Scrabble" and "celebrated omelette au Cantal" suggest that the "event" of line 27 is some sort of house party, but a house party is of limited duration whereas this happening is characterized by "The roar of time plunging unchecked through the

[12] *The Well-Tempered Critic* (Bloomington: Indiana University Press, 1963), pp. 69-70.

sluices / Of the days, dragging every sexual moment of it / Past the lenses." Perhaps the "event" is an Encounter Group session? A religious retreat? A stay in a sanatorium or mental hospital? The "stockade" which "They have so much trouble remembering" suggests a prison. The forest setting—"branches of Norfolk Island pine," "fuzz of dust under trees," "darkened trunks"—implies that some kind of ancient rite is taking place. At the same time, the forest borders on "the next / Street," and "More chairs / Were brought, and lamps were lit," as "the meeting was called to order." Perhaps this is a political rally; on the way home, the "you" speaks into the night "like a megaphone." But in that case, why are the participants of the "event" called "Troubadours"? Dozens of provocative and possible stories suggest themselves.

The pronouns, as always in Ashbery, create confusion for readers who look for logic and continuity. Here the poet's own explanation, which I cited in Chapter Two, is helpful:

> The personal pronouns in my work very often seem to be like variables in an equation. "You" can be myself or it can be another person, someone whom I'm addressing, and so can "he" and "she" for that matter and "we" . . . . my point is also that it doesn't really matter very much, that we are somehow all aspects of a consciousness giving rise to the poem and the fact of addressing someone, myself or someone else, is what's the important thing at that particular moment rather than the particular person involved. I guess I don't have a very strong sense of my own identity and I find it very easy to move from one person in the sense of a pronoun to another and this again helps to produce a kind of polyphony in my poetry which I again feel is a means toward a greater naturalism.[13]

[13] See Janet Bloom and Robert Losada, "Craft Interview with John Ashbery," *New York Quarterly*, 9 (Winter 1972), 24-25.

Once it is understood that for Ashbery, "we are somehow all aspects of a consciousness giving rise to the poem," that identity is fluid and fragmented, the shifting pronouns ("They—"you"—"I") become less vexing. The point is that the poet is at once a participant ("ex-president / Of the event") and an observer; he views the incidents recorded both from outside and inside, from the vantage point of the past as well as the present and projected future. This is the "polyphony" Ashbery speaks of.[14] Or, to use the analogy of film, we have shifting perspectives on certain phenomena that are themselves on the brink of dissolving. Thus, when the narrator says, "I still remember / How they found you after a dream, in your thimble hat, / Studious as a butterfly in a parking lot," he seems to be addressing himself, but the "I-you" dichotomy creates distance, the present self remembering its former incarnation as solitary reader. Or again, the studious "you" who wears a "thimble hat" may be a close friend or lover. In either case, the import of the little scene remains unclear for the analogy to the "butterfly in the parking lot" is purely fanciful, evoking what Ashbery has called "Märchenbilder" (SP, 59), in this case perhaps "Thumbelina." All we can safely say is that the "I" and "you" are at once part of the "they" and yet detached from "them," just as the setting is both outdoors in the pine forest and indoors in a lamp-lit meeting room, and just as the characters are simultaneously up-to-date (with "sentiments / Emblazoned on T-shirts") and medieval: "Troubadours" dreaming under their "thimble hat[s]."

The logic of "The Other Tradition" is thus that of a dream; there is no way we can say "precisely what is going on." But the "way of happening" is carefully worked out. However open the meaning of individual lines or passages may be, images do coalesce to create, not a coherent nar-

[14] For a musical analysis of Ashbery's "polyphony," see Lawrence Kramer, " 'Syringa': John Ashbery and Elliot Carter," in *John Ashbery: Essays on the Poetry* (Ithaca: Cornell University Press, 1980), pp. 255-271.

rative with a specific theme, but a precise tonality of feeling.

Consider the title of the poem. Some readers have remarked that Ashbery titles are annoying because they seem to have nothing to do with the words that follow. But in most instances, the title resonates, not just with images from the poem which it names, but from earlier ones. "The Other Tradition," for example, was introduced in *Three Poems*:

> There was, however, a residue, a kind of fiction that developed parallel to the classic truths of daily life (as it was in that heroic but commonplace age) as they unfolded with the foreseeable majesty of a holocaust. . . . It is this "other tradition" which we propose to explore. The facts of history have been too well rehearsed . . . to require further elucidation here. But the other, unrelated happenings that form a kind of sequence of fantastic reflections as they succeed each other at a pace and according to an inner necessity of their own—these, I say, have hardly ever been looked at from a vantage point other than the historian's and an arcane historian's at that. The living aspect of these obscure phenomena has never to my knowledge been examined from a point of view like the painter's: in the round. . . .
>
> (TP, 55-56)

This passage provides us with interesting clues. Not the "facts of history" but the "other, unrelated happenings that form a kind of sequence of fantastic reflections"—this is the subject of the poem. Not, in Aristotle's terms, "what actually happened," but "what could and would happen either probably or inevitably." Ashbery wants to examine the "living aspect of these obscure phenomena . . . from a point of view like the painter's: in the round." So, when we return to the poem, we see that Ashbery has created a "Märchenbild" that is rather like a Max Ernst *frottage*. In fairy tales, form is fixed (the plot begins with "Once upon a time" and moves, through a series of turns and counterturns—spells, enchantments, mistaken identities, accidents—to its dénouement: "they lived happily ever after"), but content is peculiarly fluid; events that are highly concrete and particular are open to any number of interpretations. So, in "The Other Tradition," Ashbery has created a dream plot that "each reader can adapt . . . to fit his own set of particulars."

Does this imply that the poem can mean anything one likes? Not at all. However one interprets the "event" Ashbery relates—rite, orgy, meeting, rally, party, retreat, Encounter Session, or a combination of these—clearly "The Other Tradition" is a kind of Proustian memory poem in which the narrator relives an especially haunting incident, a turning-point, whether real or imaginary, from his past. As Ashbery says of Raymond Roussel's poem "La Vue," "the poet, like a prisoner fascinated by the appearance of the wall of his cell, remains transfixed by the spectacle before his eyes."[15] One thinks immediately of Plato's cave, whose inhabitants, having had a fleeting glimpse of the light outside, now contemplate the flickering shadows of passing objects, "the fragments of a buried life you once knew," as Ashbery puts it in *Three Poems* (TP, 86). The event is "over," and the poet can only look at the cave wall, trying to find some pattern in the perpetually shifting shapes before him. So objects are outlined: "More chairs / Were brought, and lamps were lit." "For a moment," as Ashbery says of Stein's *Stanzas in Meditation*, "the story becomes startlingly clear as though a change in wind had suddenly enabled us to hear a conversation that was taking place some distance away." Then the images grow faint until "forgetting / Rescues them at last, as a star absorbs the night." And so they fade into the light of common day.

It has been suggested, notably by Alfred Corn, that poems like "The Other Tradition" are to be understood as "imitations of consciousness." "Their ambition," says Corn, "is to render as much psychic life as will go onto the

[15] "On Raymond Roussel," *Portfolio and Art News Annual*, 6 (Autumn 1962); rpt. in *Raymond Roussel, How I Wrote Certain of My Books*, ed. and trans. Trevor Winkfield (New York: Sun, 1977), p. 51.

page—perceptions, emotions, and concepts, memory and daydream, thought in all its random and contradictory character, patterned according to the 'wave interference' produced by all the constituting elements of mind."[16] But how "random" is the "psychic life" put down on the page here? It seems to me that, on the contrary, Ashbery's dream structure is highly formalized. For the chronology of the "event" provides Ashbery with a particular procedure, a way of incorporating the contradictions between "I" and "they," between indoors and outdoors, parking-lot and forest, sunlight and drizzle, omelettes and booster shots, noise and silence, union and separation, the "sexual moment" and the solitary absorption in "your book." Ashbery's is, we might say, a world where "A" can always be "B," where "silence / Moved halfway up the darkened trunks, / And the meeting was called to order."

Here Ashbery's remarks on Raymond Roussel, whom Cocteau called "the Proust of dreams," are apposite:

> What [Roussel] leaves us with is a work that is like the perfectly preserved temple of a cult which has disappeared without a trace, or a complicated set of tools whose use cannot be discovered. . . .
>
> [His] language . . . seems always on the point of revealing its secret, of pointing the way back to the "republic of dreams" whose insignia blazed on his forehead.[17]

Language always on the point of revealing its secret—this pattern of opening and closing, of revelation and re-veiling, of simultaneous disclosure and concealment is the structural principle of the Ashbery poem. Like Duchamp's *Large Glass*, such an enigma text endlessly generates the impulse that makes the reader yearn for completion and understanding. In Roger Cardinal's words, "the receiver knows that a signal *is* being emitted, but his connection with the

[16] "A Magma of Interiors," *Parnassus: Poetry in Review*, 4 (Fall/Winter 1975), 224.

[17] "On Raymond Roussel," p. 55.

transmitter seems to be on a faulty line." It is in this sense that Roussel's work is like "a complicated set of tools whose use cannot be discovered." To read such a text, says Cardinal, "is like being given a key only to learn that the locks have been changed."[18]

II

To invent persuasive "mysteries of construction" is by no means easy, as anyone who has read the countless imitations of Ashbery currently breaking into print knows. Too much disclosure produces contrivance; too much concealment, unintelligibility and boredom. In Ashbery's early poems, these twin dangers are not always avoided. Consider "The Instruction Manual," which appeared in *Some Trees*. Ashbery recalls that he wrote this poem when he was working for McGraw-Hill in New York as a writer and editor, not quite of instruction manuals but of college textbooks: "The poem really ends with me returning to the boring task I have to do, where the poem began. It leads back into me, and is probably about the dissatisfaction with the work I was doing at the time. And my lack of success in seeing the city I wanted most to see, when I was in Mexico. Mostly because the name held so much promise: Guadalajara."[19]

"The Instruction Manual" begins:

As I sit looking out of a window of the building
I wish I did not have to write the instruction manual
  on the uses of a new metal.
I look down into the street and see people, each
  walking with an inner peace,
And envy them—they are so far away from me!
Not one of them has to worry about getting out this
  manual on schedule.
And, as my way is, I begin to dream, resting my

[18] "Enigma," *20th Century Studies*, 12 (December 1974), 45, 56.

[19] See "Interview with John Ashbery," *San Francisco Review of Books*, 12.

elbows on the desk and leaning out of the window a
little,
Of dim Guadalajara! City of rose-colored flowers!
(ST, 14)

Bored with the dreary instruction manual he has to prepare, the poet conjures up vivid and exotic images of Guadalajara, with its "flower girls, handing out rose- and lemon-colored flowers," its bandstand musicians "in their creamy white uniforms," its "houses of pink and white, and its crumbling leafy terraces." The poem's structure is that of a travelogue: here is the poorer quarter, there is the market, here is an old woman sitting in a patio, and so on. Finally the narrator exclaims:

How limited, but how complete withal, has been our
experience of Guadalajara!
We have seen young love, married love, and the love
of an aged mother for her son.
We have heard music, tasted the drinks, and looked at
colored houses.
What more is there to do, except stay? And that we
cannot do.
And as a last breeze freshens the top of the weathered
old tower, I turn my gaze
Back to the instruction manual which has made me
dream of Guadalajara.
(ST, 18)

The reality-dream-reality structure of "The Instruction Manual" is a version of the Greater Romantic Lyric as Meyer Abrams and others have defined it. A determinate speaker in a particular setting (looking out of the window of the building) is moved by a certain stimulus—in this case, the pages of the instruction manual—to reverie or daydream. "Such a poem," writes Abrams, "usually rounds upon itself to end where it began, at the outer scene, but with an altered mood and deepening understanding which is the result of the intervening meditation."[20] Although Ashbery's speaker does not achieve the epiphany toward which the Greater Romantic Lyric usually builds (his dream of Guadalajara is a pleasant escape fantasy rather than a transforming psychic event), "The Instruction Manual" does have the out-in-out form characteristic of Romantic poems like "Tintern Abbey" or "Frost at Midnight." Indeed, its three-act division—Before the Dream, the Dream, and After the Dream—is so neat that one might suspect Ashbery of parodying an established genre, especially since the long Whitmanesque lines that frame the daydream itself here express the very opposite of Romantic ecstasy. The speaker seems to be yawning.[21]

"The Instruction Manual" is not, in any case, a representative Ashbery poem, which is probably why it has been so frequently anthologized. Even in his earliest work, Ashbery rarely makes things so easy for himself or for his reader. In the opening poem of *Some Trees*, "Two Scenes," the interplay of fact and fantasy is much more complex:

I

We see us as we truly behave:
From every corner comes a distinctive offering.
The train comes bearing joy;
The sparks it strikes illuminate the table.
Destiny guides the water-pilot, and it is destiny.
For long we hadn't heard so much news, such noise.
The day was warm and pleasant.
"We see you in your hair,
Air resting around the tips of mountains."

[20] "Structure and Style in the Greater Romantic Lyric," in *From Sensibility to Romanticism: Essays Presented to Frederick A. Pottle*, ed. Frederick W. Hilles and Harold Bloom (New York: Oxford, 1965), p. 528. See also Robert Langbaum, *The Poetry of Experience* (New York: Norton, 1957), Chapter One, passim.

[21] On this point, see David Shapiro, *John Ashbery*, Columbia Introductions to Twentieth-Century American Poetry (New York: Columbia University Press, 1979), p. 37.

II

A fine rain anoints the canal machinery.
This is perhaps a day of general honesty
Without example in the world's history
Though the fumes are not of a singular authority
And indeed as dry as poverty.
Terrific units are on an old man
In the blue shadow of some paint cans
As laughing cadets say, "In the evening
Everything has a schedule, if you can find out what it
is."

(ST, 9)

The opening line, "We see us as we truly behave," immediately recalls the Wallace Stevens of "What we see is what we think," or "We make, although inside an egg / variations on the words spread sail" ("An Ordinary Evening in New Haven"). The phrase "dry as poverty" in line 14 echoes Stevens' "The Ordinary Women": "Then from their poverty they rose, / From dry catarrhs. . . ." Like Stevens, Ashbery is fond of using abstract nouns in prepositional constructions: "A day of general honesty," "Without example in the world's history," "the fumes are not of a singular authority," and so on. Like Stevens, he has a predilection for qualifiers ("This is perhaps a day"; "Everything has a schedule, if you can find out what it is"), and he prefers intransitive and copulative verbs to transitive ones.

Yet even in this early "Stevensian" poem,[22] Ashbery turns the Stevens mode on its head by cutting off the referential dimension. "Two Scenes" is not like, say, "Credences of Summer," the reverie of a particular speaker who "meditates / With the gold bugs, in blue meadows, late at night," the time being midsummer when "the mind lays by its

[22] The "abiding influence of Stevens" on Ashbery is a theme running through all of Harold Bloom's commentaries on Ashbery: see especially, "John Ashbery: The Charity of the Hard Moments," *Figures of Capable Imagination* (New York: The Seabury Press, 1976), pp. 169-208.

trouble and considers," it being "a long way / To the first autumnal inhalations."[23]

Ashbery's poem rejects any such continuities. "Two Scenes" presents us with "clear visual images," to use Eliot's phrase about Dante, but Ashbery's are "clear visual images" that have no discernible referents. The "laughing cadets," the "water-pilot," the "tips of mountains"—these are arresting images of some mysterious truth half-glimpsed, but their signification is purposely left blurred and open. In the first dream scene, there are references to light, sparks, warmth, hair, water, and mountains; in the second, to rain, fumes, a canal, drought, poverty, and paint cans. How the second evolves out of the first is an "absorbing puzzle." One can invent a story about a "train bringing joy," possibly carrying a group of "laughing cadets" into the mountains, possibly passing a canal where a "water-pilot" waves to them. I am reminded of the train emerging from the flowering Russian steppes, so gorgeously filmed in *Dr. Zhivago*. But many other films or fictions come to mind. "Everything has a schedule if you can find out what it is," but the trouble is that you can never find out. We cannot even identify the "you" of line eight: "We see you in your hair." The only certainty is that, as in "The Other Tradition," everything shifts ground before our eyes: the "sparks" that "illuminate the table" go out; the "Air resting around the tips of mountains" gives way to a "fine rain anoint[ing] the canal machinery," and when the rain dries up, strong fumes appear, perhaps from the "blue shadow" of the old man's "paint cans." The "distinctive offering" promised at the outset never seems to come. And yet the cadets are "laughing." Maybe the "preparatory dream" (TP, 7) will return. In its fidelity to "a way of happening" rather than to "what happens," "Two Scenes" anticipates Ashbery's later work.

But before that later work came into being, Ashbery wrote the poems collected in *The Tennis Court Oath* (1962). Here the balance sometimes tips the other way: disclosure

[23] *The Palm at the End of the Mind, Selected Poems and a Play*, ed. Holly Stevens (New York: Alfred A. Knopf, 1971), pp. 287-292.

is so totally blocked that the reader is all but excluded from the world of the text; one's connection with the transmitter seems to be, not on a faulty line which allows for expectation and suspense, but on no line at all. The collage poem "Europe" is a case in point. Its 111 sections are chiefly cut-ups from a childrens' book called *Beryl of the Bi-Planes*, which Ashbery found on a Paris quai. Here are the first five sections:

1.

To employ her
construction ball
Morning fed on the
light blue wood
of the mouth
                    cannot understand
(feels deeply)

2.

A wave of nausea—
numerals

3.

a few berries

4.

the unseen claw
Babe asked today
The background of poles roped over
into star jolted them

5.

filthy or into backward drenched flung heaviness
lemons asleep pattern crying

(TCO, 64)

As we make our way through successive sections, the story of Beryl's zeppelin ride and parachute jumps, her narrow escape from a bomb threat, and the mysterious detective story about "Ronald Pryor" and a man named Collins, appear in bits and pieces. We can, if we care to, reconstitute the plot of the pulp novel which is Ashbery's source. Thus, if we begin with items like the "construction ball" of #1 and the "poles roped over" of #4, we find a connection to the shining "instruments" of #37, the "steel bolts" of #107, and the grand Morse Code finale of #111. But there is no further range of suggestiveness, no "language on the point of revealing its secret." Once we have put all the pieces on the table and have reassembled the jigsaw puzzle, the game is over. And this is precisely what "Europe" is—an amusing game, a kind of Surrealist *cadavre exquis*.

Ironically, the opacity of "Europe," its resolute refusal to relate meanings, is not attributable to its excessive disjunctiveness, as Harold Bloom, who calls the poem a "fearful disaster,"[24] seems to think. I would argue that it is, on the contrary, too one-dimensional, which is to say that it is not "disjunctive" enough. For here we don't have disparate images or voices coming together so as to form startling new conjunctions; rather, all the references are drawn from the same circle of discourse and so the seeming discontinuities are all on the surface. I shall have more to say of this later when I take up Ashbery's extraordinary new collage poem, the fifty-page "Litany."

"Europe" aside, *The Tennis Court Oath* contains many fine poems, especially the hallucinatory " 'They Dream Only Of America' " (TCO, 13), which I have discussed elsewhere.[25] Reading this "detective poem" is, as in the case of Rimbaud's *Illuminations*, like overhearing a conversation in

[24] *Figures of Capable Imagination*, p. 172. Bloom further says: "The Ashbery of *The Tennis Court Oath* may have been moved by De Kooning and Kline, Webern and Cage, but he was not moved to the writing of poems. Nor can I accept the notion that this was a necessary phase in the poet's development, for who can hope to find any necessity in this calculated incoherence?" (p. 175).

[25] " 'Transparent Selves,' " *Yearbook of English Studies*, pp. 186-187.

which one can make out individual words or phrases but has no clear idea what the speakers are talking about. Thus we have no trouble understanding a sentence like "This honey is delicious / *Though it burns the throat*," but we cannot tell who is saying these words to whom or why he or she should feel this way about honey. Or again, it makes no sense, rationally speaking, to compare a lake to a "lilac cube," but within the context of " 'They Dream,' " where we also find "thirteen million pillars of grass" and where those who hide "from darkness in barns . . . can be grown-ups now," such comparisons come to seem perfectly natural.

In the great series of Dream Songs that begins with "These Lacustrine Cities" (1966), landscape becomes increasingly fragile, the movement in and out of dream more fluid. Consider the following prose passage from "The New Spirit," which is the first section of *Three Poems*. The subject, in a very general way, is the rebirth of the self that comes when one falls in love.

> At this point an event of such glamor and such radiance occurred that you forgot the name all over again. It could be compared to arriving in an unknown city at night, intoxicated by the strange lighting and the ambiguities of the streets. The person sitting next to you turned to you, her voice broke and a kind of golden exuberance flooded over you just as you were lifting your arm to the luggage rack. At once the weight of the other years and above all the weight of distinguishing among them slipped away. You found yourself not wanting to care. Everything was guaranteed, it always had been, there would be no future, no end, no development except this steady wavering like a breeze that gently lifted the tired curtains day had let fall. And all the possibilities of civilization, such as travel, study, gastronomy, sexual fulfillment—these no longer lay around on the cankered earth like reproaches, hideous in their reminder of what never could be, but were possibilities that had always

> existed, had been created just for both of us to bring us to the summit of the dark way we had been traveling without ever expecting to find it ending. Indeed, without them nothing could have happened. Which is why the intervening space now came to advance toward us separately, a wave of music which we were, unable to grasp it as it unfolded but living it. That space was transfigured as though by hundreds and hundreds of tiny points of light like flares seen from a distance, gradually merging into one wall of even radiance like the sum of all their possible positions, plotted by coordinates, yet open to the movements and suggestions of this new life of action without development, a fixed flame.
>
> (TP, 37)

Ashbery's prose sounds deceptively reasonable and straightforward. One sentence follows another imperturbably: "At this point . . . ," "At once . . . ," "And all the possibilities . . . ," "Indeed. . . ." The tone is quiet, the language chaste, subdued, and given to abstraction: "glamor," "radiance," "the ambiguities of the streets," "the possibilities of civilization," "reproaches hideous in their reminder of what never could be," "the summit of the dark way." Adverbs of time abound: "all over again," "at night," "no longer," "gradually," "yet"; and similes, rarely used in the early work, are prominent: "these no longer lay around on the cankered earth like reproaches," "Hundreds of tiny points of light like flares seen from a distance," "one wall of even radiance like the sum of all their possible positions."

But the seeming continuity of Ashbery's paragraph is deceptive. What looks like a retrospective account of a specific event in the poet's life is decomposed at every turn so as to ensure fidelity to dream process, for to escape "the familiar interior which has always been there. . . . is impossible outside the frost of a dream, and it is just this major enchantment that gave us life to begin with, life for each other" (TP, 11). When asked why he used prose in *Three Poems*, Ashbery explained:

> The prose is something quite new. . . . suddenly the idea of it occurred to me as something new in which the arbitrary divisions of poetry into lines would get abolished. One wouldn't have to have these interfering and scanning the processes of one's thought as one was writing; the poetic form would be dissolved, in solution, and therefore create . . . more of a surrounding thing like the way one's consciousness is surrounded by one's thoughts. And I was also very attracted by the possibility of using very prosaic elements, conversation or journalese, what libraries classify as "non-fiction"; to extract what's frequently poetic and moving in these forms of communication which are very often apparent to us and which haven't been investigated very much in poetry.[26]

To "dissolve" the "poetic form," all the while "extracting what's frequently poetic" from the so-called "prosaic"—this is not, as reviewers of *Three Poems* have often maintained, simply to put down everything that happens to come into one's mind. Rather, the feat is, in Auden's words, "to arouse authentic non-logical relations that cause wonder." The syntax of Ashbery's first sentence, for example, looks straightforward: a simple subject-predicate unit followed by a subordinate result clause. But the "result" is a mystery, for we know neither what the "name" is that "you forgot . . . all over again," nor when "At this point" might have been. In the preceding section, Ashbery has alluded to the sudden disappearance of Rumpelstiltskin, "furious that you guessed the name," but in the new context—"At this point"—there is no certainty that the reference is still to the Grimm fairy tale.

Perhaps, then, the next sentences will shed light on "the event of such glamor and such radiance." We read on, expecting to find out what it was that happened. In the dream sequence that follows, the poet, distanced as "you," finds himself arriving in an unknown city at night, intoxicated by the "strange lighting." Something happens as if

[26] *New York Quarterly* Interview, p. 27.

in slow motion: "The person sitting next to you turned to you, her voice broke and a kind of golden exuberance flooded over you just as you were lifting your arm to the luggage rack." In this privileged moment, "At once the weight of the other years and above all the weight of distinguishing among them slipped away." The effect is Proustian but with a difference: in Ashbery's poem, the connection between stimulus and response is never established. The gesture of lifting one's arm to the luggage rack is not comparable to the tasting of the *petite madeleine* or the tying of the shoestring, particular actions that bring back to life a buried past in which these same actions occurred. In "The New Spirit," we have, as in " 'They Dream Only of America,' " or "These Lacustrine Cities," parts that belong to no whole—an absent totality. For we never come to know the larger story in which the arm, raised to the luggage rack, and the breaking voice of "The person sitting next to you" play a role.

Here it is illuminating to compare Ashbery to Beckett. The dream sequences in *How It Is* usually involve a specific narrative or a series of concrete images. The difficulty in reading them is that there is no way of knowing what such a narrative or image sequence means. When, for example, we come upon the lines:

> it does and I see a crocus in a pot in an area in a basement a saffron the sun creeps up the wall a hand keeps it in the sun this yellow flower with a string I see the hand long image hours long. . . .
>
> (H, 21)

we cannot explain why this particular "yellow flower with a string," held by an unknown hand arrests the poet's attention. Ashbery's procedure is rather different. He gives the reader fewer particulars, but then makes large conceptual statements that seem to depend on those particulars, scanty as they are. Thus the "golden exuberance" experienced during the incident with the luggage rack leads to the abstract formulation: "You found yourself not wanting to care." But immediately we ask, "care about *what* and *why*?"

In this context of absent causality, even familiar things become unfamiliar. The breeze that gently lifts "the tired curtains day had let fall," for instance, is, of course, the Romantic symbol of rebirth, an influx of inspiration, a renewal of creativity. Yet here it is hard to say who has been reborn or what changes result on account of the "correspondent breeze." The "possibilities of civilization" now lie open to the poet and his beloved; "without them," he declares, "nothing could have happened." But then nothing does happen. The "Which is why" clause that follows promises a connection where none exists. One can only say that at certain moments, unpredictable and unaccountable, the self is deflected from the "summit of the dark way we have been traveling" and experiences "the intervening space" coming toward it as a "wave of music." And when this happens, the "space [is] transfigured as though by hundreds and hundreds of tiny points of light like flares seen from a distance."

This last passage recalls Stevens: for example, the "fragrant portal, dimly starred" of "The Idea of Order at Key West." But Stevens' impassioned address to his friend ("Oh! Blessed rage for order, pale Ramon"), in which these words are embedded is a response to a particular landscape seen in a particular context and therefore transfigured, whereas Ashbery's "wave of music," like Beckett's "llama emergency dream" in *How It Is*,[27] has an erotic cast. The death of the "incandescent period" (TP, 38) is the death of love, a dissolution that seems to puzzle the poet as much as it does the reader, "For we never knew, never knew, what joined us together" (TP, 10). To describe "loving" is impossible, but as the speaker of "The Recital" observes, what matters is "our private song, sung in the wilderness, nor can we leave off singing" (TP, 108).

[27] (New York: Grove Press, 1964), p. 14.

III

In his later poems, Ashbery's landscapes of desire are increasingly presented in the guise of what Frank O'Hara calls "charming artifice."[28] Medieval romance, Elizabethan pageant, comic books, Arthur Rackham fairy-tale, Disney World T-shirts, flowered wallpaper, frosted wedding cakes, "stage machinery," "grisaille shepherdesses," "terrorist chorales"—all these coalesce in the dream theater of *Houseboat Days* (1977), on whose dust jacket, designed by R. J. Kitaj, we find a portrait of a graceful lady in a long-sleeved dress, immobile at the oar of a stylized boat, silhouetted against the shadowy two-dimensional forms of mountains, lake, and cloudy sky.

In keeping with this new emphasis on art as artifice, one of the loveliest poems in the book is called "Pyrography"; the process of burning designs on wood and leather with a heated tool here becomes the process of imprinting burning traces of memory and vision on a consciousness so fluid and amorphous that the "heated tool" is likely to slip on its surface. The poem begins:

Out here on Cottage Grove it matters. The galloping
Wind balks at its shadow. The carriages
Are drawn forward under a sky of fumed oak.
This is America calling:
The mirroring of state to state,
Of voice to voice on the wires,
The force of colloquial greetings like golden
Pollen sinking on the afternoon breeze.
In service stairs the sweet corruption thrives;
The page of dusk turns like a creaking revolving stage
in Warren, Ohio.

(HD, 8)

The scene is present-day Chicago, the heart of the nation

[28] See "Apollinaire's Pornographic Novels," *Standing Still and Walking in New York*, ed. Donald Allen (Bolinas: Grey Fox Press, 1975), p. 157.

("This is America calling"), but curiously it is also a fairy-tale world in which "The carriages are drawn forward under a sky of fumed oak." This contrast of old and new is nicely reflected in the stanza's meter which oscillates between the formality of "In service stairs the sweet corruption thrives," a perfect iambic pentameter line with inverted word order and heavy alliteration, and the prosaic inflection of "The page of dusk turns like a creaking revolving stage in / Warren, Ohio."

In the second stanza, the "we" who are also "they" set out on a journey across the great American continent, first by boxcar through the "gyrating fans of suburbs" and "the darkness of cities," and then the scene suddenly dissolves and the travelers are moving up the Pacific coast to Bolinas, where "The houses doze and seem to wonder why." Along the way, they meet, in an echo of Baudelaire's "Le Voyage," the "disappointed, returning ones," but "the headlong night" beckons and it is too late to take warning and turn back. Indeed, as the journey continues, we proceed, not westward or north to Canada, but into an imaginary world. A city has evidently been erected, "built . . . / Partly over with fake ruins in the image of ourselves: / An arch that terminates in mid-keystone a crumbling stone pier / For laundresses, an open-air theater, never completed / And only partially designed" (HD, 9). Where are we? Like Rimbaud's "Villes," or Ashbery's own "lacustrine cities," these cities cannot be specified; they emerge as part of a theater decor upon which the curtain may fall any minute. So the poet asks:

How are we to inhabit
This space from which the fourth wall is invariably missing,
As in a stage-set or dollhouse, except by staying as we are,
In lost profile, facing the stars. . . .

(HD, 9)

This question has haunted Ashbery from the beginning. He has known, all along, that "Everything has a schedule, if you can find out what it is," the difficulty being that you can never find out. Just so, the question posed in "Pyrography" is rhetorical, for the poet knows that the only way to inhabit a "space from which the fourth wall is invariably missing" is to accept it as the "stage-set or doll-house" it really is, to realize that, in Yeats's words, "Man can embody truth but he cannot know it."

And yet one longs to counter the "strict sense / Of time running out, of evening presenting / The tactfully folded-over bill." And so one continues the journey, despite all warnings from "the disappointed, returning ones," this time into the haunted landscape of the past:

A long period of adjustment followed.
In the cities at the turn of the century they knew
  about it
But were careful not to let on as the iceman and the
  milkman
Disappeared down the block and the postman shouted
His daily rounds. The children under the trees knew
  it
But all the fathers returning home
On streetcars after a satisfying day at the office undid
  it:
The climate was still floral and all the wallpaper
In a million homes all over the land conspired to hide
  it.
One day we thought of painted furniture, of how
It just slightly changes everything in the room
And in the yard outside, and how, if we were going
To be able to write the history of our time, starting
  with today,
It would be necessary to model all these unimportant
  details
So as to be able to include them; otherwise the
  narrative

Would have that flat, sandpapered look the sky gets
Out in the middle west toward the end of summer. . .

(HD, 9-10)

Here memories of Ashbery's Rochester childhood blend with "Märchenbilder" and present-day images to create a hallucinatory picture of absence. Everyone seems to know "it"—whatever "it" is—but "it" must be kept from the iceman, milkman, and postman. Fathers, "returning home / On streetcars after a satisfying day at the office undid it"; "the wallpaper / In a million homes conspired to hide it." This mysterious "it," the poem implies, must be included in all accounts of "the history of our time." Without "these unimportant details," the narrative "Would have that flat, sandpapered look the sky gets / Out in the middle west toward the end of summer." And of course we already know *that* look from the opening lines of the poem.

The journey, it turns out, is not only a journey across the American continent or back into "cities at the turn of the century," but the eternally present "journey" one lives through each day of one's life. Change is the keynote: thus the "still floral" climate instantly dissolves into the floral wallpaper found "In a million homes all over the land"; the "painted furniture" "just slightly changes everything in the room," and one cannot "save appearances / So that tomorrow will be pure" (HD, 10). Such rationalistic schemes invariably fail for "The parade is turning into our street." As in Rimbaud's "Parade," these dreams are haunted by a procession of unidentifiable and hence frightening figures in "burnished uniforms." And now the scenic dissolves come faster and faster: the "street" gives way to the image of "The land / pulling away from the magic, glittering coastal towns." Cottage Grove and Bolinas, boxcars and trams, boats and circling kites—all coalesce and their fragments are etched, as if with a heated tool, into the contours of the poet's psyche. And the poem concludes:

The hunch is it will always be this way,

The look, the way things first scared you
In the night light, and later turned out to be,
Yet still capable, all the same, of a narrow fidelity
To what you and they wanted to become:
No sights like Russian music, only a vast unravelling
Out toward the junctions and to the darkness beyond
To these bare fields, built at today's expense.

(HD, 10)

"Pyrography," which is to say *poetry*, thus involves a continuous attempt at "unravelling / Out toward the junctions," an attempt just as continuously blocked as the stage-set disappears from sight. Just when the language "seems . . . on the point of revealing its secret," the mirror clouds over. For the designs burnt into the surface by the pyrographer's tool lose their sharp outlines after a time. Yet the artist continues to erect his crumbling stone piers and open-air theaters, to invent "forgotten showtunes" for his "Street Musicians," in an effort to redeem the "bare fields, built at today's expense." For

The phenomena have not changed
But a new way of being seen convinces them they
have.

(TP, 39)

This "new way of being seen" is nowhere more startling than in Ashbery's ambitious new sixty-eight-page poem called "Litany" (1979). Here the poet returns to the collage technique of "Europe," but the text he now "cuts up" is not someone else's novel but, so to speak, his own poem even as he is in the process of composing it. In "Litany," we meet familiar Ashbery paradigms: the "journey *en bateau*" of "Daffy Duck in Hollywood" and "Pyrography," the house party or cell-group meeting of "The Other Tradition," the disquisitions on art objects of "Self-Portrait in a Convex Mirror." The landscapes too are the familiar ones: the sleepy nondescript small town, somewhere in the Middle West, the Pacific coast, the fake Palladian buildings one sees in stage sets, fields of flowers, fairytale castles with balustrades and towers, comic-book animal farms, battle scenes from old war movies, "forest prisms." Ashbery's "strange juxtapositions" (Auden's term) recall Rimbaud's famous catalogue of "decadent" art works in the *Saison en enfer*:

> J'aimais les peintures idiotes, dessus de portes, décors, toiles de saltimbanques, enseignes, enluminures populaires; la littérature demodée, latin d'église, livres érotiques sans orthographe, romans de nos aïeules, contes de fées, petits livres de l'enfance, opéras vieux, refrains niais, rhythmes naïfs.

> (I loved absurd paintings, door panels, stage sets, backdrops for acrobats, sign-boards, popular engravings; literature that is out of fashion, Church Latin, erotic books with bad spelling, novels of our grandmothers, fairy tales, little books of childhood, old operas, silly refrains, artless rhythms.)[29]

If Ashbery's poem incorporates such irreverent and nonpoetic material, in what sense is it a litany? According to the OED, a *litany* is "an appointed form of public prayer, usually of a penitential character, consisting of a series of supplications, deprecations, or intercessions in which the clergy lead and the people respond, the same formula of response being repeated for several successive clauses." Ashbery's litany maintains the prayer-response form: the poem is written for two voices, presented on the page in double columns using different typefaces. But here the two voices do not stand for the prayer of the clergy and the response of the faithful. On the contrary, although there is a certain "response" element in "Litany," which I shall talk about later, on the whole voices A and B are generally interchangeable, both usually dealing with the same material, although from different points of view. Indeed, the Author's Note tells us that "The two columns of

[29] Rimbaud, *Œuvres*, ed. Suzanne Bernard (Paris: Garnier, 1960), p. 228.

'Litany' are meant to be read as simultaneous but independent monologues."[30]

"Simultaneous but independent" is nicely noncommittal: it suggests that we can read "Litany" in almost any sequence we like. Instead of following column A from page to page and then turning to column B, we can often move from A to B or B to A on the same page, generating different narratives and image clusters as we go along. In creating a text that can be read both across and down, and sometimes even diagonally, Ashbery has fulfilled his own earlier aim of producing "an open field of narrative possibilities" (TP, 41).

Consider the following passage, taken from the center of Part II (L, 49). The context is a parodic disquisition on the relation of art to reality. In column A, the narrator is arguing that no portrait can ever capture the inner reality of its subject anyway, and so, paradoxically, landscape, into which we can project ourselves, is the truer representation. In column B, the plot of a film that the narrator and his lover have seen "a dozen or more times" is considered to be more "real" than the actual "plot" of their own lives, which remains a mystery. Monologue A is chatty and discursive:

> Right. That's why landscapes are more
> Familiar, more what it's all about—we can see
> Into them and come out on the other side. With
> People we just see another boring side of ourselves. . . .

Monologue B is closer to the landscape of dream:

> *In the sea of the farm*
> *The dream of hay whirls us toward*
> *Horizons like those only*
> *Imagined, with no space, no groove*
> *Between the sky and the earth. . . .*

[30] See *As We Know*, p. 2. Since "Litany" occupies more than half of this volume and it is the only poem in the collection I refer to, in subsequent references I use the abbreviation L.

The two monologues can, of course, be read independently. But when we read them horizontally as well as vertically, we discover a number of new narrative possibilities. Suppose, for instance, that when I come to line 15, I move from A to B:

Portraits, on the other
Hand, are a different matter—they have no
Bearing on the human shape, their humanitarian
Concerns are foreign to us, who dream
And know not we are humane, though, as seen
In the sea of the farm
The dream of hay whirls us toward
Horizons like those only
Imagined, with no space, no groove
Between the sky and the earth, metallic,
Unfleshed, as though, as children,
Each of us might say how good
He or she is, and afterwards it is forgotten,
The thought, the very words.

Here the connecting link between the two columns is the word "dream" in the first. The "reality" of portraiture is rejected in favor of a dream vision, in which earth and water blend, the hay whirling "*us toward / Horizons*" where there is "*no space, no groove / Between the sky and the earth.*" For a fleeting moment, the harmony of childhood is restored.

Or again, we may begin with the "lost horizon" image in column B and move from there to the parallel sequence in A:

In the sea of the farm
The dream of hay whirls us toward
Horizons like those only
Imagined, with no space, no groove
Between the sky and the earth, metallic,
Right. That's why landscapes are more
Familiar, more what it's all about—we can see
Into them and come out on the other side.

Here the moment of vision quite naturally leads to the explanation, "That's why. . . ." Of course "landscapes" are "what it's all about," for when the line *"Between the sky and the earth"* disappears, we are able to see into the life of things, to "come out on the other side."

In reading "Litany," we thus become collaborators, choosing those plots and meditational sequences that most appeal to us. But this is not to say that we can read the poem any way we like. For, whether we read the two monologues on page 49 vertically or horizontally, we never get very far away from the same underlying "plot." Ashbery, in other words, creates a form that allows for a good measure of free play, but the larger "puzzle scene" nonetheless has its own particular contours.

However we splice the parts, "Litany" is, first and foremost, a penitential poem, playing on the conventions of intercession, supplication, and deprecation. Thus religious vocabulary—"prayer," "psalm," "angel," "chant," "church," "cathedral spire," "rite," "scrolls," "temple," "holy," "preordained," "liturgical," "eternity," "petitioner," "God's road"—floats to the surface of the text repeatedly only to disappear once more as if the presence of these words were accidental, having no connection to the context in which they appear. For of course there is no one to intercede for this poet, no one to whom he may pray and who will listen to his words of self-depreciation. The response to the "prayers" of the A voice can come only from within; the B voice, as we have seen, is not even the poet's alter ego since the two are largely indistinguishable. Moreover, the one feature of litany this poem almost never manifests is the very central one of *repetition*. On the rare occasions when the formula is invoked, as on page 22 where we read:

For all those with erysipelas
And all the wrinkles on the forehead
And the cheeks that come from within, like reverse scars

For all those wearing old clothes
With the dormant look of expectation about them

For the women ironing
And who cut into lengths of white cloth. . . .

we are taken aback, as if a sudden intrusion had spoiled the moment, inhibiting the free play of the text.

Indeed, one way to read "Litany" is as a serious parody of Eliot's *Four Quartets*, whose phrasing is heard again and again:

there was
Never anything but this,
No footfalls on the mat-polished marble floor,
No bird-dropping, no fates, no sanctuary.

(L, 15)

The moment
Not made of itself or any other
Substance we know of, reflecting
Only itself. Then there are two moments. . . .

(L, 18)

When the winter is over, and the sodden spring
That goes on even longer, a pitcher of water
Drawn deep from the well is to be
The reward and the end of just about everything. . . .

(L, 62)

. . . . and gradually leads us, each of us,
Back to the fragment of sense which is the place
We started out from. Isn't it strange
That this was home all along, and none of us
Knew it?

(L, 63)

In Ashbery's 1980 version of the *Quartets*, the fire and the rose can never become one, nor can the poet ever come in contact with "the still point of the turning world." He only knows that "time flows round again / With things I did in it, / I wish to keep my differences / And to retain my kinship / To the rest" (L, 2-3). Accordingly, the "suppliant" of Part I expresses his longing for simplification:

For someone like me
The simple things
Like having toast or
Going to church
Are kept in one place.

(L, 1)

But at the same time, the poet knows that he cannot keep these "simple things" "in one place," that he cannot make it cohere. Indeed, while the A voice expresses this wish, the B "response" is:

So this must be a hole
Of cloud
Mandate or trap
But haze that casts
The milk of enchantment

Over the whole town. . . .

And so the "simple things" like "having wine and cheese" are seen as through a haze filter and become Other; the "having toast" and "Going to church" give way to the "*milk of enchantment.*" The setting of both monologues is the same small town, but while in the first, "The parents of the town / Pissing elegantly escape knowledge / Once and for all," in the second, the narrator starts to imagine "*whatever / Could be happening / Behind tall hedges / Of dark, lissome knowledge.*"

This movement in and out of dream characterizes the whole poem. In Part I, whose subject is, in very general terms, the childhood world, there is consistent rapid-fire modulation from "wooden fences" to "towers of lightning high over / The Sahara desert," from an "old apple tree" to "wisteria . . . in league / With the Spanish minstrels," from dust blowing through open windows to a "caravan / In slow motion" of "Elephants and wolves / Painted bright colors." If the poet dwells in an ordinary town on a lake shore, he also seems to be at home in "A colossal desert full of valleys and melting canyons" or in "Greek coves barely under the water."

The repeated prayer for deliverance from the past and the stated longing for "the flutes and premises of the future" must, accordingly, be construed as false leads. For in the course of "Litany," both poet and reader come to see that there is no way of distinguishing the past from the present or future, or the "real" from the fictive. In a related poem entitled "No Way of Knowing," we read:

The body is what this is all about and it disperses
In sheeted fragments, all somewhere around
But difficult to read correctly since there is
No common vantage point, no point of view
Like the "I" in a novel. And in truth
No one never saw the point of any. . . .

(SP, 56)

Accordingly, one must be open to possibilities. So, in Part II of "Litany," while voice A "photographs all things," B reads *"some poem"* that reminds him of the *"dark, wet street . . . Gleaming, ecstatic, with the thin spear / Of faerie trumpet-calls"* (L, 17). On the same page, A talks of the "enormous summer nights opening / Out farther and farther, like the billowing / Of a parachute," while B remarks that *"It's getting dark at seven now"* and evokes a rainy autumnal world. Yet, just as we can read across as well as down, so we discover that Ashbery also reverses roles: it is the voice of the A column that remembers "the hours in the rain-drenched schoolroom," while B speaks of "*the summer job in the department store.*"

Such cross-cutting is not just arbitrary. To be alive in the late twentieth century is, for Ashbery, to recognize that *"So many points of view, so many details . . . are probably significant" (L, 35).* One can make a good case for a New England vacation (L, 22), where "the ocean that came crashing almost / Into the back yard did not seem ill-disposed," and where even though "No one offered you a drink and there were no / Clean glasses and the supper / Never appeared on the table, it was / Strangely rewarding anyway." But one can just as well argue (the B column on the same page), that, what with *"an increasingly mobile populace"* filling up the trailer parks, it's better to stay home:

and the mountains are
Now so breathtakingly close to the city
That it's like taking a vacation
Just to stay home and look at them
That's all one can do.

(L, 22)

The ultimate absurdity! For if present-day technology has brought the mountains within easy travel distance of the city, it has also created a world in which one is not likely to see further from one's window than the building across the street or the smog floating above it. But then, one can always dream of mountains. . . .

The form of "Litany," Edmund White has observed, "is the ideal transcription of Ashbery's sense of things: a mental space humming with signal and noise, focus and blur. Anthropologists have suggested that the human cortex may be so large not because of an evolutionary pressure toward intelligence but rather because of the need in an animal so sociable, for a 'computer' that might select meaning out of constant and random chatter."[31] In this sense, Ashbery's "hymn to possibility" is indeed a litany for the computer age. If it renounces the phrasal repetition indigenous to the form, it is because things no longer happen in precisely the same way twice. As Ashbery puts it in "Self-Portrait in a Convex Mirror":

Today has no margins, the event arrives
Flush with its edges.

(SP, 79)

[31] "Two-Part Inventions" (review of *As We Know*), *The Washington Post Book World*, 25 November 1979, p. 4.

CHAPTER EIGHT

"No More Margins": John Cage, David Antin, and the Poetry of Performance

—Permission granted. But not to do whatever you want.
—John Cage, *A Year from Monday*

I

IF, as John Ashbery suggests in "Self-Portrait in a Convex Mirror," "Today has no margins, the event arrives / Flush with its edges," perhaps the very notion of the poem as "preconceived object,"[1] as a set of words arranged on the page according to plan, needs to be reassessed. In Chapter Six of the *Poetics*, Aristotle lists the six constituent parts of tragedy (for him the supreme form of poetry) as *mythos* (plot), *ethos* (character), *dianoia* (thought), *lexis* (diction), *melopoeia* (rhythm and song), and *opsis* (spectacle). Romantic and Modernist theory elevated the second, fourth, and fifth of these elements: poetry, it was and still is assumed, involves the presentation of a self (the "ethical argument") in terms of appropriate *lexis* and *melopoeia*. In practice, lexis means connotative, multi-layered language and symbolic imagery, whereas ethos has generally been

[1] The phrase is John Cage's:

> The early works have beginnings, middles, and endings. The later ones do not. They begin anywhere, last any length of time. . . . They are therefore not preconceived objects and to approach them as objects is to utterly miss the point. They are occasions for experience. . . .

"Composition as Process" (1958) in *Silence* (Middletown: Wesleyan University Press, 1961), p. 31. Subsequently cited as S. Wesleyan is also the publisher of *A Year from Monday* (1967), cited as YFM, and *M, Writings '67-'72* (1973), cited as M.

construed as some form of psychological depth. In the past few decades, however, the pendulum has begun to swing. Performance, which Michel Benamou calls "the unifying mode of the postmodern,"[2] is, by definition, an art form that involves *opsis*; it establishes a unique relationship between artist and audience. More important, performance poetry, as it has been practiced by such artists as John Cage, Jackson Mac Low, Jerome Rothenberg, and David Antin, reintroduces narrative into the lyric structure, whereas *dianoia*, declared out of court in Symbolist aesthetic, is curiously coming in by the back door.

I present this schematic account of the Aristotelian model only to remind the reader that *poiesis* can be many different things. This is, I think, a necessary reminder, for contemporary criticism has been peculiarly uncomprehending of if not downright hostile to such compositions as the lecture-poetry of John Cage and the "talk poems" of David Antin. When William Spanos, the enterprising editor of *Boundary 2*, wanted to publish Antin's *"what am i doing here?"*, an improvisation first performed at the San Francisco Poetry Center in 1973 and only then transcribed on the typewriter and presented on the page without left and right margins and with spaces of varying length to mark natural pauses, his co-editor, Robert Kroetsch, was highly skeptical. In a letter to Antin (5 October 1974), subsequently published as part of a fascinating three-way debate among Antin, Spanos, and Kroetsch on the meaning and value of Antin's text and, by implication, on the nature of poetry in general, Kroetsch makes what are surely typical objections:

> 1. The talk-poem . . . assumes that to write at all is somehow to create art. To justify this assumption you have to negate imagination. . . .
>
> 2. Your talk-poem becomes poem as pure content. It is

[2] "Presence as Play," in *Performance in Postmodern Culture*, ed. Michel Benamou and Charles Caramello (Milwaukee: Center for Twentieth Century Studies, 1977), p. 3.

> not a solution to but an avoidance of the problem of form. In art I look for the tension of opposing forces. . . .
>
> 3. Your poetry as "uninterruptable discourse" is uninterruptable simply in the sense that a nervous lecturer is uninterruptable.
>
> 4. Your stance is a naive one. Naive in its avoidance of selection. . . . Naive . . . in assuming that to talk about writing a poem is to write one. . . .[3]

These four reservations boil down to one simple objection: Antin's "talk pieces," which he himself describes as "notations of scores of oral poems with margins consequently unjustified,"[4] have no form; they merely go on and on. For not only do the talk poems do away with meter; they even avoid that last stronghold of contemporary free verse—lineation. Moreover, Antin's discourse jumps from topic to topic as does ordinary talk. It thus seems "Naive in its avoidance of selection." The same charge is regularly levelled against John Cage: witness the following anecdote he tells:

> London publisher sent blank ("Fill out") so I'd be included in survey of contemporary poets of the English language. Threw it out. Week later urgent request plus duplicate blank arrived. "Please return with a glossy photo." Complied. July, August, September. Publisher then sent letter saying it'd been decided I'm not significant poet after all: If I were, everyone else is too.[5]

I am not sure that the way to answer such charges is to argue, as does Spanos, that Antin's "*what am i doing here?*"

[3] David Antin, "A Correspondence with the Editors, William Spanos and Robert Kroetsch," *Boundary 2: The Oral Impulse in Contemporary American Poetry*, 3 (Spring 1975), pp. 626-627. Subsequently cited as OI.

[4] *Talking at the Boundaries* (New York: New Directions, 1976), headnote, unpaginated. Subsequently cited as TB.

[5] Cited by Richard Kostelanetz, "Cagean Poetry," in *John Cage*, ed. Richard Kostelanetz (New York: Praeger, 1970), p. 168.

"reverberates with echoes of the past (the oral poetry of Homer, Plato's Dialogues . . . the whole Parry and Lord *Singer of Tales* context) and is at the same time utterly situated in the present: McLuhan, the French *parole* vs. *écriture* debate, Heideggerian phenomenology" (OI, 602). Such enthusiasm is misleading: Antin is not exactly a Homer or a Socrates and, in fact, his talk poetry does not exploit the formulaic patterns described by Alfred Lord in *The Singer of Tales*. As for Heidegger, in the course of the correspondence, Antin expresses his marked distaste for the German philosopher:

> Anyone who starts with "Being" as goal has already reduced the possibility of travelling. He always it seems knew what Being was and could produce it from his hip pocket when necessary. . . .
>
> (OI, 624)

Spanos is much closer to the mark when he tries to convince Kroetsch that the Antin text has "a structural rhythm—an interspersion of 'story' and 'speculation'," and a speaking voice that generates "the sense of exploration" (OI, 601). He is also on to something important when he remarks: "Just as all the prose writers of the *Modern* period wanted to make poems out of their prose, so a lot of contemporary poets want to make prose out of their poetry" (OI, 607). But before we take up the question of voice and structural rhythm, which Spanos does not pursue in the correspondence, we might pause to consider a "simple" statement Cage makes in response to those who scoff at the reductiveness of his "music":

> There are people who say, "if music's that easy to write, I could do it." Of course they could, but they don't.
>
> (S, 72)

This is an aphorism to ponder long and hard. It *is* easy to copy a piece like *4' 33"* (the 1952 Cage composition originally "performed" by David Tudor, who simply sat at the piano for four minutes and thirty-three seconds, his only action being to close the piano cover three times so as to indicate the start of a "movement" and then to open it again at the end of a specified time period),[6] but how many of us would have conceived of the idea in the first place? Again, it may seem easy to talk into a tape recorder and then transcribe one's words, avoiding all margins and leaving blank spaces between word groups. Yet we don't in fact do it. For what is really "easy," in the context of the present, is to write little epiphany poems in free verse, detailing a "meaningful" experience. I am walking, let us say, in the snow, and I notice strange footprints: I am reminded of the day when. . . . Or to take an actual example:

The Moth

The papaya colored moth flickering in sun
Outside the seventh-story window
tapped the window twice going up

Urging the beige building to unfold
and rise, the landscape to flutter.
The world was bitten through its cloud wrappings.

Moth the color of banana squash,
moth in the gusts above sour traffic. I tell you
there was a bloom of dust on our faces
an eccentric lurching in our hearts.[7]

That, I would posit, is *easy*. And "they" do "do it" in a thousand dreary little magazines and chapbooks. But as for the "mere noise" of Cage or the "ordinary talk" of Antin, we will have to look again. And perhaps the best way to begin is with beginnings. Cage's are well known and I shall not rehearse them here, nor do I plan to discuss his work as a composer except insofar as it relates to poetry

[6] See Calvin Tompkins, "John Cage," in *The Bride and the Bachelors, Five Masters of the Avant-Garde* (1965; rpt. New York: Penguin Books, 1976), pp. 118-119.

[7] Ben Saltman, "The Moth," in *Beyond Baroque*, No. 792 (Summer 1979), 22.

and poetics.[8] But Antin's poetic origins provide some interesting perspectives on the improvisatory mode he was to develop in the seventies.

II

Among David Antin's earliest poems are a group of translations from André Breton (1958-1959).[9] Like Ashbery, who also translated Breton,[10] Antin originally turned to France, to such poets as Blaise Cendrars (for whom his son is named), Alfred Jarry, and Tristan Tzara, as well as to Breton, because he found the local scene so dispiriting. "The great ones were the early ones and then they died somehow, and by a mechanism completely mysterious to me, they were replaced by others who were supposed to be their heirs."[11] Here Antin commemorates Gertrude Stein, his favorite American "great one" of the early twentieth century, by adopting her own syntax; the "heirs" he refers to are, as we know from his famous essay "Modernism and Postmodernism" in *Boundary 2*, such neo-Symbolist poets as W. D. Snodgrass, Anthony Hecht, Richard Wilbur,

[8] Calvin Tompkins' essay on Cage in *The Bride and the Bachelors* is an excellent introduction. See also Richard Kostelanetz, *John Cage*, for a useful chronological survey of Cage criticism as well as interviews and extracts from his writings. The book has a catalogue of Cage's compositions (by instrument and chronology), a bibliography of his writings, and a checklist of writings about Cage up to 1969.

[9] The following were published in *Floating World*, 4 (1962), 7-12; "A Man and Woman Absolutely White" ("Un Homme et une femme absolument blancs"); "Free Union" ("L'Union libre"); "The Air of Water" ("Au beau demi-jour"); "A Branch of Nettle Enters by the Window" ("Une branche d'ortie entre par la fenêtre"); "Knot of Mirrors" ("Nœud de miroirs"). All but "The Air of Water" are reprinted in Michael Benedikt's anthology, *The Poetry of Surrealism* (Boston: Little, Brown, 1974). Benedikt also includes Antin's "Go-for-Broke" ("Cours-les toutes"). For the French text, see André Breton, *Poèmes* (Paris: Gallimard, 1948).

[10] See "From *The Immaculate Conception*, by André Breton and Paul Eluard," *Locus Solus*: Collaborations Issue, 2 (Summer 1961), 53-66.

[11] David Antin, "An Interview conducted by Barry Alpert," Bloomington, Indiana, 3 November 1973, in *Vort #7*, David Antin-Jerome Rothenberg Issue (1975), 4. This interview is subsequently cited as IBA.

and Karl Shapiro.[12] In a letter to Nicolas Calas (17 September 1964), Antin draws a distinction between *image* and *symbol* that recalls Ashbery's opposition of Reverdy's "transparent images" to the "symbolic" ones of Eliot's followers.[13] Blake's "sick rose," Antin argues, is not an "image" at all: "It is an emblem. Nobody has the slightest idea that we are dealing with a particular dicotyledonous flower. From the very start it is quite obvious that the word 'rose' in the context of European poetry has come to mean 'BEAUTY,' just as Mallarmé's damned swan is no swan at all but 'THE POET.' "

Pound's definition, "An image is that which presents an intellectual and emotional complex in an instant of time," is, Antin believes, more satisfactory:

> Image poetry is not a means of saying one thing and meaning something else. It is an art of presentation somewhat like the film, only it is not essentially visual. When Rimbaud gives the vowels their colors, he has no rationalizations for them. If there was a middle term that ever connected green to U, it has been deliberately suppressed, and not to create a guessing game for critics, but because Rimbaud wanted to produce two simultaneous successions, one of colors, one of vowels—in the absence of translational meaning. . . . The absence of connection was precisely necessary to create a charged space between the vowels and the colors. Furthermore, I do not think it would make the least bit of difference if a different order of colors were assigned to the vowels—the essential effect would not be significantly altered, any more than that of the Rauschenberg combine is affected by rearrangements of the pebbles.[14]

Here Antin's strong anti-Symbolist reading of Rimbaud

[12] "Modernism and Postmodernism: Approaching the Present in American Poetry," *Boundary 2*, I, 1 (Fall 1972), 98-133.

[13] "Reverdy en Amérique," *Mercure de France: Pierre Reverdy Issue*, 344 (January/April 1962), 111-112, and pp. 35-36 above.

[14] Unpublished letter to Nicolas Calas, 17 September 1964; reprinted by permission of the author.

allies him to Breton, who regarded Rimbaud as the father of modern poetry, the first poet to resolve Symbolist dualism.[15] In *Les Vases communicants* (1932), Breton argues that the pointing function of the symbol limits the field of figuration, whereas "Le moindre objet, auquel n'est pas assigné un role symbolique particulier, est susceptible de figurer n'importe quoi" (the least object which is not assigned a particular symbolic role can come to represent anything).[16] Breton's strategy, as Antin sees it, is "to detach objects from the world with a kind of surgical precision, depriving them of their commonplace (and misleading) contexts." "Misleading," because in Antin's view, the commonplace world is itself a fiction, being "legislated" and "negotiated" rather than "experienced."[17] Thus, when a so-called banal object—say, Duchamp's urinal—is deliberately and systematically detached from its usual context and put to unexpected use (in this case, turned on its side, labelled "Fountain," and signed R. Mutt), it is defamiliarized, becoming a node of radiating energy.

There is a further link between Antin and Breton. Of all the Surrealists, Breton was held to be the most "prosaic"; indeed, even some of his greatest admirers have regarded him as not being a "real" poet at all, questioning his belief that it is not through *form* that prose is distinguishable from verse but through the process of thought that permeates the work in question. Anna Balakian has observed that Breton developed three distinct forms of writing: (1) the free verse poem, (2) the critical essay or manifesto, written in straightforward logical prose, and (3) the "analogical prose" of such works as *Poisson soluble*, *Nadja*, and *Les Vases communicants*. Unlike the prose poem, such "analogical prose" often has the dimensions of a short novel. But unlike the novel, "it proceeds not on the basis of narrative sequence or systematic description, but it is free of both time and place and moves in accordance with word and image

[15] See Anna Balakian, *André Breton, Magus of Surrealism* (New York: Oxford, 1971), pp. 17-18.

[16] *Les Vases communicants* (1932; Paris: Gallimard, 1955), p. 148.

[17] Letter to the author, 22 July 1979.

associations, not as elliptically as free verse but analogically even in the discussion of objects, events, and states of being."[18]

The relation of such "analogical prose" to Antin's talk pieces will become apparent later. But even the translations of the more "normal" poems like "Un Homme et une femme absolument blancs" and "Une Branche d'ortie entre par la fenêtre" suggest that Antin is less concerned with the mechanics of the Surrealist image (he often makes up his own equivalent as when he turns the "calfats" [caulkers] "qui boivent" of "L'Union libre" into "steeplejacks"),[19] than with Breton's way of defamiliarizing ordinary objects and events and generating narrative momentum.

Consider Antin's rendition of "Cours-les-toutes" (1938), which he calls aptly "Go for Broke." It begins:

> In the heart of the Indian territory of Oklahoma
> There is a man sitting
> Who has the eyes of a cat circling a clump of
> couchgrass[20]

The reference to Oklahoma, the "eyes of a cat," and "couchgrass" recall for a moment Wallace Stevens' famous "Earthy Anecdote":

> Everytime the bucks went clattering
> Over Oklahoma
> A firecat bristled in the way.

But in the Breton poem, there is no formal pattern created by the tension of such opposites as clattering bucks and bristling firecat. Rather, we find ourselves reading a sort of parody Western in which the narrator's observations seem to have little to do with what is happening. Thus we cut from:

[18] Balakian, *André Breton*, p. 61.

[19] See Breton, *Poèmes*, p. 66; Antin, "Free Union," in Benedikt, *Poetry of Surrealism*, p. 133; and cf. IBA, 8.

[20] See Benedikt, *Poetry of Surrealism*, p. 140. Antin's translation omits one line of Breton's poem ("Comètes fixes dont le vent décolore les cheveux"), but on the whole, this is a literal translation.

A man encircled
Who sees through his window
The council of lying inflexible divinities . . .
Spanish style virgins inscribed in a right isoceles
   triangle

to the absurd comment that

The gasoline billows out over the continents
Like Eleonor's hair

And from

A man with his head wrapped in the stockings of the
   setting sun
And the hands of a trunk fish

to

This country is like a huge nightclub
With its women from the ends of the earth
Whose shoulders roll the galleys of all seas

The effect is dizzying: who is this "encircled" man with the "circling" cat eyes, and what does he have to do with nightclubs or with Eleonor's hair?[21] The image of the female Atlases holding what we might call the *vases communicants* of the world's seas on their shoulders is absurd. Or is it? For this "Indian territory of Oklahoma" really *is* a sort of natural nightclub in which erotic games and business transactions occur without warning. As the "story" unfolds, "the man they have drawn a circle around / Like a chicken," turns out to be the cock of the walk:

The agent passes each month
Places his hat on the bed covered with a veil of arrows
And from his sealskin bag
Spreads the latest manufacturers' catalogues
Turned by the hand that opened and closed them
   when we were children

[21] David Antin's wife is named Eleonor so that we also have a private double entendre here.

Here Antin, following Breton, fuses past and present, reality and dream. The matter-of-fact statement, "The agent passes each month," is qualified by the image of "the bed covered with a veil of arrows." Whatever such a "veil" may be, the Indian chief, as we now know him to be, seems to be well protected against all comers. And now, from the sealskin bag, emerges one of those catalogues "Turned by the hand that opened and closed them when we were children." The Oklahoma wilderness, it seems, is really our own commonplace world. Perhaps the story of the Indian chief is a child's dream. Or perhaps "gasoline billows out over the continent" because the "dispossessed chief" has discovered oil wells on his land. He seems, in any case, to turn into a great capitalist entrepreneur, first considering the purchase of "a wedding limousine / With fins extending ten yards / For the train," and finally acquiring the ultimate American Dream Machine in the form of "one / Fast / Black / Car":

> Crowned with mother-of-pearl eagles
> Inscribed in all of its angles with rinceaux of salon
> fireplaces
> Like waves
> A carriage that could only be moved by lightning
> Like the one in which the princess Acanthe wanders
> with shut eyes
> A giant sedan chair of gray snails
> And tongues of fire. . . .
> A fast fish trapped in algae
> Trying to free itself with pulsations of its tail
> A great state or funeral limousine
> For the last parade of a sainted emperor to come
> Out of fantasy
> That would outmode all life
>
> (pp. 141-142)

And so this "dispossessed chief who is somewhat ours" and who "carries / The flamboyant name of Go-for-Broke," is urged to make the most of it:

Run your luck that is a volley of bells of celebration
  and alarm
Run the creatures of your dreams till they collapse
  spewing on their white collars
Run the ring without the finger
Run the head of the avalanche

The germs of Antin's improvisational style are found here. I am not referring to the individual Surrealist images (e.g., "a giant sedan chair of grey snails"), for Antin will become increasingly indifferent to such fanciful polarities. What interests him, rather, is the *conception* that animates "Cours-les-toutes"—the transformation of a bona fide Indian chief, confined to his reservation in Oklahoma, into a kind of mad race-car driver. The procedure of the poem is to deprive the image of the Noble Savage of its commonplace or cliché context, to make it strange. It also permits the reader, subject to the same political and economic laws as the Indian, to identify with him. Thus the poem functions as a serious parody of those endless tales of dispossessed Indian chiefs, victimized by the White Oppressor, or again, of the Romantic lyric of self-recognition, in which an innocent "I" comes upon a downtrodden old man, engages him in conversation, and comes away sadder and wiser. But no such "Resolution and Independence" pattern is allowed to operate here. Breton presents the flamboyant "Go-for-Broke" as just as eager for pleasure and power as the next fellow, and, what's more, the poet finds this urge, so totally at variance with the modern "Indian myth," exhilarating.

It is the sort of turn-about that delights Antin, who regards a poem as "a way of getting somewhere," an "energy construct" (IBA, 8). In "The Death of the Platypus,"[22] written at about the same time as the Breton translations, there is a similar defamiliarization of the ordinary. The source of the poem, Antin recalls (IBA, 8-9), was a newspaper story about a platypus that died in the Bronx zoo. Annoyed

[22] *Trobar*, 1 (1960), 3-4.

on the one hand by the absurdity of imprisoning in a zoo a small furry animal that no one could see anyway because it was always hiding under a bush, and, on the other, by the sentimentality of the newspaper article which suggested that the platypus had died of a broken heart, Antin constructed a catalogue poem that contains the same sort of verbal play and "contaminated feeling" we find in his Breton translations. Lulled by such lines as "And he cried for the creatures of the earth's first night," many readers, including James Wright and Robert Bly, read "The Death of the Platypus" as a serious treatment of man's failure to respond properly to nature (IBA, 10-11).[23] Yet many of the images function as false clues: "He cried for unlit stone lilies at the sea bottom" sounds pretty, but a stone lily has nothing to do with "stone" or "lily"; it is a kind of echinoderm. The same is true of "maidenhair" ("he cried . . . for the chaste maidenhairs"), an ordinary species of fern. Antin, in short, is not voicing the expected sentiment; he is examining standard ways of mourning and applying them to a variety of animals, vegetables, and minerals unfitted for survival by the evolutionary process. The last lines bring the note of absurdity to the fore:

> The platypus in his great grief cried without discretion
> or measure
> His tears sank deep into the ground where they
> corroded aluminum
> And his great heart collapsed like the quenched walls
> of the sun.

This is like a scientific parody of Donne's "Valediction: Of Weeping," in which the lovers' tears are said to flow so freely that they produce a major flood.

But by the time "The Death of the Platypus" had won a poetry prize in 1960, Antin was no longer especially interested in fantasy, even as a parodic device. More and more, his images become insistently literal and referential,

[23] Because Antin feels that the poem was admired for all the wrong reasons, he has never reprinted it; see IBA, 11.

as in "constructions and discoveries," which is about the building projects that transformed New York in the early 60s:

morning and the jib of a crane
today the air
is full of breaking things
rising and falling
full of angles and ladders
bright powder
pollen and chalkdust
in the sunlight[24]

And when, in a related poem, he examines the meaning of "Touch," Antin performs the role of scientist rather than lover: it is the "touch" of "skinned knees" that interests him, of "bricks that are rich in abrasions," "overripe fruit," "rubber bandages," "chalkdust of blackboards that never come clean," and especially the touch, unlike any other, of glass.[25]

The hard-edged literalness of these poems is coupled with an increasing distrust in the image as the embodiment of personal emotion. When questioned by Barry Alpert about his relation to the Deep Image school (which, in its inception, included Antin's closest poet-friend, Jerome Rothenberg), Antin replied:

> By the end of 1960 I knew that I was involved with something inherently linguistic, and I didn't have any idea about "deep" which was furthermore an idea I not only didn't understand but thoroughly disliked. . . . I have a terrific distrust of ideas of interiority. . . . What I wanted was a kind of precise impact. . . . [My work] wasn't aiming at psychological depths which I didn't believe in. It was aiming at perfectly straightforward experience, which I did believe in.
>
> (IBA, 13)

[24] *Chelsea*, #16 (March 1965), 104-105.
[25] *Trobar*, 4 (1962), 40.

In keeping with this new aesthetic, Antin wrote "Definitions for Mendy."[26] The loss of a close friend, who had never quite managed to fulfill even the least of his ambitions and then died rather suddenly of Hodgkin's Disease, struck Antin as wholly "unintelligible," and, as he tells Barry Alpert, "the one thing I believe a poet ought to do is respect what he doesn't understand, respect its unintelligibility" (IBA, 17). The "formal structure of grief" of traditional elegy seemed inappropriate, for Antin regarded his loss to be like anyone's loss of a loved one, neither more nor less, and he refused to mythologize it or to use it as a vehicle for self-projection. An "emotional vocabulary," he argues, "takes you on bridges past the cracks in the real, and I wanted to deal with the cracks" (IBA, 18).

Characteristically, Antin tackled the poetic problem by beginning, not with an expression of personal grief or a complaint to the gods for letting Mendy die, but with a definition of the word "loss" that he found in an insurance manual: "loss is an unintentional decline in or disappearance of / a value arising from a contingency." "Value" is further defined (from Webster's) as "an efficacy a power a brightness / it is also a duration" (D, 5).

So it goes throughout the poem, in which valid argument forms are filled with false and inconsistent statements, invalid forms with true statements, and the syllogism, as Hugh Kenner notes, is shown to resemble "a verse form more closely than it does a tool."[27] For how, in fact, do we reason?

take a glass of water
hold it against a wall

[26] *Definitions* (New York: Caterpillar Press, 1967), pp. 5-14. Subsequently cited as D.

[27] "Antin, Cats, &c.," *Vort*, 7 (1975), 90. Kenner is referring not to "Definitions for Mendy," but to "Stanzas," Antin's most extended poem to explore the vagaries of logic; see *Meditations* (Santa Barbara: Black Sparrow Press, 1971), pp. 52-65.

it is not pure water
it is almost pure wall

(D, 8)

Of course, because we see the wall through the glass and water is invisible. But from this "logical" deduction, it is only a step to the false conclusion that the water *is* the wall, and so "water is a barrier / a glass of water is between us / you are there and i am here" (D, 8). Or again, because "a glass of water falling / is a falling body of water" (major premise), and "all bodies fall / at a rate that increases uniformly / regardless of their form or weight / at the same altitude and latitude" (minor premise), it "follows" that Mendy's falling body and the falling body of water are one.

There is, the poem implies, no "meaningful" way of dealing with Mendy's death; it remains, and must remain, incomprehensible. For one cannot transcend certain facts:

the eye cannot discriminate true intensities of light
only their ratios
similarly the ear
cannot distinguish among sounds that are very high or
  low
in the dark all cats are black
what color are they in a blinding light

(D, 13)

Conceptually, "Definitions for Mendy" looks ahead to the talk poems, but Antin has still to master what Northrop Frye calls the "associative rhythm," the forward movement of speech when it is allowed to evolve according to its own laws. Thus the personal vignettes about Mendy (his visit to David when he told him he was dying; their listening to Bach and Webern together and coming back "in the rain"), and the imagistic passage about spring renewal ("yellow branches of willow / small flames of forsythia") are felt to be intrusions; they do not follow naturally from the pattern of definition and counter-definition the speaker puts before us. Rather, these passages still seem to be "framed" as obligatory lyrics; they are placed where they are according to a plan that antedates the poem as actual discourse. In other words, the "uninterruptable" mode of the talk poems would not permit "yellow / branches of willow" to be introduced unless something that had just been said had generated the image. For it is characteristic of speech to be fragmented and associative rather than to have precise beginnings and endings as do the strophes of "Definitions for Mendy."

The inventory structure used in "Mendy" and many other poems of this period is also at odds with the rhythm of speech:

duration
it is a stone
it is a fact
it does not move
it has no place into which it could move
it has no place to move out of
it is a stone
it is a fact
it is a stone on which water has dropped
it is a fact
it is hard
it is smooth

(D, 11)[28]

The formality of such clausal repetition gets in the way of Antin's poetics of process. In his own terms, such a structure is still a "bridge" over the "crack in the real." The next step was to remove such "bridges" as the forsythia passage and to find a rhythm suitable for talking. And here I turn to John Cage, whose *Silence* (1961) furnished Antin not only with the "glass of water" image of "Definitions for Mendy,"[29] but with a way of creating verbal-visual compositions that lead to the "seamlessness" of improvisation.

[28] Cf. in *Code of Flag Behavior* (Los Angeles: Black Sparrow Press, 1968), the following: "A list of the delusions of the insane" (pp. 22-23), "W. S. Male" (p. 26), and "history" (pp. 30-34).

[29] The line, "is there enough silence here for a glass of water," followed

III

Cage's *Silence* is subtitled *Lectures and Writings*, but this tells us little about its remarkable format. In the Foreword, Cage tells us:

> For over twenty years I have been writing articles and giving lectures. Many of them have been unusual in form . . . because I have employed in them means of composing analogous to my composing means in the field of music. . . . As I look back, I realize that a concern with poetry was early with me. At Pomona College, in response to questions about the Lake poets, I wrote in the manner of Gertrude Stein, irrelevantly and repetitiously. . . . Since the *Lecture on Nothing* (1949), there have been more than a dozen pieces that were unconventionally written, including some that were done by means of chance operations and one that was largely a series of questions left unanswered. When M. C. Richards asked me why I didn't one day give a conventional informative lecture, adding that that would be the most shocking thing I could do, I said, "I don't give these lectures to surprise people, but out of a need for poetry"
>
> (S, x).

But in what sense can the lectures, essays, and diaries collected in *Silence, A Year from Monday* (1967), and *M* (1973) be considered poetry? The unconventional arrangement (in both directions for performance and visual layout) of these compositions is not, I shall argue, their most interesting feature. Still, something should be said of Cage's format. The most famous of his texts is probably the "Lecture on Nothing" (given at the Arts Club in New York in 1949 and first published in 1959), which has the following structure:

There are four measures in each line and twelve lines

by a long space (D, 7), is an ironic allusion to Cage's "Lecture on Nothing"; see *Silence*, p. 110; cf. Barry Alpert, "Post-Modern Oral Poetry: Buckminster Fuller, John Cage, and David Antin," *Boundary 2*, III (Spring 1975), 665-681.

> in each unit of the rhythmic structure. There are forty-eight such units, each having forty-eight measures. The whole is divided into five large parts, in the proportion 7, 6, 14, 14, 7. The forty-eight measures of each unit are likewise so divided. The text is printed in four columns to facilitate a rhythmic reading. Each line is to be read across the page from left to right, not down the columns in sequence. This should not be done in an artificial manner . . . but with the *rubato* which one uses in everyday speech.
>
> (S, 109)

Here is the first subset:

I am here , and there is nothing to say

If among you are

those who wish to get somewhere , let them leave at

any moment . What we re-quire is

silence ; but what silence requires

is that I go on talking .

(S, 109)

Lecture on Nothing and the corresponding *Lecture on Something* (1951) are heavily influenced by Gertrude Stein's mode of repetition, especially the middle section of the former, which takes sentences like "If anybody is sleepy let him go to sleep," "I have the feeling that we are getting nowhere," and "It is not irritating to be where one is. It is only irritating to think one would like to be somewhere else," and places them in constantly shifting contexts.

All Cage's "lectures" are in some way related to this format. "Composition as Process" (1958) has three parts. The first, "Changes," is based on the duration of his *Music of Changes*, each line of the text, whether speech or silence, requiring one second for its performance. These "one second" lines (some contain only one or two words plus the first syllable of a third word) are arranged in four columns on the page, to be read sequentially, and the lengths of the paragraphs are determined by chance operations (S, 18). The second part, "Indeterminacy," is written in "normal" paragraphs, but the type is, in Cage's words, "excessively small" so as "to emphasize the intentionally pontifical character of the lecture" (S, 35), and each section begins with the identical sentence, "This is a lecture on composition which is indeterminate with respect to its performance," and then proceeds to give an example. The third part, "Communication," consists entirely of questions and quotations, for example:

> Do we have a mythology?
> Would we know what to do if we had one?
>
> (S, 42)

Here are some other compositional strategies. "Eric Satie" (1958) is printed in double columns as an imaginary conversation between Satie (italics) and Cage (roman). This arrangement may well have influenced Ashbery in the composition of "Litany." "2 Pages, 122 Words of Music and Dance" (1957) uses chance operations to generate the words, and the placement depends upon imperfections in the sheets of paper upon which Cage happened to be working (S, 96). "On Robert Rauschenberg" (1961), one of Cage's most interesting pieces, consists of a series of lyric meditations, rather like short prose poems, on various facets of the artist's work. The sections may be read in any order, but here is the first, as printed:

> Conversation was difficult and correspondence virtually ceased. (Not because of the mails which continued.) People spoke of messages, perhaps because they'd not heard from one another for a long time. Art flourished.
>
> (S, 98)

Again, "Where Are We Going? and What Are We Doing?" (1961) contains four simultaneous lectures, designated in print by four different typefaces. On the page, these are arranged in double columns and the structure is fugal, the second voice coming in only after four measures of the first, and so on.

Since 1965, Cage has been writing installments of what

he calls *Diary: How To Improve The World (You Will Only Make Matters Worse)*. He describes the format as follows:

> It is a mosaic of ideas, statements, words, and stories. It is also a diary. For each day, I determined by chance operations how many parts of the mosaic I would write and how many words there would be in each. The number of words per day was to equal, or by the last statement written, not to exceed one hundred words. . . . I used an IBM Selectric typewriter to print my text. I used twelve different type faces, letting chance operations determine which face would be used for which statement. So too, the left marginations were determined, the right marginations being the result of not hyphenating words and at the same time keeping the number of characters per line forty-three or less.
>
> (YFM, 3)

There is a touch of gimmickry in these elaborate typographic games and mathematical rules, especially since there is no real connection between the typeface of a given word group and the meaning it conveys. Indeed, this really *is* a diary, a series of jottings about daily life and opinions put down as they happen to occur to Cage. The best we can say for the constant shifts in visual appearance and the jagged right margins is that these devices demand special attention from the reader. But the diaries still observe a prose norm; they are written in perfectly coherent sentences.

The first genuinely improvised talk Cage gave is called "Talk I" and was performed by the Once Group in Ann Arbor, Michigan in 1965 (YFM, 141-144). But even here, he wrote down the topics he was interested in talking about, and the transcript of the talk is just a set of words and phrases scrambled across the page in all directions and in different typefaces. A similar mode is that of the "Statement on Ives" (1965), in which a talk for the Canadian Broadcast Corporation is transcribed by using triangles to indicate breathing, circles to represent swallowing, and scribbles for the "uh"s and other noises (YFM, 41).

The formal features I have described so far, whether mathematical or visual or guides for oral performance, have gained Cage a good deal of notoriety, but they are not in themselves the mainspring of his poetic art. Rather, we must look at the system of relationships that goes beyond such obvious devices as the number of characters per line, the columnar arrangements, or the use of varying typefaces. In "Experimental Music" (1957), Cage observes:

> There is no such thing as an empty space or an empty time. There is always something to see, something to hear. In fact, try as we may to make a silence, we cannot.

And then Cage goes on to tell the story (which he will repeat again and again) about the time he entered an anechoic chamber at Harvard and yet heard "two sounds, one high and one low," the high one being, so the engineer told him, his nervous system in operation, the low one, the circulation of the blood. "Until I die," Cage concludes, "there will be sounds" (S, 8).

It is this conviction that nature not only abhors but rejects a vacuum that generates the structure of *Silence* and the later books. For if "Art is the imitation of nature in her manner of operation" (S, 100), the artist's book cannot have an empty space or an empty time. Accordingly, the "lectures" in *Silence* do not so much begin or end as they *continue*, expository discourse giving way, at unexpected junctures, to the non-fictional narrative of Cage's versions of Zen *koans*.[30] Further, the gap between "story" and "lecture"

[30] The *koan* is a theme or statement of question given to the Zen student for solution, which will lead him to a spiritual insight. In its classic Buddhist form, a new monk would be presented with an illogical question or problem by the head of the monastery, who would then monitor his response. If the novice struggled to construct a response using logical thought processes, he failed; if he intuitively and non-discursively grasped the truth within the koan, he passed. The irrationality intrinsic to the koan is thus "resolved" in the enlightenment of *satori*. In Cage's versions, however, the stress is less on *satori* than on the irrationality or absurdity itself. See D. T. Suzuki, *Essays in Zen Buddhism, First Series* (1949; rpt. New York: Grove Press, 1978), pp. 18-32, 255; Thomas Hoover, *Zen Culture* (New York: Random House, 1978), pp. 59-61.

is bridged by italicized headnotes and afterwords,[31] so that the net effect is one of what Cage calls "UNIMPEDEDNESS AND INTERPENETRATION":

> SO THAT WHEN ONE SAYS THAT THERE IS NO CAUSE AND EFFECT, WHAT IS MEANT IS THAT THERE ARE AN INCALCULABLE INFINITY OF CAUSES AND EFFECTS, THAT IN FACT EACH AND EVERY THING IN ALL OF TIME AND SPACE IS RELATED TO EACH AND EVERY OTHER THING IN ALL OF TIME AND SPACE.
>
> (S, 46-47)

The relationship of narrative to conceptual statement in Cage's verbal structures is especially interesting. In "Experimental Music," he writes:

> And what is the purpose of writing music? One is, of course, not dealing with purposes but dealing with sounds. Or the answer must take the form of paradox: a purposeful purposelessness or a purposeless play. This play, however, is an affirmation of life—not an attempt to bring order out of chaos . . . but simply a way of waking up to the life we're living, which is so excellent once one gets one's mind and one's desires out of its way and lets it act of its own accord.
>
> (S, 12)

A "purposeless play" that wakes us up to the very "life we're living"—this is precisely the mode of the "Zen stories." Some are autobiographical, some are anecdotes told to Cage by his friends, and some derive from the Zen literature. Here are four varied and typical examples:

> (1) It was a Wednesday. I was in the sixth grade. I overheard Dad saying to Mother, "Get ready: we're going to New Zealand Saturday." I got ready. I read

[31] The influence of these italicized bridge-passages on those found in Antin's *Talking at the Boundaries* is unmistakable. The titles of the talk poems also owe something to Cage's titles: compare "*what am i doing here?*" (Antin) to "Where Are We Going? and What Are We Doing?" (Cage).

everything I could find in the school library about New Zealand. Saturday came. Nothing happened. The project was not even mentioned, that day or any succeeding day.

(S, 6)

(2) One day I went to the dentist. Over the radio they said it was the hottest day of the year. However, I was wearing a jacket, because going to a doctor has always struck me as a somewhat formal occasion. In the midst of his work, Dr. Heyman stopped and said, "Why don't you take your jacket off?" I said, "I have a hole in my shirt and that's why I have my jacket on." He said, "Well, I have a hole in my sock, and, if you like, I'll take my shoes off."

(S, 95)

(3) A crowded bus on the point of leaving Manchester for Stockport was found by its conductress to have one too many standees. She therefore asked, "Who was the last person to get on the bus?" No one said a word. Declaring that the bus would not leave until the extra passenger was put off, she went and fetched the driver, who also asked, "All right, who was the last person to get on the bus?" Again there was public silence. So the two went to find an inspector. He asked, "Who was the last person to get on the bus?" No one spoke. He then announced that he would fetch a policeman. While the conductress, driver, and inspector were away looking for a policeman, a little man came up to the bus stop and asked, "Is this the bus to Stockport?" Hearing that it was, he got on. A few minutes later the three returned accompanied by a policeman. He asked, "What seems to be the trouble? Who was the last person to get on the bus?" The little man said, "I was." The policeman said, "All right, get off." All the people on the bus burst into laughter. The conductress, thinking they were laughing at her, burst into tears and said she refused to make the trip to Stockport. The inspector then arranged for an-

other conductress to take over. She, seeing the little man standing at the bus stop, said, "What are you doing there?" He said, "I'm waiting to go to Stockport." She said, "Well, this is the bus to Stockport. Are you getting on or not?"

(S, 271)

(4) There was an American man from Seattle who went to Japan to buy screens. He went to a monastery where he had heard there were very special ones and managed to get an interview with the Abbot, who, however, didn't say a word during the entire time they were together. Through an interpreter, the American made known his desires, but received no comment of any kind from the Abbot. However, very early the next morning, he received a telephone call from the Abbot himself, who turned out to speak perfect English and who said that the American could not only have the screen he wanted for a certain price, but that, furthermore, the monastery possessed an old iron gate that he could also purchase. The American said, "But what on earth would I do with an old iron gate?" "I'm sure you could sell it to a star in Hollywood," the Abbot replied.

(YFM, 135)

Perhaps the first thing that strikes one about these stories is their radical empiricism, their stubborn and insistent literalness. In each case, the facts are plainly given—"It was a Wednesday," "One day I went to the dentist"—as if to emphasize that these things really happened. Indeed, Cage insists again and again that "No thing in life requires a symbol since it is clearly what it is: a visible manifestation" (S, 136). In his collage-essay on Rauschenberg, he gives a slight twist to Williams' famous aphorism "No ideas but in things!":

. . . object is *fact*, not symbol. If any thinking is going to take place, it has to come out from inside the Mason jar which is suspended in *Talisman*, or from the center of the rose (is it red) or the eyes of the pitcher. . . . Not ideas but facts.

(S, 108)

But "facts" in what sense? Unlike the typical joke, the Cagean "koan" does not have a point. It is not social satire directed against a particular class or ethnic group. It does not fuse humor and pathos as does, say, a Chaplin film, because it is oddly unemotional. We don't, I think, feel for the boy who thinks his parents will take him to New Zealand or for the patient in the dentist's chair, nor do we know what any of the characters, including the author himself, are thinking. Rather, what strikes us about the Cagean story is its peculiar non-sense. The seemingly straightforward narrative leads into a labyrinth. For although each proposition made is reasonable in itself, the statements don't add up.

Take the story of "the American man from Seattle who went to Japan to buy screens." What happens seems normal enough: the interview with the Abbot conducted with the help of the interpreter. Even the twist that the silent Abbot turns out to speak perfect English is not at all improbable: we have all had this kind of experience. And the further twist that the Abbot emerges as a shrewd businessman, ready to palm off his old iron gate on the American, is also not unlike the things that really have happened to us. Nevertheless, the conclusion "I am sure you could sell it to a star in Hollywood" is absurdly funny. Who would have thought that this silent monastic type really had an eye on the Hollywood market? Yet the conclusion is not quite a punch line that unravels the joke. For many things in the story remain inexplicable. If the Abbot really knows English, why does he go through the charade of using an interpreter? Is it to lead the businessman on, or does he actually change his mind about the screens? Again, why should the Abbot of a Japanese monastery want to make shrewd business deals? Is he offering the man from Seattle the iron gate in order to test him? Or is he perhaps a Hollywood fraud himself?

There are no answers to such questions, and we must remember that the largest collection of Cage's stories appears under the title *Indeterminacy* (S, 261-273).[32] The neutral, almost bland surface structure of the Cage story is what John Ashbery would call "an open field of narrative possibilities."

Consider the little autobiographical anecdote about New Zealand. What insight does it give us? Perhaps the child must learn that his father's statements are not to be taken literally, that it is just a manner of speaking. On the other hand, perhaps the child is right: people should mean what they say. For why does the father say to the mother, "Get ready: we're going to New Zealand Saturday"? Does he have anything in mind? Is he perhaps speaking in code, referring to a secret between himself and his wife? Does "going to New Zealand" mean making love? Or is the father trying to test his son in some way, trying to teach him that the readiness is all? Anything is possible and yet the story is not at all far-fetched; it is the sort of thing that happens. Similarly, in the dentist story, each statement makes sense but the sequence is pure nonsense. Dentist and patient play the role of two Zen masters, engaged in polite exchange. In their comic game of one-upmanship, neither expects to

[32] According to Cage's headnote, when "Indeterminacy" was first given as a "lecture" in Stockholm, it consisted of thirty stories (1958). "The following spring, back in America, I delivered the talk again, at Teachers College, Columbia. For this occasion I wrote sixty more stories and there was a musical accompaniment by David Tudor." This performance was brought out as a Folkways recording (FT-3704). Cage explains:

> In oral delivery of this lecture, I tell one story a minute. If it's a short one, I have to spread it out; when I come to a long one, I have to speak as rapidly as I can. The continuity of the stories as recorded was not planned. . . . My intention in putting the stories together in an unplanned way was to suggest that all things—stories, incidental sounds from the environment, and, by extension, beings—are related, and that this complexity is more evident when it is not oversimplified by an idea of relationship in one person's mind." (S, 260)

The text as printed in *Silence* has fifty-four stories.

get the "right" answer to his formulation of the question; the patient's "explanation" and the dentist's analogy (a false one: socks are normally covered by shoes, shirts not necessarily covered by jackets; again, socks often have a hole or two, shirts don't) are equally absurd.

The poise between sense and non-sense is especially notable in the anecdote about the Stockport bus. The whole procedure is typical of daily life: the foolish delay so as to evict a single passenger, the legalistic maneuvers of the conductress, driver, and inspector, the unexpected arrival of the new passenger, with the comic twist that the policeman can get a response whereas the conductress couldn't. But the real humor of the story hinges on the indeterminacy of the word "last." Who *is* the "last person to get on the bus"? Cage sets up the equation: $N - 1 = N + 2$ (where N is the number of passengers the bus can safely carry). For what happens is that instead of getting rid of the extra passenger ($N - 1$), circumstances work out so that the bus finally carries $N + 2$. And these circumstances are themselves equivocal. What happens may be purely accidental. On the other hand, it almost seems as if the passengers were acting as a collective entity, using the "little man" to fool the authorities. Either way, "due process" turns out to be no sort of process at all.

There is no way of governing such absurdity, but one can learn to use it. It is only fitting that Cage's narratives regularly generate expectations that they never quite fulfill or that they give way, for no seeming reason, to the format of "lecture" or lyric, as when a mesostic is embedded in the diary form of *M*. For, as Antin says of Cage's "process pieces," a "system of representation" is replaced by a "system of exemplification, in which the method of presentation, referred to the materials presented, becomes a model from which meaning is inferred."[33] In Cage's art of "exemplary presentation," the meaning inferred is that we can only know *how* things happen ("nature in her manner of

[33] "Some Questions about Modernism," *Occident*, 8 (Spring 1974), 31.

operation") but never quite *what* happens, much less *why*. *Silence* celebrates the quintessential non-sensicality of the universe, a non-sensicality that Cage curiously enjoys. "The very life we're living . . . is so excellent once one gets one's mind and one's desires out of the way and lets it act of its own accord." This is the central conception behind the "purposeless play" and chance operations of Cage's language constructions, and we should note that, despite his description of himself as a formalist,[34] Cage is, like Antin, a poet for whom *dianoia* supercedes *ethos*, a poet of what we might call "the new didacticism."

IV

"An improvisation," says David Antin, "is not 'in prose' which is an image of the authority of 'right thinking' conveyed primarily through 'right printing'—justified margins, conventional punctuation, and regularized spelling."[35] This notion of the text is, we have seen, already present in Cage, as is the renewed interest in "exemplary" narrative. Nevertheless, as I noted earlier, Cage's lectures and diaries are not really improvisations; with rare exceptions, they are written prior to oral delivery and their syntax is still that of prose—that is, their basic unit is the sentence. (The *sound texts* that begin with "Mureau" [1970] represent a rather different phenomenon, which I take up later.) If we go back to the distinction Northrop Frye makes between verse, prose, and the "associative rhythm," we can see that Antin's talk pieces, being *ex post facto* scores of oral poems, are not composed in sentences at all. Frye observes:

[34] In the Foreword to *Silence*, Cage says: "As I see it, poetry is not prose simply because poetry is in one way or another formalized. It is not poetry by reason of its content or ambiguity but by reason of its allowing musical elements (time, sound) to be introduced into the world of words" (S, x). It is easy to misinterpret this and related statements. Cage is not repudiating conceptual thought but the traditional way of conveying meaning in poetry—that is, by indirection, figuration, semantic complexity.

[35] See TB, dust jacket.

> One can see in ordinary speech . . . a unit of rhythm peculiar to it, a short phrase that contains the central word or idea aimed at, but is largely innocent of syntax. It is much more repetitive than prose, as it is in the process of working out an idea, and the repetitions are largely rhythmical filler. . . . In pursuit of its main theme, it follows the paths of private association, which gives it a somewhat meandering course.[36]

In its pure form, the "associative rhythm" is, of course, subliterary: "it seldom appears without some kind of verse or prose disguise" (p. 72). In the first case, when we get a move toward verse, we find "a series of phrases, with no fixed metrical pattern, the influence of verse being shown in the fact that the phrases are rhythmically separated from one another, not connected by syntax as in prose." Such minimal formalization of the associative rhythm is usually called "free verse," and we find it in all of Antin's early poems, for example in "Definitions for Mendy":

a fâlse kéy will nót tûrn a trúe lóck
fâlse háir will nót tûrn gréy
méndy will nót come báck

(D, 5)

But suppose the associative rhythm appears in the opposite or "prose disguise":

> Associative rhythms move toward prose in much the same way that they move toward verse. Criticism does not appear to have any such term as "free prose" to describe an associative rhythm influenced, but not quite organized, by the sentence. But that free prose exists is clear enough, and in fact it develops much earlier than free verse.
>
> (p. 81)

[36] *The Well-Tempered Critic* (Bloomington: Indiana University Press, 1963), p. 21.

As early examples of "free prose," Frye cites Burton's *Anatomy of Melancholy*, Swift's *Journal to Stella*, and Sterne's *Tristram Shandy*. Beckett's *The Unnamable* is an important modern exemplar of the "associative monologue" (p. 56); so, I might add, are *How It Is* and *Fizzles*.

It is in this tradition we must locate Antin's talk poems. "The associative rhythm," Frye remarks, "represents the process of bringing ideas into articulation in contrast to prose or verse, which normally represent a finished product" (p. 99). Just so, Antin's improvisatory talk poetry is, in an even more radical sense than Cage's "interpenetrating" lecture-story format, a process-oriented art. The associative rhythm is, by definition, "intensely continuous" (p. 56); or, to use Antin's own term which Robert Kroetsch found so objectionable, it is "uninterruptable discourse."

How does it work in practice? Let me take up, one by one, the formal features that characterize Antin's talk poems. In what follows, I shall stress form precisely because the usual objection is that Antin's poetry doesn't have any.

(1) In Antin's associative monologues, there are no complete sentences, the trick being, in the words of Charles Olson, to "keep it moving as fast as you can." The famous precept that "ONE PERCEPTION MUST IMMEDIATELY AND DIRECTLY LEAD TO A FURTHER PERCEPTION" is put into action. Consider the following passage from "*is this the right place?*"

> when i came here in the plane this time
> and ive come back and forth so many times now im beginning
> to suffer from air shock between flights when i got on the plane
> i had the feeling i started out early in the day it was
> about 12 oclock to be on a plane 12 oclock on a plane is in
> some ways the worst possible time to get on a plane because
> what happens is you start out in the daylight and you
> wind up in the night and there never was any day and its odd you
> feel that youre travelling into the past though technically youve
> gone into the future and lost the present

Notice that the first two "when" clauses are left suspended, there being no main clause, for the speaker immediately interests himself in what it was like *when* he got on the plane. Again, the proposition, "It was about 12 oclock" leads, not to the expected account of what happened at twelve o'clock but to a comic sequence about the peculiar feelings attendant upon boarding an eastbound flight at noon. And so it goes, with rapid-fire shifts from one idea or image to another. In associative monologue, parenthetical utterance (e.g., "and ive come back and forth so many times now . . .") can assume a primary role and vice versa, continuity being supplied by the repetition of word groups: in this case, "in the plane," "on the plane," etc.

(2) Unlike prose, Antin's "score" cannot be scanned or skimmed. Here a simple exercise might be helpful. Take one of Antin's own essays, say the article "Modernism and Postmodernism" in *Boundary 2*, and select a random page. When I open to page 107, I find a fifteen-line paragraph roughly in the center of the page, whose first sentence is: "For better or worse 'modern' poetry in English has been committed to a principle of collage from the outset, and when 'history' or 'psychoanalysis' are invoked, they are merely well-labeled boxes from which a poet may select ready-made contrasts." Now *there* is a statement I can copy out in my notebook, to be used at some future time when the characteristics of "modern" poetry are to be discussed. If I want, I can now skim over Antin's discussion of how "history" and "psychoanalysis" are used in the collage forms of Modernism, and go on to the next paragraph, which begins with the assertion that in the hands of "the Nashville critics and the poets who followed them," the principle of collage is treated reductively. And this is, of course, the way we read such essays.

In reading the talk poems, it is impossible to scan in this way. If I take the passage from "*is this the right place?*" cited above and glance down the page, I cannot decide where to focus. The words "plane," "time," and "art," recur again and again; I also see something about a "bloody mary" and a "merger of conglomerates." But the fragmentation of phrasing, the suspension of meaning, and the repetition of words, always in a slightly altered context, precludes the possibility of deriving key "ideas" from this text or summarizing its contents. There is no short cut; I must simply read the whole thing. Accordingly, Kroetsch's original request that Antin cut "*what am i doing here?*" by at least half (see OI, 598) was, as Antin remarked at the time, "not only impossible . . . but directly antithetical to [the piece's] significance" (OI, 599). In Gertrude Stein's words, "Cézanne conceived the idea that in composition one thing was as important as another thing. Each part is as important as the whole."[37]

But, the skeptical reader will object, if we do have to read these talk pieces word for word, isn't it boring? Here three other principles come in:

(3) The talk poem incorporates as many different threads as will allow it to retain its improvisatory quality, yet those threads are all relational. "A 'word,' " says Antin in "Some Questions about Modernism," "will in its metonymic capacity evoke a 'neighborhood' of related 'words,' " the neighborhood depending not only on actual contiguity but also on the social context of the discourse (see *Occident*, 20-21).

As an example of Antin's particular kind of metonymic structuring, let us consider the opening pages of "*remembering recording representing*" (1973):

> before coming here i stopped at a number of places   ive been
> travelling a lot   im beginning to feel a little travel shock at this
> point   ive gone east from california to philadelphia   from
> philadelphia to new york   from new york to bloomington
> and now im here from bloomington   and when i was in
> bloomington i was introduced to a painter   a very good
> skilfull painter   in the positive sense of that term   a
> figure painter and he was working   on a large painting   on a

[37] "A Transatlantic Interview 1946," in Robert Haas (ed.), *A Primer for the Gradual Understanding of Gertrude Stein* (Santa Barbara: Black Sparrow Press, 1976), p. 15.

diptych i guess maybe eight feet high and each
part of it maybe four feet wide and the painting was very
formally devised with borders painted around both sections in
the manner of a medieval painting and in one part of the diptych
there was a woman seated and in the other part a man standing and they were each of them in a house that looked
like it would have been one house joined across the two panels
except that the borders of both panels split them from each
other and outside of the great window or windows of the room
or rooms housing them were landscape elements and
the two landscapes were somewhat disjunctively chosen
looking through the window on the womans side there was a
section of a freeway that began and ended without going anywhere
that began abruptly in the midst of some countryside and
terminated as suddenly and on the other side the mans
there was what seemed like a more rural landscape and this
felt confusing somehow as if on the womans side you were
looking into a room in italy out onto an american countryside
while on the other side it seemed you were looking from an
american room into italy and this seemed so because the
woman on the left hand side was clearly an italian woman or
she was dressed as an italian woman in a stylized black italian
dress the kind of chic black low-necked dress that a fashionable
european woman might wear or might have worn several years ago
and she was hunched over a table it might have been the
kind of severe black dress worn by an unfashionable female member
of a family of impoverished country gentry or wealthier peasants
anyway she was hunched over this table and it looked as if she
was drawing lemons or something of that order that is
she was looking away from the man and down at a piece of paper
and making a drawing on the far side of her section of the painting
and the drawing was projecting over the border on that side of
the diptych in the manner of certain 15th century paintings
which might have somebody pursuing something say inside
the painting and the prey passing over the border of the painting
which is a painted border and there is this ambiguity about
where the painting ends and the world begins now in this other
part of the painting the man was holding up his hand i think
and looking it seemed somewhat in the direction of the woman
now there were things about this painting i didnt understand
in some sense it looked very low pressure the way a lot of
painting looks in america that is it looked as if it was not urgent

about anything   painting is embarrassed to be about anything
its been embarrassed for a long time   theres a grave sense of
embarrassment before the possibility of being about in painting
which they call being literary   and literary is a bad term for
a painter because everyone knows that if you paint a painting of anything it shouldnt be about anything but painting   so that a
figurative painting must be an abstract painting in disguise   so
that if you were to ask someone   a painter   about a woman
in his painting say he would probably tell you it was a figure not a
woman   maybe   or maybe even just a pattern he needed
there in that color or those colors to support his plastic values   i
mean "who is that woman?"   what a thing to say   if you said
that in 1953 the painter probably wouldnt have answered you at all
but this is 1973 and im brave   so i ask the painter "who is
that woman?" and he answers   nervously "i like to think of that
as my wife"   actually i didnt ask him anything of the sort   he
volunteered   kind of playfully   that he liked to think of the
woman in the painting as his wife   and i said "oh?" or something
noncommittal and he said yes   "we have a place in italy   in
fiesole   and i spend half the year here and half the year there
my wife stays there all year round and then we join each other
in the spring"   having some image of what it is to live with someone or to be married and have a wife   the half year seemed rather
difficult to sustain   i know people have sustained longer intervals
but it seemed to impose some character on the painting that made
me wonder whether we were dealing with an abstract painting or not
the separation of the two parts of the diptych interested me and
i wasnt sure that i could say anything to him about it because he was
very nervous   yet he had said "of course i like to think that this
is like my wife and this is me" he said later   and then he said
"and i like to think thats italy and thats america   but of course
thats for me   i wouldnt want anybody to think its important"
and so i pretended i didnt think it was important i said of course
drank some wine and ate some peanuts and i looked at the painting
there were a lot of objects in the painting   quotes i mean
from oh trompe loeil paintings from herculaneum and pompeii
and other things that were floating around in the painting
looking   reminiscent   and they made the painting look less
important   more like other paintings   for example   you
couldnt see what the woman looked like   she was looking down
and the painter had in a rather characteristically chic manner
deformed her shoulder   hes an extraordinarily competent painter

and he always deforms his people   usually people who are painting
representational paintings which they suppose to be partial abstractions impose a signal upon the painting so that you will recognize
that it is not a painting of something   but rather a painting
so what they tend to impose is what you could call the art
deformation upon the picture   so that you wont be inclined to
say "what is that a picture of?" but "what does that painting mean?"
perhaps   well she had this sort of hunched back and i knew of
course that that didnt mean that his wife had a hunchback   in
fact i was pretty certain his wife didnt have a hunchback   and
the man in the painting looked peculiar too   he was standing
very stiff   looking as if he had been stylized   as if the painter
had realized that paintings should be done in certain ways not intended to make his figure too much like a man   but let me take
that back   he made it look as much like a man as any painter
might   but he also made it as wooden as any kind of man he
could conceivably make while still having you recognize that it
looked like a man   though this was not a "picture" of a man that
you were looking at but a "painting" in which there was a reference
to a man and a reference to a woman   you might call this kind of
stylization lexical   which is to say that it was the kind of image
you might see in certain kinds of indian painting of the 18th and 19th
centuries   there is this style which tells you how to shape images
of things   and you reach for each image like out of some bag
and you pull out a "cow" and a "man" and you put them
together   you sort of make simple sentences with these images
you make "cow" "man" landscapes   "the man follows the
cow up the hill" say   for which you need an image also of a "hill"
and an order   in which the cow and the man face toward the hill
with the cow "higher up"   for which you need a conventional
sign indicating "higher up"   like placing the cow higher up on
the paper say   and you need to put one foot in front of the other
so someone will read "walking"   but while the painting   this
painting   had the kind of lexical stylization of this kind of sentence building painting it didnt read like that   i mean this was
not the ramayana you realize   for while everything in the
painting seemed to say just "read this"   it wasnt at all clear what
you were supposed to read or whether there was anything for you
to read there at all   while the purpose of such a style   in indian
painting say   is just to tell you to concentrate on reading and
then to give you the sentences they want you to read   so if this
wasnt the ramayana   or some other story   which the painter

had assured me it wasnt   why were these things looking this way?
  i wasnt entirely clear   yet i did know   that when one has
considered the whole issue of representing in this culture   how i

In this associative monologue, repetition is central, not just as "rhythmical filler," as Frye puts it, but in Gertrude Stein's sense of beginning over and over again. As in Stein's 1912 portrait of Picasso, which may well have been in Antin's mind when he performed "*remembering recording representing*," both narrator and audience come to understand a given word or word group only in the course of its repetition in varied contexts. Not the appearance of a word but its reappearance is what counts.

The word "painting," with its cognates "paint and painter," appears more than fifty times in the passage, and we gradually realize that Antin's subject is the status of painting as an image of the "real." In what sense does a painting represent the external world? And how do we interpret an image, whether in painting or in a photograph? Which is more "real," a visual image or a mental one? All these questions, which are explored later in the talk poem, are introduced by what seems to be a matter-of-fact account of a particular painting made by

a painter
a very skilfull painter
a figure painter and he was working   on a large
  painting

who is never called by name.

These opening references immediately place the painter from Bloomington, Indiana in a less than flattering light. Antin now moves metonymically from the painter himself to his painting, which is described factually as "a diptych . . . maybe eight feet high," whose two parts are each "maybe four feet wide," and we learn that "the painting was very formally devised with borders painted around both sections in the manner of a medieval painting." Now the narrator turns from the facts about the painting to a description of its subject matter. There is no change in his tone, so that the listener (or reader) assumes that the information about to be divulged is of the same order as the fact that the diptych is eight feet high and has borders. But such metonymic structuring turns out to be comically deceptive. For when Antin assumes that the woman in the left part of the diptych must be an Italian woman in a room looking out on America, whereas the man in the right part is an American, located in the same room but looking out over Italy, we are being treated to an inference based on nothing more than that the landscape on the woman's side has a freeway in it while that on the man's side looks rural. Indeed, the only way the narrator knows about the Italian-American split he reads into the painting is that, later on, the "skilfull competent figure painter" tells him, "of course i like to think that this is like my wife and this is me," and that, since his wife stays in Italy all year while he spends six months in America, "i like to think thats italy and thats america   but of course   thats for me   i wouldnt want anybody to think its important."

But before we come to this "explanation," the process of making inferences based on false clues continues. The woman on the left is assumed to be Italian because of these descriptions:

(1) "she was dressed as an italian woman   in a stylized black italian dress"
(2) "the kind of chic black low-necked dress that a fashionable european woman might wear or might have worn several years ago"
(3) "the kind of severe black dress worn by an unfashionable female member of a family of impoverished country gentry or wealthier peasants"

By the time we come to this third qualification, the "black dress" has become a meaningless signifier, pointing to whatever we want to make of it.

The same thing happens when Antin digresses metonymically from the physical appearance of the woman to what she does:

(1) "she was hunched over a table" (this first observation is embedded in the account of the black dress cited above)
(2) "she was hunched over this table and it looked as if she was drawing lemons"
(3) "the painter had in a rather characteristically chic manner deformed her shoulder"
(4) "she had this sort of hunched back"
(5) "and I knew of course that that didn't mean that his wife had a hunchback"
(6) "in fact i was pretty certain his wife didn't have a hunchback"

Here, as in the case of the word "painting," repetition works to deflate the image of the "figure painter" from Bloomington. And, at the same time as one metonymic sequence moves from the painting to the subject of the painting to an account of what the people in the painting might be doing, a second series takes up its "art history" features: "diptych"—"medieval" borders—images that project over the border "in the manner of certain fifteenth-century paintings"—"quotes" from "trompe loeil paintings from herculaneum and pompeii." These historical allusions are then contrasted to the images found in Indian painting: a man, one of whose feet is placed in front of the other, is "walking"; if the "cow" on his right is placed higher up in the painting than he is, he is following the cow up the hill, and so on.

By the time we reach the bottom of page 96, where Antin refers to the "whole issue of representing in this culture," we realize that the patterns of association used in the seemingly random anecdote about the "competent" figure painter from Indiana have forced us to look at the whole question of "art" in a new way. For consider the issues raised by the seemingly point-by-point "description" of the painting and of the painter's response to it. First, why does a "competent" painter who wants to convey a particular emotion—his sense of separation from his wife in Italy—disown the "importance" of the image? Why does he assume that a painting has only formal value? On the other hand, why, if he does want to portray something "real"—himself and his wife in their separate places—does he use historical elements like the diptych, the medieval borders, or the *trompe l'oeil* devices seen at Pompeii? Again, how should the viewer respond to such a painting? Does he look for the hidden meaning? Try to infer what the black dress means? Or does he admire the "lexical" stylization? Does he perhaps "read" the painting as a Surrealist work in the vein of Magritte, who regularly places "realistically" drawn figures in non-corresponding, contradictory landscapes?

The larger questions generated by these local ones are: what does it mean, in our society, to be a "skillful" painter? And, if a painting is meant to be "read," why doesn't it use the kind of signifiers one finds in the cow / man landscapes of Buddhist painting? To put it another way, is "painting" the same thing in Indiana as it is in India?

The narrator of "*remembering recording- representing*" does not claim to have answers to these questions. His aim is not to construct a coherent argument, as he would if he were writing an essay, but to *present* and *expose*. Clearly, the force of the repetition of "painter," "painting," "painted" in the contexts provided is to create a sense of absurdity: the Italian-American connection, as depicted here, seems at once foolish and pathetic. Out of this sense of absurdity, Antin now goes on to generate a number of related narratives and commentaries, all of which deal in some way with the "issue of representing in this culture," the relation of art to reality. Thus the digressive comment on page 94, "a figurative painting must be an abstract painting in disguise," leads to the consideration of the "realism" of photography. The notion that a photograph can be used as "an absolute validation principle," say, in an adultery case in court, is undercut by the narrator's mental image of his father, who died when he was two:

and i have only two images
of his existence   or only two that i can remember   i remem-

ber seeing him from the end of a corridor i was passing through
i could see him through the open door of the bathroom and he
had one foot up on the bathtub   i think he was shining his shoes
now that i think of it maybe there was another   he was
passing in front of a window   i mean these are not what you tend
to think of as a loaded image   theyre not the sort you think of
as describing   as a rich experience   they have   the first
one anyway   because its the one i remember most clearly   the
transient quality of fact   a child passing through a corridor catch-
ing a glimpse of his father doing some neutral thing   by some
accident remembered   shining his shoes one foot up on a bathtub   i say a neutral thing because i detest the vulgarity of mind
the imperialism of that psychology that would unmotivatedly
provide some trivial to me psychological need that would pretend
aggressively   to explain the remembrance of this scene
because i can believe in this unfunctional scanning   a kind
of casual registration of the world

This image, inconsequent as it is, turns out to be much more powerful than the "silver framed photograph" on his mother's dresser, a photograph "of a man with a serious oval face his hair peaked at the brow holding in his arm a small boy who was sitting on his lap holding a stick" (TB, 104). For this photograph strikes Antin as oddly unreal. For one thing, the child's hair is "golden and curled," whereas his own hair, until he lost it, was "black and wavy" (TB, 105). For another, the man with the oval face could just as easily have been his father's identical twin brother. Of course his mother and his other uncle insist that the photograph is of David and his father, but should he believe them? Various anecdotes that question their veracity now follow in what looks like a digression, but the central focus on the relation of the Image to the Real is never lost.

Throughout the improvisation, Antin performs an elaborate juggling act, and we realize only as we approach the ending that he is keeping all the balls up in the air. "*remembering recording representing*" begins with the image of a self-conscious painting; it "digresses" on such topics as Renaissance perspective, camera oscura, the daguerrotype, Dada collage, the photography of Stieglitz; and it ends with the image of Antin carrying around "a great big view camera" and ringing doorbells. His plan is to offer to take a picture of every person who answers. But because he knows how difficult it is to capture the "reality" of other people, he decides to set up a system of second chances. If the people don't like the first print:

> and then
> you tell me whether its right or not and maybe we can do it over"
> or maybe i should go in with a video camera instead of a view
> camera and ask these people if they want to tell me what they
> think its like their life and i shoot it and show it to them so
> they can give me their second thoughts about it because maybe
> they think their first thoughts werent right it seems to me
> most people would want to take a crack at that making their
> own self portrait especially if they arent worried about their
> lack of readiness or competence and have a chance for second thoughts
> except perhaps in that part of the art world where no one has
> second thoughts about his life because you cant have second
> thoughts where there are no first ones

Only at this point, when Antin turns off the tape recorder (or we come to the end of the page), do we realize that we have come full circle from self-portrait (that of the figure painter and his wife) to self-portrait (our "true lives" as we conceive of them, recorded by the video camera). "*remembering recording representing*" is not just "talk" or "pure content"; its complex elaboration of metonymic threads creates a *projective* or *generative* stance. In the talk poem, that is to say, *dianoia* can emerge only from the process of discovery enacted by the associative rhythm.

Such three-ring performance is not easy. At one extreme, the talk may be too linear, too concerned with the exposition of a particular theme; the discussion of linguistics found in the first ten pages or so of "Tuning" (1977)[38] seems to me to be a case in point. At the other extreme, the diverse materials—childhood memories, anecdotes about art shows, speculations on Homeric nar-

[38] "and ive called this talk tuning," *Alcheringa*, 3 (1977), 92-125.

rative, and so on—may fail to generate the necessary cross-references. The radio talk piece "*whos listening out there*,"[39] for example, is organized by roll call: Antin invokes the names of various people who may be "listening out there": Timmy, who used to take care of the Antins' garden in San Diego when he wasn't stoned, Jeanie, their first baby-sitter, an elderly neighbor named Mrs. Harris, a doctor visiting San Diego who invited them to an irritating party, and finally his step-sister Anita, whom he hasn't seen since she was a child. The story of Anita is one of the most poignant narratives in the talk poems, and I shall say more of it below. But although this story is related to those of Timmy and Jeanie by the theme of youth, the overall structure of the piece is somewhat mechanical, no doubt because Antin is reacting to the medium. Confronted by the anonymous radio audience, he cannot quite interweave his arguments and plots as he does in a live performance. The continuity essential to the associative rhythm is not always maintained.

(4) From what has been said so far, it is implicit that *narrative* (but not fiction) is an integral feature of the talk poem. Pure exposition, rumination, meditation—these undercut the poet's emphasis on self-discovery as a continuing process. Like Cage's narratives, Antin's are exemplary, but they are much looser than the Cage *koans*. An Antin story often weaves in and out of the expository discourse in which it is embedded; or again, it may fragment in mid-air, in keeping with Antin's distrust of memory and perception as guides to what has actually "happened." So, in "Real Estate,"[40] the inquiry into the meaning of the words "currency," "legal tender," and "real estate" seems to get lost as we are given a series of comic narratives about various Antin relatives who did or did not own real estate. These "stories," like Cage's, are funny in themselves, but, in considering in what sense, if any, a little hotel in the Catskills, bought by his eccentric uncle, is a "real" estate,

[39] (College Park: Sun & Moon Press, 1979).

[40] *New Directions in Prose and Poetry 38*, ed. J. Laughlin (New York: New Directions, 1979), pp. 6-22.

Antin leads us right back to the possible meanings of his title.

The Anita story in "*whos listening out there*," which I mentioned a moment ago, is an extended autobiographical memoir. If "*remembering recording representing*" recalls Gertrude Stein's Picasso portrait, this story brings to mind Stein's *Melanctha*. The events themselves are perfectly commonplace. Nat, the widowed father of a little blonde girl named Anita, works in a girdle factory in New York; he meets and courts David's widowed and overworked mother. During the courtship period, he wears suits and gold cuff links, plays the ukelele, and takes Antin's mother out to dinner. But after their marriage he settles down, first in front of the phonograph and then, when television is born, in front of the TV, and makes a life of watching the variety shows, fights, and ball games. The adolescent David, having no room of his own in which to sleep or study, has to witness these celluloid events. One evening, Nat invites his supervisor Mitch to have dinner and then watch the Louis-Charles fight on TV. It is a real occasion and David's mother makes her special spaghetti dish. But after dinner, Nat and Mitch ignore her and get on with their TV-viewing, which is intense, noisy, and combative: Nat takes Joe Louis' victory for granted, Mitch remains skeptical, and so, when Louis loses, the evening ends on a sour note. A few years later, when David is at college, Nat dies of cancer. One day his mother phones to tell him that she is sending Anita back to her aunts, that she "wasn't going to be a widow all over again with another child to raise." David sees Anita once more, and they tell each other sentimentally that they must keep in touch. But he never sees her again; later he hears that she has worked for the government and married a marine who died in Vietnam, "and now she lives in leucadia and shes probably listening to this program right now."

In summary form, this story sounds both pedestrian and pointless: a "slice of life" set in working-class Jewish Brooklyn. Yet, although it has none of Cage's riddling concise-ness, Antin's narrative exhibits a similar tension between the flat literalism of its surface and the odd indeterminacy of its meaning. For, as in the case of *Melanctha*, the patient, indeed exhaustive, "constatation of fact," as Pound would call it, functions as a kind of inverse naturalism. Throughout the story, the one constant is that everyone is trying—and failing—to talk to someone else: the mother wants to get Nat's attention away from his TV, Nat wants to convince Mitch that Louis is the Champ, and so on. But the further irony is that these futile talk rituals are part of a larger and perhaps even more frustrating talk format: the radio piece, in which the narrator can make no real contact with his audience.

In this context, how are we to interpret the motives of Antin's "characters"? When the mother decides to send Anita back to her aunts, are we to conclude that she is basically cold-hearted? Or that her decision is typical of her place and time? Or perhaps that the dinner for Mitch, recounted at such length, was the last straw? Such questions are not only unanswerable; they are, so to speak, unaskable because the "reality" of the speaker's world is created only by his discourse about it.

An Antin narrative depends heavily on what we might call the misplaced synecdoche. In the talk poems, everything is rigidly subordinated to the creation of a language field that, as Cage puts it, would imitate the operational processes of nature, that is to say, the actual way in which the mind experiences the outside world. We don't come to "know" Nat or Anita any more than we "know" the uncle from Argentina in "Real Estate" or Stein's Melanctha. Rather, we witness certain fragmented gestures, words, and actions that provide a matrix for the speaker's talking. The images are highly particularized, but, as in Gertrude Stein, the parts refer to no whole. Behind the decision to get rid of Anita made by David's mother or the manic behavior of "Dick" at the wheel of the " '53 Chrysler" in "*what am i doing here?*" there is an absent totality. The nonsensicality embodied in Cage's Stockport bus story is also

Antin's, but where Cage is impersonal, cryptic, and elliptical, providing beginnings, middles, and endings that are, in fact, nothing of the sort, Antin is repetitive and digressive, placing himself squarely at the center of his serial discourse.

(5) This brings me to the question of self-projection. The generation of a particular *voice* is, I would posit, the one "fictional" element Antin allows himself. He regularly presents himself as a kind of passive register, although his knowledge of art or language or science is a persistent element, hovering at the edges of his discourse. The "I" of the talk poetry is consistently "confused" or "puzzled" or "surprised." He sees the things around him as if for the first time. In "*is this the right place?*" for example, the Antins are making their way across the country to San Diego, their future home, when their little boy is taken sick. Here is Antin's account of what happened when they finally arrived in Solana Beach and were referred to the local medical center:

> in california a medical center is unlike anything youve ever seen
> unless youre a californian   medical centers depend on red-
> wood trees   because theyre made out of redwood trees and ice-
> plant   because what they do is level off an area   whatever was
> there they take a bulldozer and level it off   if there were euca-
> lyptus trees they knock them down they push things out of the way
> and then what they dont cover with redwood and blacktop they
> cover with iceplant   wherever you go theres iceplant   its a
> kind of squishy water-retaining plant that flowers very prettily
> its a bizarre plant and its rubbery and it forms a lawn all over
> southern california   and no matter what you do southern
> california is characterized by iceplant   it grows like crazy
> normally there would be a coastal desert   but there is this
> iceplant and theres the medical center

This is a good example of the way Antin "detaches objects from the world" in the Breton manner. To define a medical center as a place made of redwood and iceplant has nothing whatever to do with informational content but everything to do with the poet's first impressions of the strange new world which is Southern California. So absorbed is the listener (or reader) in this particular story, that it occurs to us only afterward that nowhere in "*is this the right place?*" do we ever find out what happened to the sick child. Was a doctor ever found? Within the context of the talk poem, it doesn't matter. For the narrator now focuses on "a man called a dentist a strange morose man" whom he happens upon in the "medical center," a man "who looked at me disapprovingly as though he was silently trying to persuade me to go away so he could go back to looking at his iceplant" (TB, 35). This image leads to a consideration of different vocational patterns, different ways of solving the problem posed by the question, "*is this the right place?*" The "real" David Antin would, of course, be able to tell his auditor how the child's problem was resolved, but within the frame of the talk poem, Antin adopts the stance of slightly bewildered observer, trying to infer meanings from the sights and sounds of what he takes to be the external—if not the "real"—world.[41] The humor of the talk poetry is, of course, generated by this stance: Antin trying to decide who the woman in the black dress depicted in the diptych might be, or why lawcourts won't admit drawings as admissible evidence in adultery suits when they do so admit photographs, plays the straight man for his own clowning.

V

A talk poem like "*remembering recording representing*" ends when the sixty-minute "frame" provided by the tape

[41] This stance is often misunderstood; in a review of *Talking at the Boundaries* (*The American Book Review*, 1 [December 1977], 11-12), David Bromige objects to the "monotony of feeling" in the talk poems; "The pervasive feeling-tone in this book is of a refusal to feel, to dwell inside any experience." But to "dwell inside" experience is not necessarily "to feel," in the sense of confessional poetry; Antin's experiences are ideational, and "feeling" is purposely subordinated to concept.

recorder is over; this, we should note, is the only framing device that explicitly controls the poet's associative monologue.[42] Yet we could argue that its form is no more disorderly than that of a Pound Canto, which similarly becomes what Leo Steinberg has called "a running transformer of the external world, constantly ingesting unproccessed data to be mapped in an overcharged field."[43] In both cases, mapping proceeds according to the principle of contiguity: one cannot move from A to any B, but only to the B that will create some kind of connection. This is what Antin means when he tells Barry Alpert: "To me shaping into a poem means steering it—the talk—into open water and not all kinds of talking—talking situations—have open water possibilities" (IBA, 30). Or, as John Cage puts it in "Seriously Comma" (1966):

> (Fish) species, separated and labeled, isn't what an aquarium is now. It's a large glass water-house with unidentified fish freely swimming. Observation—Discovery.
> (YFM, 29)

In the past decade, Cage has himself experimented with the "open water possibilities" of such a new "aquarium." "Mureau" (1970), the most unconventional text in *M* (see pp. 35-56), is described by Cage as follows:

> It is a mix of letters, syllables, words, phrases, and sentences. I wrote it by subjecting all the remarks of Henry David Thoreau about music, silence, and sounds he heard that are indexed in the Dover publication of the *Journal* to a series of I Ching chance operations. The personal pronoun was varied according to such operations and the typing was likewise determined. Mureau

[42] In conversation, David Antin has told me that he does, however, make some changes when he transcribes a talk poem on the typewriter. The basic structure and movement remain the same, but he may add a related narrational unit or clarify a point.

[43] *Other Criteria: Confrontations with Twentieth-Century Art* (New York: Oxford, 1972), p. 88.

> is the first syllable of the word music followed by the second of the name Thoreau.
>
> (*M*, Foreword)

Why Thoreau? In a preface to "Empty Words," the sequel to "Mureau" (first performed in 1973), which again submits Thoreau's prose to decomposition according to chance operations, and includes slide projection of images based on Thoreau's drawings in the *Journal*, Cage says: "Other great men have vision. Thoreau had none. Each day his eyes and ears were open to see and hear the world he lived in. Music, he said was continuous: only listening is intermittent."[44]

At the outset of the performance,[45] Cage appears onstage and explains that the piece will have four movements: (1) phrases, words, syllables, and letters; (2) words, syllables, and letters; (3) syllables and letters; and finally (4) only letters (which is to say, sounds). During the fourth part, we are further told, Thoreau's drawings will be projected on the screen.

During the first three movements, the lights are on and Cage begins by reciting and chanting recognizable phrases. But almost immediately, the language is, in his words, "demilitarized":[46] linguistic units are broken down and become increasingly nonsensical, until, in the long fourth part, the audience hears only sounds in all possible combinations. Silence now becomes an obsessive element, the effect of the sound/silence pattern being wholly hypnotic.

Meanwhile, the first image is projected onto the screen. It arrives quite imperceptibly, just as the strange sounds break the silence. At first, we see almost nothing; the slight

[44] See *Empty Words, Writings '73-'78* (Middletown: Wesleyan University Press, 1979), p. 3.

[45] I attended the performance of "Empty Words" (Part IV) at the Los Angeles County Museum of Art on 27 March 1979.

[46] Cage made this reference in the prefatory comments to the performance I attended. See also *Empty Words*, p. 11: "Language free of syntax: demilitarization of language."

form appearing in the lower righthand rectangle of the screen might be an optical illusion. Then gradually the area is lit up and a shape appears that resembles the puzzles used in perception exercises; it is elementary yet wholly suggestive. The eye now focuses on this approximate "duck" shape as the chant continues, and the listener/viewer is increasingly put in a meditational state, a kind of trance. Altogether, there are four visual images: (1) the "duck"; (2) three dotted cylinders rather like ears of corn but connected to one another; (3) a jagged half-moon; and (4) an imperfect horseshoe that looks as if it were not drawn quite correctly.

While we see and don't see these images (they appear and disappear as slowly as possible and there are temporal intervals between projection), we are treated to a series of sounds that includes such types as: (1) guttural animal sounds, (2) exercises in the use of voiced and voiceless stops, (3) spirant series, (4) a "French" network exploiting sounds like "ce" and "ton," (5) sound units made up of the ending of one word and the beginning of another, (6) crescendos and diminuendos, (7) miniature chants. Throughout, we perceive approximations of musical intervals. No two "phrases" are the same yet there is continuous patterning. At first, the stress is on decomposition, but toward the end of the performance sounds once again coalesce and begin to approximate syllables and words. The relationship of sound to silence and of both to visual image creates a unique and complex rhythm. The auditor is gradually drawn into the performance; one wants to articulate one's own sounds, to create one's own phonemic patterning.

The "score" of "Empty Words," recently published,[47] is,

[47] *Empty Words* has four parts, each with an introductory text. Part I was published in George and Susan Quasha's *Active Anthology* 1974; Part II in *Interstate 2*, ed. Carl D. Clark and Loris Essay (Austin, Texas, 1974); Part III in *Big Deal 3* ed. Barbara Baracks (Spring 1975); and Part IV in *WCH WAY*, ed. Jed Rasula (Fall 1975). For the full text, see *Empty Words*, pp. 11-78.

like the earlier one of "Mureau," fairly uninteresting, for everything here depends on Cage's enormous register, his astonishing timbre, his individual timing and articulation. Such dependence on *opsis* (much greater than in the case of Antin's talk poems, where the scores can be read and reread with great profit) is, of course, a limitation; we have to attend the performance in order to respond to Cage's language construct.

Nevertheless, I would argue that "Empty Words," which is a direct outgrowth of Beckett's short verbal compositions like *Ping* and *Fizzles*, is an important work of art. Like Gertrude Stein's "Susie Asado," it is poised between compositional game and reference, for all the time that we perceive only sounds, denuded of meaning, we are reminded in odd ways that this is after all a composition derived from Thoreau and that both words and images are on the verge of representing something. Further, "Empty Words" is not a work that combines the verbal and the visual or the verbal and the musical. It *is*, in the literal sense, verbal and visual and musical. As such, it is a fascinating experiment in *poiesis*.

Does this mean that "poetry" is reduced to the utterance of meaningless sounds, of animal cries interspersed with "mere" silence? Not at all. "Empty Words" is Cage's way of making us look at the world we actually inhabit, the sights and sounds we really see. So, from the opposite direction, Antin's talk poems force us to become aware of our natural discourse, to become sensitive to the way we actually talk and hence think. In this sense, both Cage's texts and Antin's talk poems are highly *conceptual* art forms. In the very indeterminacy of their sound, their imagery, and their narration, they challenge us, once again, to take up *ideas*. When, in other words, the poetry of indeterminacy, of anti-symbolism, has reached its outer limit, it comes back once more to such basic "literary" elements as the hypnotic sound pattern, the chant, the narrative account, the conceptual scheme. In the poetry of the future, we are likely to find more emphasis on these elements. The so-called "belatedness" of our poetry—belated with respect to the Romantic tradition only—may turn out to be its very virtue. "America," said John Cage, "has an intellectual climate suitable for radical experimentation. We are, as Gertrude Stein said, the oldest country of the twentieth century. And I like to add: in our air way of knowing nowness" (S, 73).

Index

Library of Congress Cataloging in Publication Data

Perloff, Marjorie.
The Poetics of Indeterminacy.

Includes index.
1. American poetry—20th century—History and criticism. 2. American poetry—French influences. 3. Rimbaud, Jean Nicholas Arthur, 1854-1891—Influence. 4. Art and literature. 5. Arts, Modern—20th century. I. Title.
PS323.5.P47 811'.5'09 80-8569
ISBN 0-691-06244-7

DATE			

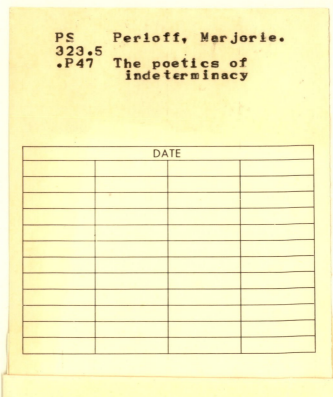